S. O. Houghton

THE EXPEDITION
OF THE DONNER PARTY

AND ITS TRAGIC FATE

BY
ELIZA P. DONNER HOUGHTON

Introduction to the Bison Books Edition
by Kristin Johnson

UNIVERSITY OF NEBRASKA PRESS
LINCOLN AND LONDON

Introduction © 1997 by the University of Nebraska Press
Manufactured in the United States of America

First Bison Books printing: 1997
Most recent printing indicated by the last digit below:
10   9   8   7   6   5   4   3   2   1

Library of Congress Cataloging-in-Publication Data
Houghton, Eliza Poor Donner.
The expedition of the Donner Party and its tragic fate / by Eliza
P. Donner Houghton.
p.   cm.
Originally published: Chicago: A. C. McClurg, 1911.
Includes bibliographical references and index.
ISBN 0-8032-7304-5 (pa: alk. paper)
1. Donner Party.   I. Title.
F868.N5H8   1998
978—dc21
97-25362   CIP

Reprinted from the original 1911 edition by A. C. McClurg &
Co., Chicago.

To
My Husband and my Children
and to
My Sister Georgia
This Book is Lovingly Dedicated

INTRODUCTION

Kristin Johnson

What shapes a life? In the modern Western world many of us have abandoned the concept of destiny, of a power that decrees our fate at birth. Instead, we tend to see our life's course as the result of many factors, of circumstances and events that create who we are and what we become. For some this process is so subtle they cannot say exactly what led them to their present state; others have made conscious decisions; and still others feel they have been at the mercy of events that have jerked them from path to path. And for some, a single experience looms over all others and shadows the entire course of their lives.

In this last category we might place the author of this book. Eliza Poor Donner was a child of three in April 1846 when her large and prosperous extended family left Illinois. A year later she was an orphan depending on the charity of strangers in California. What she underwent was not, of course, a single event but a yearlong experience known to history as "the Donner Party."

That experience is recounted in this book. Briefly, a party of emigrants led by George Donner had nearly completed its long and arduous journey to California when an early snowfall trapped the travelers in the Sierra Nevada. Caught unprepared and low on supplies, the emigrants were forced to spend the winter in hurriedly contrived shelters. Donner, his brother Jacob, and their families camped in the Alder Creek Valley, about seven miles east of the main body of emigrants at what is now Donner Lake.

INTRODUCTION

With the Donner families were several other individuals, including young Jean Baptiste Trudeau, usually called John Baptiste. When relief parties from the California settlements reached the starving emigrants they found George Donner near death. His wife Tamsen, still hale, was caught in a dilemma. She chose to stay with her husband and sent her children ahead to safety. She never rejoined them.

When it was all over, nearly half the eighty-one emigrants had died, including all the adults in the two Donner families. The Donner Party became a legend, not because of the emigrants' sufferings but because of the dire extremity to which some of them had been reduced. The specter of cannibalism haunted the survivors for the rest of their lives.

George Donner's five daughters all survived. Homes were found for all of them. Eliza and Georgia, at four and five the youngest, were especially close and insisted on staying together. An elderly Swiss couple named Brunner took them in. They lived first near Sutter's Fort, later moving to Sonoma. The Brunners were kind to the little girls, but Mrs. Brunner was strict and often capricious.

Eliza and Georgia revered their mother's memory. They had a few of her possessions, which they regarded almost as holy relics, and though grateful to their guardians, they refused to call Mrs. Brunner "mother," a name "too sacred" to apply to anyone but Tamsen Donner. Eliza's longing was manifested in her secret hope that perhaps her mother was only lost, that she had made her way down from the mountains and was looking for her daughters.

While the girls were growing up, they would sometimes hear adults recount dreadful tales of the Donner Party. At first Eliza felt keenly indignant, but later one "Picayune" Butler caused her "hours of suffering" by telling her shocking things about the Donner Party—that her father's body had been mutilated, that her mother had been murdered and devoured, that the emigrants had killed and eaten their own children. Eliza attempted to deny the stories, but was told that she was too young to remember anything.

INTRODUCTION

> Oh, how I longed to be grown, to have opportunities to talk with those of the party who were considered old enough to remember facts, and would answer the questions I wanted to ask; and how firmly I resolved that when I grew to be a woman I would tell the story of my party so clearly that no one could doubt its truth!

As time went on, the Donner disaster receded from popular memory. Eliza was discreet about her personal history, though occasional references still pained her.

On October 10, 1861, Eliza Donner married Sherman Otis Houghton, a widower with a baby daughter. Houghton, fifteen years older than Eliza, was a lawyer who had served as mayor of San Jose, where the Houghtons lived for the next twenty-five years. They had seven children, the youngest of whom died as a toddler. Mrs. Houghton kept busy with family and church duties, and she had many social obligations to meet as well. In 1871 Mr. Houghton was elected to Congress, serving until 1875. His wife enjoyed the years in Washington and acquired a social aplomb that would later serve her well.

During her adolescence and early adulthood Mrs. Houghton was no doubt too busy with her present to dwell much on her past. In February 1879, however, she received a letter that would change her life. Her correspondent was Charles Fayette McGlashan of Truckee, California, a town that had sprung up near the scene of the tragedy at Donner Lake. McGlashan, a lawyer, also edited the *Truckee Republican* and had rashly promised his readers a history of the Donner Party. His letter to Eliza Houghton was part of his energetic campaign for information.

Mrs. Houghton's response was wary. She had "a deep interest in having the truth told," she wrote, but she did "not wish to furnish information for a sentimental newspaper story." McGlashan quickly convinced her of his sincerity and they began a lifelong friendship and a voluminous correspondence.[1]

Once reassured, Mrs. Houghton was eager to set the record straight and over the next six months letters sped between San Jose and Truckee. McGlashan corresponded with many other Donner Party survivors, but his relationship with Mrs. Houghton was unique. A deep rapport sprang up between them. "How is it that you understand my disposition so much better than any of the others?" McGlashan wondered. The aspiring historian was effusive in his praise as his informant gently but firmly made her wishes known. He gratefully accepted her suggestions and accommodated her requests as much as possible.

History of the Donner Party: A Tragedy of the Sierra came out in July 1879. Both McGlashan and Mrs. Houghton regarded it as a collaboration, referring to it in their letters as "our book." Eliza had actually written some of the text. She no doubt regarded her work with McGlashan as the fulfillment of her childhood resolution to tell the truth about the Donner Party when she grew up, and she was satisfied with the result. The book portrayed the emigrants as victims of misfortune who had overcome great hardships, instead of the depraved monsters of earlier stories. Tamsen Donner was presented as a noble and heroic woman who had sacrificed her life for her husband, and the charge that she had been murdered was discredited. McGlashan did not shrink from describing some acts of cannibalism, but was discreetly silent on incidents involving the Donner families.

McGlashan's history was well received and this time the attention Mrs. Houghton attracted because of her past was sympathetic, even gratifying. In 1880 President and Mrs. Rutherford B. Hayes visited San Jose and Mrs. Houghton helped arrange the festivities. When Governor Leland Stanford introduced Sherman Houghton to Mrs. Hayes as the husband of one of the Donner Party, the word spread quickly. Eliza wrote McGlashan, "I was really an object of curiosity. All were glad to meet me, and showed me many attentions." The Houghtons accepted the governor's impromptu invitation to join the presidential party as it continued to Monterey. Afterward the couple shared their amusement at how Mrs. Houghton had outshone her husband.

Since Mrs. Houghton was so pleased with the success of McGlashan's book, why did she later write her own? The seed of discontent was sown in 1884, when, late in the afternoon of November 11, Mrs. Houghton received an unexpected visitor. Jean Baptiste Trudeau, or Truvido, as he now called himself, had applied for membership in the Society of California Pioneers and met Eliza's husband in the process.[2] Mr. Houghton brought him home for a visit, but time was short, so the two old acquaintances arranged to meet again.

The following day when Mrs. Houghton saw John approach the house she hastened to admit him. She spent the afternoon enthralled by his description of life at Alder Creek during that winter thirty-eight years previously. He confirmed her memory of an incident which her sisters had dismissed, and spoke feelingly of her parents, of his great regard for them, and of his regret for having abandoned them. He asked her to read parts of McGlashan's history to him and attested to its general truth, though he amended some details. He had done the heavy work at the camp, he emphasized, and categorically denied that the Donners had eaten human flesh.

Mrs. Houghton quickly wrote to McGlashan, describing the meeting in detail and asking if this "missing link" should not be added to his history. She was preoccupied by the incident and wrote about it again on November 22, adding many details to her previous account. It was not until December 7 that she could write:

> I am my old self again. The nummed feeling and dreamy mood which followed John Baptiste['s] visit has worn off . . . John's visit has been a blessing to me. I am comforted, and satisfied. The missing link which he has given me completes the chain of events which I have prayed for and sought for many, many years . . . I cannot tell you how thankful I am that I have lived to see the History of the Donner Party complete.

But for what answer had Mrs. Houghton prayed all those

years? What missing link had John Baptiste supplied? His devotion to her parents had touched her deeply, and she was also grateful for his labor, which had ensured her own survival; but was this enough to leave her feeling that the truth had yet to be told? The news that shook her must have been the denial of cannibalism at Alder Creek. Years earlier she had been tormented by gruesome stories of maneating and the implication that her family had been involved. McGlashan had simply sidestepped the issue, but here at last was vindication.

John Baptiste had lied, however. There can be little doubt that at least some of the Donners had eaten the only food remaining to them. In addition to contemporary statements by rescuers and passersby, Eliza's sister Georgia had related several incidents to McGlashan indicating that the three youngest Donner girls, including Eliza, had been given human flesh to eat. In 1847 John himself had boasted about his cannibalism, but in 1884 his well-intentioned statement to the contrary was so sincere that Mrs. Houghton could not doubt him. She did not wish to.

John Baptiste's revelations were so important to Mrs. Houghton that she copied her letters to McGlashan, with a few alterations, to preserve them for her children.[3] The decision to write a book came later. Her life went on. The Houghtons moved to Southern California in 1886. Their children grew up and began their own lives. One son died in 1893. It was not until 1898 that Mrs. Houghton broached the subject in a letter to her old friend in Truckee. Her friends had been urging her to record her early experiences in California, she wrote, but she had not yet made up her mind. She would consider the suggestion carefully, discuss it with her family, read and study, and present nothing for publication until she was sure it was correct.

Over the next thirteen years she worked on the project, persevering despite her domestic and social activities, her husband's health problems, and her own bouts with rheumatism. She read all she could find on the Donner Party, and sought further information from her sisters and advice from McGlashan. Finally, in 1911, the A. C. McClurg Company of Chicago published *The Expedition of the Donner Party and Its Tragic Fate*.

The book did well. The reviews were favorable, McGlashan sent congratulations, and once again Mrs. Houghton attracted attention because of her association with the Donner Party. Now, however, she was a recognized authority, and often gave talks and readings. She had wanted to call her book *The Story of the Donner Party by a Donner*, but the publisher dissuaded her. To strengthen her identification with the book, Mrs. Houghton published it under the name "Eliza P. Donner Houghton," a form which she used increasingly in public, especially after her husband's death in 1914.

In the years following her book's publication Mrs. Houghton kept busy with the various organizations to which she belonged, which included the Red Cross, the Native Daughters of the Golden West, and the Daughters of the American Revolution. She took an active interest in the construction of the pioneer monument at Donner Lake, whose unveiling she attended in 1918. Being a Donner Party survivor had been a source of pain to her as a child, but in her old age it became a point of pride.

Eliza Donner Houghton lived to see her childhood vow fulfilled. When she died of heart disease on February 19, 1922—seventy-five years to the day after the first rescue party reached Donner Lake—the Donner Party had attained a heroic stature in the history of California, a legacy of the diligence of one woman in redeeming the reputations of her beloved parents and her former companions in misfortune.

The Expedition of the Donner Party and Its Tragic Fate differs from Mrs. Houghton's earlier collaboration with McGlashan in several respects. It contains more information on the Donner family, naturally, but also describes the early stages of the company's journey to California in much greater detail—McGlashan, as a Truckee resident, had emphasized the events in the Sierra. Mrs. Houghton treated John Baptiste kindly and wove many of the details he had told her into the text. Despite its title, only the first half of the book deals with the Donner Party; the remainder describes Mrs. Houghton's youth until her marriage in 1861. In an appendix she analyzed and dismissed the horror tales that had so upset her as a child as well as the charge that her mother had been murdered.

Mrs. Houghton's book was received with respect. After all, the author was not only a survivor of the disaster, the daughter of Captain Donner, and the wife of a prominent citizen; she was also highly regarded in her own right, an intelligent, articulate woman, devoted to her family and active in her community. Her integrity was beyond question.

Mrs. Houghton's apparent authority is somewhat misleading, however. Her status as a survivor may have enhanced her credibility, but it also impaired her objectivity, and although a survivor, she was not necessarily a witness, for much of her information about the Donner Party can be traced to published sources, John Baptiste's statement, and her older sisters' recollections. Some of her narrative reflects her own memories, but how much she remembered, and how accurately, is open to question. Her writing style is therefore problematic: she wrote definitively, as if she remembered events, when in fact she had probably reconstructed most them. While her account is not as authoritative as it sounds, it nevertheless has the ring of truth and an emotional depth missing from many other accounts of the Donner disaster.

The problem of style is a distinct drawback, but it only underlines the obvious: *The Expedition of the Donner Party and Its Tragic Fate* is not a scholarly history, but rather one individual's attempt to come to grips with the tragedy that shaped her life. The work is a significant contribution to the literature of the Donner Party: it is the source of several favorite anecdotes, many secondary writers have cited it, and it represents an important stage in the evolution of the Donner story, bridging the gap between McGlashan's *History of the Donner Party* (1879) and George R. Stewart's *Ordeal by Hunger* (1936).

INTRODUCTION

In addition, *The Expedition of the Donner Party and Its Tragic Fate* is a period piece of considerable charm. It richly evokes a vanished period in California's history, and its phrasing and sentiments reveal much about the mentality of the time. Of special interest are the photographs of members of the Donner family, few of which have been reproduced elsewhere. The book also satisfies in part the curiosity of many readers who have wondered what happened to the survivors after their rescue. Finally, it offers a unique insight into the heart and mind of the remarkable woman whose labor of love became a classic of Western Americana.

NOTES

1. McGlashan's letters to Mrs. Houghton are preserved in the Sherman Otis Houghton Collection at the Huntington Library, San Marino, California. They were published in *From the Desk of Truckee's C. F. McGlashan*, ed. M. Nona McGlashan and Betty H. McGlashan (Fresno: Truckee-Donner Historical Society, 1986). Eliza Donner Houghton's side of the correspondence is among the Charles Fayette McGlashan Letters and Papers held by the Bancroft Library, University of California, Berkeley.

2. Mrs. Houghton first reported John Baptiste's surname as "Truvido," which is known from other sources, but later changed it to "Tribodó." In her book it appears as "Trubode."

3. This second version can be found among the Eliza (Donner) Houghton Papers at the Huntington Library, along with Mrs. Houghton's scrapbooks and a wealth of other documents and memorabilia.

Eliza P. Donner Houghton

PREFACE

OUT of the sunshine and shadows of sixty-eight years come these personal recollections of California — of the period when American civilization first crossed its mountain heights and entered its overland gateways.

I seem to hear the tread of many feet, the lowing of many herds, and know they are the re-echoing sounds of the sturdy pioneer homeseekers. Travel-stained and weary, yet triumphant and happy, most of them reach their various destinations, and their trying experiences and valorous deeds are quietly interwoven with the general history of the State.

Not so, however, the "Donner Party," of which my father was captain. Like fated trains of other epochs whose privations, sufferings, and self-sacrifices have added renown to colonization movements and served as danger signals to later wayfarers, that party began its journey with song of hope, and within the first milestone of the promised land ended it with a prayer for help. "Help for the helpless in the storms of the Sierra Nevada Mountains!"

And I, a child then, scarcely four years of age, was too young to do more than watch and suffer with other children the lesser privations of our snow-beleaguered camp; and with them survive, because the fathers and mothers hungered in order that the children might live.

Scenes of loving care and tenderness were emblazoned on my mind. Scenes of anguish, pain, and dire distress were branded on my brain during days, weeks, and months of famine,— famine which reduced the party from eighty-one souls to forty-five survivors, before the heroic relief men from the settlements could accomplish their mission of humanity.

Who better than survivors knew the heart-rending circumstances of life and death in those mountain camps? Yet who can wonder that tenderest recollections and keenest heartaches silenced their quivering lips for many years; and left opportunities for false and sensational details to be spread by morbid collectors of food for excitable brains, and for prolific historians who too readily accepted exaggerated and unauthentic versions as true statements?

Who can wonder at my indignation and grief in little girlhood, when I was told of acts of brutality, inhumanity, and cannibalism, attributed to those starved parents, who in life had shared their last morsels of food with helpless companions?

Who can wonder that I then resolved that, " When I grow to be a woman I shall tell the story of my party so clearly that no one can doubt its truth "? Who can doubt that my resolve has been ever kept fresh in mind, by eager research for verification and by diligent communication with older survivors, and rescuers sent to our relief, who answered my many questions and cleared my obscure points?

And now, when blessed with the sunshine of peace and happiness, I am finishing my work of filial love and duty to my party and the State of my adoption, who can wonder that I find on my chain of remembrance countless names marked, " forget me not "? Among the many to whom I became greatly indebted in my young womanhood for valuable data and gracious encouragement in my researches are General William Tecumseh Sherman, General John A. Sutter, Mrs. Ulysses S. Grant, Mrs. Jessie Benton Frémont, Honorable Allen Francis, and C. F. McGlashan, author of the " History of the Donner Party."

My fondest affection must ever cling to the dear, quaint old pioneer men and women, whose hand-clasps were warmth and cheer, and whose givings were like milk and honey to my desolate childhood. For each and all of them I have full measure of gratitude, often pressed down, and now overflowing to their sons and daughters, for, with keenest appreciation I learned that, on June 10, 1910, the order of Native Sons of the Golden West laid the corner stone of " Donner Monument," on the old emigrant trail near the beautiful lake which bears the party's name. There the Native Sons of the Golden West, aided by the Native Daughters of the Golden West, propose to erect a memorial to all overland California pioneers.

In a letter to me from Dr. C. W. Chapman, chairman of that monument committee, is the following forceful paragraph:

"The Donner Party has been selected by us as the most typical and as the most varied and comprehensive in its experiences of all the trains that made these wonderful journeys of thousands of miles, so unique in their daring, so brave, so worthy of the admiration of man."

ELIZA P. DONNER HOUGHTON.

LOS ANGELES, CALIFORNIA,
  September, 1911.

CONTENTS

CHAPTER I

PAGE

THE PACIFIC COAST IN 1845 — SPEECHES OF SENATOR BENTON AND REPORT OF CAPT. FRÉMONT — MY FATHER AND HIS FAMILY — INTEREST AWAKENED IN THE NEW TERRITORY — FORMATION OF THE FIRST EMIGRANT PARTY FROM ILLINOIS TO CALIFORNIA — PREPARATIONS FOR THE JOURNEY — THE START — ON THE OUTSKIRTS OF CIVILIZATION 1

CHAPTER II

IN THE TERRITORY OF KANSAS — PRAIRIE SCHOONERS FROM SANTA FÉ TO INDEPENDENCE, MO. — LIFE *en route* — THE BIG BLUE — CAMP GOVERNMENT — THE *Blue Rover* 11

CHAPTER III

IN THE HAUNTS OF THE PAWNEES — LETTERS OF MRS. GEORGE DONNER — HALT AT FORT BERNARD — SIOUX INDIANS AT FORT LARAMIE 21

CHAPTER IV

FOURTH OF JULY IN AN EMIGRANT PARTY — OPEN LETTER OF LANSFORD HASTINGS — GEORGE DONNER ELECTED CAPTAIN OF PARTY BOUND FOR CALIFORNIA — ENTERING THE GREAT DESERT — INSUFFICIENT SUPPLY OF FOOD — VOLUNTEERS COMMISSIONED BY MY FATHER TO HASTEN TO SUTTER'S FORT FOR RELIEF 30

CONTENTS

CHAPTER V

BEWILDERING GUIDE BOARD — SOUL-TRYING STRUGGLES — FIRST SNOW — REED-SNYDER TRAGEDY — HARDCOOP'S FATE 39

CHAPTER VI

INDIAN DEPREDATIONS — WOLFINGER'S DISAPPEARANCE — STANTON RETURNS WITH SUPPLIES FURNISHED BY CAPT. SUTTER — DONNER WAGONS SEPARATED FROM TRAIN FOREVER — TERRIBLE PIECE OF NEWS — FORCED INTO SHELTER AT DONNER LAKE — DONNER CAMP ON PROSSER CREEK 54

CHAPTER VII

SNOWBOUND — SCARCITY OF FOOD AT BOTH CAMPS — WATCHING FOR RETURN OF McCUTCHEN AND REED . 64

CHAPTER VIII

ANOTHER STORM — FOUR DEATHS IN DONNER CAMP — FIELD MICE USED FOR FOOD — CHANGED APPEARANCE OF THE STARVING — SUNSHINE — DEPARTURE OF THE " FORLORN HOPE " — WATCHING FOR RELIEF — IMPOSSIBLE TO DISTURB THE BODIES OF THE DEAD IN DONNER CAMP — ARRIVAL AND DEPARTURE OF FIRST RELIEF PARTY 68

CHAPTER IX

SUFFERINGS OF THE " FORLORN HOPE " — RESORT TO HUMAN FLESH — " CAMP OF DEATH " — BOOTS CRISPED AND EATEN — DEER KILLED — INDIAN *Rancheria* — THE " WHITE MAN'S HOME " AT LAST . . . 77

CHAPTER X

RELIEF MEASURES INAUGURATED IN CALIFORNIA — DISTURBED CONDITIONS BECAUSE OF MEXICAN WAR — GENEROUS SUBSCRIPTIONS — THREE PARTIES ORGANIZE —

CONTENTS

" First Relief," under Racine Tucker; " Second Relief," under Reed and Greenwood; and Relay Camp under Woodworth — First Relief Party Crosses Snow-Belt and Reaches Donner Lake . 91

CHAPTER XI

Watching for the Second Relief Party — " Old Navajo " — Last Food in Camp 100

CHAPTER XII

Arrival of Second Relief, or Reed-Greenwood Party — Few Survivors Strong Enough to Travel — Wife's Choice — Partings at Donner Camp — My Two Sisters and I Deserted — Departure of Second Relief Party 104

CHAPTER XIII

A Fateful Cabin — Mrs. Murphy Gives Motherly Comfort — The Great Storm — Half a Biscuit — Arrival of Third Relief — " Where is My Boy? ". . 109

CHAPTER XIV

The Quest of Two Fathers — Second Relief in Distress — Third Relief Organized at Woodworth's Relay Camp — Divides and One Half Goes to Succor Second Relief and Its Refugees; and the Other Half Proceeds to Donner Lake — A Last Farewell — A Woman's Sacrifice 115

CHAPTER XV

Simon Murphy, Frances, Georgia, and I Taken from the Lake Cabins by the Third Relief — No Food to Leave — Crossing the Snow — Remnant of the Second Relief Overtaken — Out of the Snow — Incidents of the Journey — Johnson's Ranch — The Sinclair Home — Sutter's Fort 123

CONTENTS

CHAPTER XVI

ELITHA AND LEANNA — LIFE AT THE FORT — WATCHING THE COW PATH — RETURN OF THE FALLON PARTY — KESEBERG BROUGHT IN BY THEM — FATHER AND MOTHER DID NOT COME 132

CHAPTER XVII

ORPHANS — KESEBERG AND HIS ACCUSERS — SENSATIONAL ACCOUNTS OF THE TRAGEDY AT DONNER LAKE — PROPERTY SOLD AND GUARDIAN APPOINTED — KINDLY INDIANS — " GRANDPA " — MARRIAGE OF ELITHA . . 138

CHAPTER XVIII

" GRANDMA " — HAPPY VISITS — A NEW HOME — AM PERSUADED TO LEAVE IT 147

CHAPTER XIX

ON A CATTLE RANCH NEAR THE COSUMNE RIVER — " NAME BILLY " — INDIAN GRUB FEAST 156

CHAPTER XX

I RETURN TO GRANDMA — WAR RUMORS AT THE FORT — LINGERING HOPE THAT MY MOTHER MIGHT BE LIVING — AN INDIAN CONVOY — THE BRUNNERS AND THEIR HOME 165

CHAPTER XXI

MORAL DISCIPLINE — THE HISTORICAL PUEBLO OF SONOMA — SUGAR PLUMS 181

CHAPTER XXII

GOLD DISCOVERED — " CALIFORNIA IS OURS " — NURSING THE SICK — THE U. S. MILITARY POST — BURIAL OF AN OFFICER . . . . . . - . . . 192

CONTENTS

CHAPTER XXIII

REAPING AND THRESHING — A PIONEER FUNERAL — THE HOMELESS AND WAYFARING APPEAL TO MRS. BRUNNER — RETURN OF THE MINERS — SOCIAL GATHERINGS — OUR DAILY ROUTINE — STOLEN PLEASURES — A LITTLE DAIRYMAID — MY DOGSKIN SHOES 200

CHAPTER XXIV

MEXICAN METHODS OF CULTIVATION — FIRST STEAMSHIP THROUGH THE GOLDEN GATE — " THE ARGONAUTS " OR " BOYS OF '49 " — A LETTER FROM THE STATES — JOHN BAPTISTE — JAKIE LEAVES US — THE FIRST AMERICAN SCHOOL IN SONOMA 214

CHAPTER XXV

FEVER PATIENTS FROM THE MINES — UNMARKED GRAVES — THE TALES AND TAUNTS THAT WOUNDED MY YOUNG HEART 226

CHAPTER XXVI

THANK OFFERINGS — MISS DOTY'S SCHOOL — THE BOND OF KINDRED — IN JACKET AND TROUSERS — CHUM CHARLIE 232

CHAPTER XXVII

CAPT. FRISBIE — WEDDING FESTIVITIES — THE MASTER-PIECE OF GRANDMA'S YOUTH — SENORA VALLEJO — JAKIE'S RETURN — HIS DEATH — A CHEROKEE INDIAN WHO HAD STOOD BY MY FATHER'S GRAVE 242

CHAPTER XXVIII

ELITHA, FRANCES, AND MR. MILLER VISIT US — MRS. BRUNNER CLAIMS US AS HER CHILDREN — THE DAGUERREO-TYPE 251

CONTENTS

CHAPTER XXIX

GREAT SMALLPOX EPIDEMIC — ST. MARY'S HALL — THANKSGIVING DAY IN CALIFORNIA — ANOTHER BROTHER-IN-LAW 255

CHAPTER XXX

IDEALS AND LONGINGS — THE FUTURE — CHRISTMAS . 264

CHAPTER XXXI

THE WIDOW STEIN AND LITTLE JOHNNIE — " DAUGHTERS OF A SAINTED MOTHER " — ESTRANGEMENT AND DESOLATION — A RESOLUTION AND A VOW — MY PEOPLE ARRIVE AND PLAN TO BEAR ME AWAY 269

CHAPTER XXXII

GRANDMA'S RETURN — GOOD-BYE TO THE DUMB CREATURES — GEORGIA AND I ARE OFF FOR SACRAMENTO . . 282

CHAPTER XXXIII

THE PUBLIC SCHOOLS OF SACRAMENTO — A GLIMPSE OF GRANDPA — THE RANCHO DE LOS CAZADORES — MY SWEETEST PRIVILEGE — LETTERS FROM THE BRUNNERS 289

CHAPTER XXXIV

TRAGEDY IN SONOMA — CHRISTIAN BRUNNER IN A PRISON CELL — ST. CATHERINE'S CONVENT AT BENICIA — ROMANCE OF SPANISH CALIFORNIA — THE BEAUTIFUL ANGEL IN BLACK — THE PRAYER OF DONA CONCEPCION ARGUELLO REALIZED — MONASTIC RITES . . . 296

CHAPTER XXXV

THE CHAMBERLAIN FAMILY, COUSINS OF DANIEL WEBSTER — JEFFERSON GRAMMAR SCHOOL — FURTHER CONFLICTING ACCOUNTS OF THE DONNER PARTY — PATERNAL ANCESTRY — S. O. HOUGHTON — DEATH TAKES ONE OF THE SEVEN SURVIVING DONNERS 305

CONTENTS

CHAPTER XXXVI

NEWS OF THE BRUNNERS — LETTERS FROM GRANDPA . . 316

CHAPTER XXXVII

ARRIVAL OF THE FIRST PONY EXPRESS 321

CHAPTER XXXVIII

WAR AND RUMORS OF WAR — MARRIAGE — SONOMA RE-
VISITED 324

APPENDIX

I

ARTICLES PUBLISHED IN *The California Star* — STATISTICS
OF THE PARTY — NOTES OF AGUILLA GLOVER — EXTRACT
FROM THORNTON — RECOLLECTIONS OF JOHN BAPTISTE
TRUBODE 335

II

THE REED-GREENWOOD PARTY, OR SECOND RELIEF — REM-
INISCENCES OF WILLIAM G. MURPHY — CONCERNING
NICHOLAS CLARK AND JOHN BAPTISTE . . . 345

III

THE REPORT OF THOMAS FALLON — DEDUCTIONS — STATE-
MENT OF EDWIN BRYANT — PECULIAR CIRCUMSTANCES 352

IV

LEWIS KESEBERG 360

INDEX 373

LIST OF ILLUSTRATIONS

PAGE

S. O. Houghton . . . . . . *Frontispiece*

Eliza P. Donner Houghton vii

The Camp Attacked by Indians 8

Our Stealthy Foes 9

Governor L. W. Boggs 18

Corral Such as was Formed by Each Section for the Protection of its Cattle 19

Fort Laramie as it Appeared When Visited by the Donner Party 26

Chimney Rock 27

John Baptiste Trubode 34

Frances Donner (Mrs. Wm. R. Wilder) 35

Georgia Ann Donner (Mrs. W. A. Babcock) . . . 35

March of the Caravan 56

United States Troops Crossing the Desert . . . 57

Pass in the Sierra Nevadas of California . . . 70

Camp at Donner Lake, November, 1846 71

Bear Valley, from Emigrant Gap 78

The Trackless Mountains 79

Sutter's Fort 92

Sam Brannan's Store at Sutter's Fort 93

Arrival of Relief Party, February 18, 1847 . . . 106

Donner Lake 107

Arrival of the Caravan at Santa Fe 118

On the Banks of the Sacramento River . . . 119

Elitha Donner (Mrs. Benjamin Wilder) . . . 134

LIST OF ILLUSTRATIONS

PAGE

Leanna Donner (Mrs. John App) 134

Mary Donner 135

George Donner, Nephew of Capt. Donner 135

Papooses in Bickooses 158

Sutter's Mill, Where Marshall Discovered Gold, January
19, 1848 159

Plaza and Barracks of Sonoma 174

One of the Oldest Buildings in Sonoma 175

Old Mexican Carreta 186

Residence of Judge A. L. Rhodes, a Typical California
House of the Better Class in 1849 187

Mission San Francisco Solano, Last of the Historic Missions of California 194

Ruins of the Mission at Sonoma 195

Gold Rocker, Washing Pan, and Gold Borer . . . 206

Scene During the Rush to the Gold Mines from San
Francisco, in 1848 207

Post Office, Corner of Clay and Pike Streets, San Francisco, 1849 218

Old City Hotel, 1846, Corner of Kearney and Clay Streets,
The First Hotel in San Francisco 219

Mrs. Brunner, Georgia and Eliza Donner . . . 256

S. O. Houghton, Member of Col. J. D. Stevenson's First
Regiment of N. Y. Volunteers 257

Eliza P. Donner 257

Sacramento City in the Early Fifties 278

Front Street, Sacramento City, 1850 279

Pines of the Sierras 290

Col. J. D. Stevenson 291

General John A. Sutter 291

St. Catherine's Convent at Benicia, California . . 298

Chapel, St. Catherine's Convent 299

LIST OF ILLUSTRATIONS

The Cross at Donner Lake 310

General Vallejo's Carriage, Built in England in 1832 . 326

General Vallejo's Old Jail 327

Alder Creek 340

Dennison's Exchange and the Parker House, San Francisco 341

View in the Grounds of the Houghton Home in San Jose 356

The Houghton Residence in San Jose, California . . 357

NOTE

I WISH to express my appreciation of the courtesies and assistance kindly extended me by the following, in the preparation of the illustrations for this book: Mr. Lynwood Abbott, "Burr-McIntosh Magazine," Mr. J. A. Munk, donor of the Munk Library of Arizoniana to the Southwest Museum, Mr. Hector Alliot, Curator of the Southwest Museum, the officers and attendants of the Los Angeles Public Library, Miss Meta C. Stofen, City Librarian, Sonoma, Cal., Miss Elizabeth Benton Frémont, Mr. C. M. Hunt, Editor "Grizzly Bear," the Dominican Sisters of St. Catherine's Convent at Benicia, Cal., and Mrs. C. C. Maynard.

E. P. D. H.

THE EXPEDITION OF THE DONNER PARTY

CHAPTER I

THE PACIFIC COAST IN 1845 — SPEECHES OF SENATOR BEN-
TON AND REPORT OF CAPT. FRÉMONT — MY FATHER AND
HIS FAMILY — INTEREST AWAKENED IN THE NEW TER-
RITORY — FORMATION OF THE FIRST EMIGRANT PARTY
FROM ILLINOIS TO CALIFORNIA — PREPARATIONS FOR THE
JOURNEY — THE START — ON THE OUTSKIRTS OF
CIVILIZATION.

PRIOR to the year 1845, that great domain lying west of the Rocky Mountains and extending to the Pacific Ocean was practically unknown. About that time, however, the spirit of inquiry was awakening. The powerful voice of Senator Thomas H. Benton was heard, both in public address and in the halls of Congress, calling attention to Oregon and California. Captain John C. Frémont's famous topographical report and maps had been accepted by Congress, and ten thousand copies ordered to be printed and distributed to the people throughout the United States. The commercial world was not slow to appreciate the value of those distant and hitherto unfrequented harbors. Tales of the equable climate and the marvellous fertility of the soil spread rapidly, and it followed that before the close of 1845, pioneers on the western frontier of our ever expanding republic were preparing to open a wagon route to the Pacific coast.

After careful investigation and consideration, my father, George Donner, and his elder brother, Jacob, decided to join the westward migration, selecting California as their destination. My mother was in accord with my father's wishes, and helped him to carry out his plan.

At this time he was sixty-two years of age, large, fine-looking, and in perfect health. He was of German parentage, born of Revolutionary stock just after the close of the war. The spirit of adventure, with which he was strongly imbued, had led him in his youth from North Carolina, his native State, to the land of Daniel Boone, thence to Indiana, to Illinois, to Texas, and ultimately back to Illinois, while still in manhood's prime.

By reason of his geniality and integrity, he was widely known as "Uncle George" in Sangamon County, Illinois, where he had broken the virgin soil two and a half miles from Springfield, when that place was a small village. There he built a home, acquired wealth, and took an active part in the development of the country round about.

Twice had he been married, and twice bereft by death when he met my mother, Tamsen Eustis Dozier, then a widow, whom he married May 24, 1839. She was a native of Newburyport, Massachusetts. She was cultured, and had been a successful teacher and writer. Their home became the local literary centre after she was installed as its mistress.

My father had two sons and eight daughters when she became his wife; but their immediate family circle consisted only of his aged parents, and Elitha and Leanna, young daughters of his second marriage, until July 8, 1840, when blue-eyed Frances Eustis was born to them. On the fourth of December, 1841, brown-eyed Georgia Ann was added to the number; and on the eighth of March, 1843, I came into this world.

I grew to be a healthy, self-reliant child, a staff to my sister Georgia, who, on account of a painful accident and long illness during her first year, did not learn to walk steadily until after I was strong enough to help her to rise, and lead her to a sand pile near the orchard, where we played away the bright days of two uneventful years.

With the approaching Winter of 1845 popular interest in the great territory to the west of us spread to our community. Maps and reports were eagerly studied. The few old letters which had been received from traders and trappers along the Pacific coast were brought forth for general perusal. The course of the reading society which met weekly at our home was changed, in order that my mother might read to those assembled the publications which had kindled in my father and uncle the desire to migrate to the land so alluringly described. Prominent among these works were "Travels Among the Rocky Mountains, Through Oregon and California," by Lansford W. Hastings, and also the "Topographical Report, with Maps Attached," by Captain Frémont, which has been already mentioned.

The Springfield Journal, published by Mr. Allen Francis, appeared with glowing editorials, strongly advocating emigration to the Pacific coast, and its columns contained notices of companies forming in Southern and Southwestern States, each striving to be ready to join the "Great Overland Caravan," scheduled to leave Independence, Missouri, for Oregon, early in May, 1846.

Mr. James F. Reed, a well-known resident of Springfield, was among those who urged the formation of a company to go directly from Sangamon County to California. Intense interest was manifested; and had it not been for the widespread financial depression of that year, a large number would have gone from that vicinity. The great cost of equipment, however, kept back many who desired to make the long journey.

As it was, James F. Reed, his wife and four children, and Mrs. Keyes, the mother of Mrs. Reed; Jacob Donner, his wife, and seven children; and George Donner, his wife, and five children; also their teamsters and camp assistants,— thirty-two persons all told,— constituted the first emigrant party from Illinois to California. The plan was to join the Oregon caravan at Independence, Missouri, continue with it to Fort Hall, and thence follow Frémont's route to the Bay of San Francisco.

The preparations made for the journey by my parents were practical. Strong, commodious emigrant wagons were constructed especially for the purpose. The oxen to draw them were hardy, well trained, and rapid walkers. Three extra yoke were provided for emergencies. Cows were selected to furnish milk on the way. A few young beef cattle, five saddle-horses, and a good watch-dog completed the list of live stock.

After carefully calculating the requisite amount of provisions, father stored in his wagons a quantity that was deemed more than sufficient to last until we should reach California. Seed and implements for use on the prospective farms in the new country also constituted an important part of our outfit. Nor was that all. There were bolts of cheap cotton prints, red and yellow flannels, bright-bordered handkerchiefs, glass beads, necklaces, chains, brass finger rings, earrings, pocket looking-glasses and divers other knickknacks dear to the hearts of aborigines. These were intended for distribution as peace offerings among the Indians. Lastly, there were rich stores of laces, muslins, silks, satins, velvets and like cherished fabrics, destined to be used in exchange for Mexican land-grants in that far land to which we were bound.

My mother was energetic in all these preparations, but her special province was to make and otherwise get in readiness a bountiful supply of clothing. She also superintended the purchase of materials for women's handiwork, apparatus for preserving botanical specimens, water colors and oil paints, books and school supplies; these latter being selected for use in the young ladies' seminary which she hoped to establish in California.

A liberal sum of money for meeting incidental expenses and replenishing supplies on the journey, if need be, was stored in the compartments of two wide buckskin girdles, to be worn in concealment about the person. An additional sum of ten thousand dollars, cash, was stitched between the folds of a quilt for safe transportation. This was a large amount for those days, and few knew that my parents were carrying it with them. I gained my information concerning it in later years from Mr. Francis, to whom they showed it.

To each of his grown children my father deeded a fair share of his landed estate, reserving one hundred and ten acres near the homestead for us five younger children, who in course of time might choose to return to our native State.

As time went on, our preparations were frequently interrupted by social obligations, farewell visits, dinners, and other merrymakings with friends and kindred far and near. Thursday, April 15, 1846, was the day fixed for our departure, and the members of our household were at work before the rosy dawn. We children were dressed early in our new linsey travelling suits; and as the final packing progressed, we often peeped out of the window at the three big white covered wagons that stood in our yard.

In the first were stored the merchandise and articles not to be handled until they should reach their destination; in the second, provisions, clothing, camp tools, and other necessaries of camp life. The third was our family home on wheels, with feed boxes attached to the back of the wagon-bed for Fanny and Margaret, the favorite saddle-horses, which were to be kept ever close at hand for emergencies.

Early in the day, the first two wagons started, each drawn by three yoke of powerful oxen, whose great moist eyes looked as though they too had parting tears to shed. The loose cattle quickly followed, but it was well on toward noon before the family wagon was ready.

Then came a pause fraught with anguish to the dear ones gathered about the homestead to say farewell. Each tried to be courageous, but not one was so brave as father when he bade good-bye to his friends, to his children, and to his children's children.

I sat beside my mother with my hand clasped in hers, as we slowly moved away from that quaint old house on its grassy knoll, from the orchard, the corn land, and the meadow; as we passed through the last pair of bars, her clasp tightened, and I, glancing up, saw tears in her eyes and sorrow in her face. I was grieved at her pain, and in sympathy nestled closer to her side and sat so quiet that I soon fell asleep. When I awoke, the sun still shone, but we had encamped for the night on the ground where the State House of Illinois now stands.

Mr. Reed and family, and my uncle Jacob and family, with their travelling equipments and cattle, were already settled there. Under father's direction, our own encampment was soon accomplished. By nightfall, the duties of the day were ended, and the members of our party gathered around one fire to spend a social hour.

Presently, the clatter of galloping horses was heard, and shortly thereafter eight horsemen alighted, and with merry greetings joined our circle. They were part of the reading society, and had come to hold its last reunion beside our first camp-fire. Mr. Francis was among them, and took an inventory of the company's outfit for the benefit of the readers of *The Springfield Journal.*

They piled more wood on the blazing fire, making it a beacon light to those who were watching from afar; they sang songs, told tales, and for the time being drove homesickness from our hearts. Then they rode away in the moonlight, and our past was a sweet memory, our future a beautiful dream.

William Donner, my half-brother, came to camp early next morning to help us to get the cattle started, and to accompany us as far as the outskirts of civilization.

We reached Independence, Missouri, on the eleventh of May, with our wagons and cattle in prime condition, and our people in the best of spirits. Our party en-

THE CAMP ATTACKED BY INDIANS

OUR STEALTHY FOES

camped near that bustling frontier town, and were soon a part of the busy crowds, making ready for the great prairie on the morrow. Teams thronged the highways; troops of men, women, and children hurried nervously about seeking information and replenishing supplies. Jobbers on the street were crying their wares, anxious to sell anything or everything required, from a shoestring to a complete outfit for a four months' journey across the plains. Beads of sweat clung to the merchants' faces as they rushed to and fro, filling orders. Brawny blacksmiths, with breasts bared and sleeves rolled high, hammered and twisted red hot metal into the divers forms necessary to repair yokes and wagons.

Good fellowship prevailed as strangers met, each anxious to learn something of those who might by chance become his neighbors in line.

Among the pleasant acquaintances made that day, was Mr. J. Q. Thornton, a young attorney from Quincy, Illinois, who, with his invalid wife, was emigrating to Oregon. He informed us that himself and wife and ex-Governor Boggs and family, of Missouri, were hourly expecting Alphonso Boone, grandson of Daniel Boone; and that as soon as Boone and his family should arrive from Kentucky, they would all hasten on to join Colonel Russell's California company, which was already on the way, but had promised to await them somewhere on the Kansas River.

It was then believed that at least seven thousand emigrant wagons would go West, through Independence, that season. Obviously the journey should be made while pasturage and water continued plentiful along the route. Our little party at once determined to overtake Colonel Russell and apply for admission to his train, and for that purpose we resumed travel early on the morning of May twelfth.

As we drove up Main Street, delayed emigrants waved us a light-hearted good-bye, and as we approached the building of the American Tract Society, its agent came to our wagons and put into the hand of each child a New Testament, and gave to each adult a Bible, and also tracts to distribute among the heathen in the benighted land to which we were going. Near the outskirts of town we parted from William Donner, took a last look at Independence, turned our backs to the morning sun, and became pioneers indeed to the Far West.

CHAPTER II

D URING our first few days in the Territory of Kansas we passed over good roads, and through fields of May blossoms musical with the hum of bees and the songs of birds. Some of the party rode horseback; others walked in advance of the train; but each father drove his own family team. We little folk sat in the wagons with our dolls, watching the huge white-covered " prairie schooners " coming from Santa Fé to Independence for merchandise. We could hear them from afar, for the great wagons were drawn by four or five span of travel-worn horses or mules, and above the hames of each poor beast was an arch hung with from three to five clear-toned bells, that jingled merrily as their carriers moved along, guided by a happy-go-lucky driver, usually singing or whistling a gleeful tune. Both man and beast looked longingly toward the town, which promised companionship and revelry to the one, and rest and fodder to the other.

We overtook similar wagons, heavily laden with goods bound for Santa Fé. Most of the drivers were shrewd; all of them civil. They were of various nationalities; some comfortably clad, others in tatters, and a few in picturesque threadbare costumes of Spanish finery. Those hardy wayfarers gave us much valuable information regarding the route before us, and the Indian tribes we should encounter. We were now averaging a distance of about two and a half miles an hour, and encamping nights where fuel and water could be obtained.

Early on the nineteenth of May we reached Colonel Russell's camp on Soldiers' Creek, a tributary of the Kansas River. The following account of the meeting held by the company after our arrival is from the journal of Mr. Edwin Bryant, author of "What I Saw in California":

May 19, 1846. A new census of our party was taken this morning; and it was found to consist of 98 fighting men, 50 women, 46 wagons, and 350 cattle. Two divisions were made for convenience in travelling. We were joined to-day by nine wagons from Illinois belonging to Mr. Reed and Messrs. Donner, highly respectable and intelligent gentlemen with interesting families. They were received into the company by a unanimous vote.

Our cattle were allowed to rest that day; and while the men were hunting and fishing, the women spread the family washings on the boughs and bushes of that well-wooded stream. We children, who had been confined to the wagon so many hours each day, stretched our limbs, and scampered off on Mayday frolics. We waded the creek, made mud pies, and gathered posies in the narrow glades between the cottonwood, beech, and alder trees. Colonel Russell was courteous to all;

visited the new members, and secured their cheerful indorsement of his carefully prepared plan of travel. He was at the head of a representative body of pioneers, including lawyers, journalists, teachers, students, farmers, and day-laborers, also a minister of the gospel, a carriage-maker, a cabinet-maker, a stonemason, a jeweller, a blacksmith, and women versed in all branches of woman's work.

The government of these emigrant trains was essentially democratic and characteristically American. A captain was chosen, and all plans of action and rules and regulations were proposed at a general assembly, and accepted or rejected by majority vote. Consequently, Colonel Russell's function was to preside over meetings, lead the train, locate camping ground, select crossings over fordable streams, and direct the construction of rafts and other expedients for transportation over deep waters.

A trumpet call aroused the camp at dawn the following morning; by seven o'clock breakfast had been cooked and served, and the company was in marching order. The weather was fine, and we followed the trail of the Kansas Indians, toward the Big Blue.

At nooning our teams stood in line on the road chewing the cud and taking their breathing spell, while families lunched on the grass in restful picnic style. Suddenly a gust of wind swept by; the sky turned a greenish gray; black clouds drifted over the face of the sun; ominous sounds came rumbling from distant hills, and before our effects could be collected and returned to cover, a terrific thunderstorm was upon us.

We were three hours' distance from our evening camp-ground and our drivers had to walk and face that buffeting storm in order to keep control of the nervous cattle. It was still raining when we reached the knoll where we could spend the night. Our men were tired and drenched, some of them cross; fires were out of the question until fuel could be cut and brought from the edge of a swamp a mile from camp. When brought, the green wood smoked so badly that suppers were late and rather cheerless; still there was spirit enough left in those stalwart hearts to start some mirth-provoking ditty, or indulge in good-natured raillery over the joys and comforts of pioneering.

Indians had followed our train all day, and as we had been warned against leaving temptation within reach, the cattle were corralled early and their guards doubled. Happily, the night passed without alarm or losses. The following day we were joined by ex-Governor Boggs and companions, and lost Mr. Jordan and friends of Jackson, Missouri, who drew their thirteen wagons out of line, saying that their force was strong enough to travel alone, and that Captain Russell's company had become too large for rapid or convenient handling.

We covered fourteen miles that day over a beautiful rolling prairie, dotted with Indian lodges. Frequently their owners walked or rode beside our wagons, asking for presents.

TRADE WITH THE INDIANS

Mrs. Kehi-go-wa-chuck-ee was made happy by the gift of a dozen strings of glass beads, and the chief also kindly accepted a few trinkets and a contribution of tobacco, and provisions, after which he made the company understand that for a consideration payable in cotton prints, tobacco, salt pork, and flour, he himself and his trusted braves would become escort to the train in order to protect its cattle from harm, and its wagons from the pilfering hands of his tribesmen. His offer was accepted, with the condition that he should not receive any of the promised goods until the last wagon was safe beyond his territory. This bargain was faithfully kept, and when we parted from the Indians, they proceeded to immediate and hilarious enjoyment of the unwonted luxuries thus earned.

We were now in line with spring storms, which made us victims of frequent downpours and cyclonic winds. The roads were heavy, and the banks of streams so steep that often the wagons had to be lowered by aid of rope and chain. Fortunately our people were able to take these trying situations philosophically, and were ever ready to enjoy the novelties of intervening hours of calm and sunshine.

The staid and elderly matrons spent most of their time in their wagons, knitting or patching designs for quilts. The younger ones and the girls passed theirs in the saddle. They would scatter in groups over the plains to investigate distant objects, then race back, and with song and banter join husband and brother, driving the loose cattle in the rear. The wild, free spirit of the plain often prompted them to invite us little ones to seats behind them, and away we would canter with the breeze playing through our hair and giving a ruddy glow to our cheeks.

Mr. Edwin Bryant, Mr. and Mrs. Thornton, and my mother were enthusiastic searchers for botanical and geological specimens. They delved into the ground, turning over stones and scraping out the crevices, and zealously penetrated the woods to gather mosses, roots, and flowering plants. Of the rare floral specimens and perishable tints, my mother made pencil and water-color studies, having in view the book she was preparing for publication.

On ascending the bluff overlooking the Big Blue, early on the afternoon of the twenty-sixth of May, we found the river booming, and the water still rising. Driftwood and good sized logs were floating by on a current so strong that all hope of fording it vanished even before its depth was measured. We encamped on the slope of the prairie, near a timber of cottonwood, oak, beech, and sycamore trees, where a clear brook rushed over its stony bed to join the Big Blue. Captain Russell, with my father and other sub-leaders, examined the river banks for marks of a ford.

By sunset the river had risen twenty inches and the water at the ford was two hundred yards in width. A general meeting was called to discuss the situation. Many insisted that the company, being comfortably settled, should wait until the waters receded; but the majority agreeing with the Captain, voted to construct a raft suitable to carry everything except the live stock, which could be forced to swim.

The assembly was also called upon to settle a difference between two members of our Oregon contingent, friendly intervention having induced the disputants to suspend hostilities until their rights should be thus determined. The assembly, however, instead of passing upon the matter, appointed a committee to devise a way out of the difficulty. J. Q. Thornton's work, "Oregon and California," has this reference to that committee, whose work was significant as developed by later events:

Ex-Governor Boggs, Mr. James F. Reed, Mr. George Donner, and others, myself included, convened in a tent according to appointment of a general assembly of the emigrants, with the design of preparing a system of laws for the purpose of preserving order, etc. We proposed a few laws without, however, believing that they would possess much authority. Provision was made for the appointment of a court of arbitrators to hear and decide disputes, and to try offenders against the peace and good order of the company.

The fiercest thunderstorm that we had yet experienced raged throughout that night, and had we not been protected by the bluff on one side, and the timber on the other, our tents would have been carried away by the gale.

The Big Blue had become so turbulent that work on the prospective craft was postponed, and our people proceeded to make the most of the unexpected holiday. Messrs. Grayson and Branham found a bee tree, and brought several buckets of delicious honey into camp. Mr. Bryant gathered a quantity of wild peas, and distributed them among the friends who had spices to turn them into sweet pickles.

The evening was devoted to friendly intercourse, and the camp was merry with song and melodies dear to loved ones around the old hearthstones.

Meanwhile, Captain Russell had drawn a plan of the craft that should be built, and had marked the cottonwood trees on the river bank, half a mile above camp, that would furnish the necessary materials.

Bright and early the following morning, volunteer boat-builders went to work with a will, and by the close of day had felled two trees about three and a half feet in diameter, had hollowed out the trunks, and made of them a pair of canoes twenty-five feet in length. In addition to this, they had also prepared timbers for the frames to hold them parallel, and insure the wagon wheels a steady place while being ferried across the river.

The workers were well satisfied with their accomplishment. There was, however, sorrow instead of rejoicing in camp, for Mrs. Reed's aged mother, who had been failing for some days, died that night. At two o'clock the next afternoon, she was buried at the foot of a monarch oak, in a neat cottonwood coffin, made by men of the party, and her grave was marked by a headstone.

The craft being finished on the morning of the thirtieth of May, was christened *Blue Rover*, and launched amid cheers of the company. Though not a

GOVERNOR L. W. BOGGS

CORRAL SUCH AS WAS FORMED BY EACH SECTION FOR THE PROTECTION OF ITS CATTLE

thing of beauty, she was destined to fulfil the expectations of our worthy Captain. One set of guide-ropes held her in place at the point of embarkation, while swimmers on horseback carried another set of ropes across the river and quickly made them fast. Only one wagon at a time could cross, and great difficulty was experienced in getting the vehicles on and off the boat. Those working near the bank stood in water up to their armpits, and frequently were in grave peril. By the time the ninth wagon was safely landed, darkness fell.

The only unforeseen delay that had occurred was occasioned by an awkward slip of the third wagon while being landed. The *Blue Rover* groaned under the shock, leaned to one side and swamped one of the canoes. However, the damage was slight and easily repaired. The next day was Sunday; but the work had to go on, and the Rev. Mr. Cornwall was as ready for it as the rest of the toilers.

Much anxiety was experienced when the cattle were forced into the water, and they had a desperate struggle in crossing the current; but they finally reached the opposite bank without accident. Each family embarked in its own wagon, and the last was ferried over in the rain at nine o'clock that night. The ropes were then detached from the *Blue Rover,* and she drifted away in the darkness.

Captain Russell had despatched matters vigorously and tactfully, and when the labors of that day were completed, still had a word of cheer for the shivering, hungry travellers, whom he led into camp one mile west of the memorable Big Blue. Despite stiff joints and severe colds, all were anxious to resume travel at the usual hour next day, June the first.

CHAPTER III

IN THE HAUNTS OF THE PAWNEES — LETTERS OF MRS.
GEORGE DONNER — HALT AT FORT BERNARD — SIOUX IN-
DIANS AT FORT LARAMIE.

WE were now near the haunts of the Pawnee Indians, reported to be "vicious savages and
daring thieves." Before us also stretched the summer range of the antelope, deer, elk, and buffalo. The
effort to keep out of the way of the Pawnees, and the
desire to catch sight of the big game, urged us on at
a good rate of speed, but not fast enough to keep our
belligerents on good behavior. Before night they had
not only renewed their former troubles, but come to
blows, and insulted our Captain, who had tried to separate them. How the company was relieved of them
is thus told in Mr. Bryant's Journal:

June 2, 1846, the two individuals at variance about their
oxen and wagon were emigrants to Oregon, and some
eighteen or twenty wagons now travelling with us were bound
to the same place.

It was proposed in order to relieve ourselves from consequences of dispute in which we had no interest, that all
Oregon emigrants should, in respectful manner and friendly
spirit, be requested to separate themselves from the California, and start on in advance of us. The proposition was
unanimously carried; and the spirit in which it was made
prevented any bad feeling which otherwise might have
resulted from it. The Oregon emigrants immediately drew
their wagons from the corrals and proceeded on their way.

The Oregon company was never so far in advance that we could not hear from it, and on various occasions, some of its members sent to us for medicines and other necessaries.

Our fear of the Pawnees diminished as we proceeded, and met in their haunts only friendly Indians returning from the hunt, with ponies heavily laden with packs of jerked meats and dried buffalo tongues. At least one brave in each party could make himself understood by word or sign. Many could pronounce the one word " hogmeat," and would show what they had to exchange for the coveted luxury. Others also begged for " tobac," and sugar, and generally got a little.

A surprising number of trappers and traders, returning to the United States with their stocks of peltry, camped near us from time to time. They were glad to exchange information, and kept us posted in regard to the condition of the migrants, and the number of wagons on the road in advance. These rough-looking fellows courteously offered to carry the company's mail to the nearest post-office. Mr. Bryant and my mother availed themselves of the kindness, and sent letters to the respective journals of which they were correspondents.

Another means of keeping in touch with travelling parties in advance was the accounts that were frequently found written on the bleaching skulls of animals, or on trunks of trees from which the bark had been stripped, or yet again, on pieces of paper stuck in the clefts of sticks driven into the ground close to the trail. Thus each company left greetings and words of cheer to those who were following. Lost cattle were also advertised by that means, and many strays or convalescents were found and driven forward to their owners.

Early June afforded rarest sport to lovers of the chase, and our company was kept bountifully supplied with choicest cuts of antelope, deer, and elk meat, also juicy buffalo steak. By the middle of the month, however, our surroundings were less favorable. We entered a region of oppressive heat. Clouds of dust enveloped the train. Wood became scarce, and water had to be stored in casks and carried between supply points. We passed many dead oxen, also a number of poor cripples that had been abandoned by their unfeeling owners. Our people, heeding these warnings, gave our cattle extra care, and lost but few.

Through the kindness of the Hon. Allen Francis, U. S. Consul at Victoria, British Columbia, for a long term of years, and in his earlier career editor of *The Springfield Journal,* I have in my possession two letters written by my mother for this paper. They give a glimpse of the party *en route.* The interval of time which elapsed between the date of writing and that of publication indicates how much faster our trapper letter-carriers must have travelled on horseback than we had by ox train.

The following was published on the twenty-third of July:

THE EXPEDITION OF THE DONNER PARTY

MY OLD FRIEND:

We are now on the Platte, two hundred miles from Fort Laramie. Our journey so far has been pleasant, the roads have been good, and food plentiful. The water for part of the way has been indifferent, but at no time have our cattle suffered for it. Wood is now very scarce, but " buffalo chips " are excellent; they kindle quickly and retain heat surprisingly. We had this morning buffalo steaks broiled upon them that had the same flavor they would have had upon hickory coals.

We feel no fear of Indians, our cattle graze quietly around our encampment unmolested.

Two or three men will go hunting twenty miles from camp; and last night two of our men lay out in the wilderness rather than ride their horses after a hard chase.

Indeed, if I do not experience something far worse than I have yet done, I shall say the trouble is all in getting started. Our wagons have not needed much repair, and I can not yet tell in what respects they could be improved. Certain it is, they can not be too strong. Our preparations for the journey might have been in some respects bettered.

Bread has been the principal article of food in our camp. We laid in 150 pounds of flour and 75 pounds of meat for each individual, and I fear bread will be scarce. Meat is abundant. Rice and beans are good articles on the road; cornmeal, too, is acceptable. Linsey dresses are the most suitable for children. Indeed, if I had one, it would be acceptable. There is so cool a breeze at all times on the plains that the sun does not feel so hot as one would suppose.

We are now four hundred and fifty miles from Independence. Our route at first was rough, and through a timbered country, which appeared to be fertile. After striking the prairie, we found a first-rate road, and the only difficulty we have had, has been in crossing the creeks. In that, however, there has been no danger.

I never could have believed we could have travelled so far with so little difficulty. The prairie between the Blue and the Platte rivers is beautiful beyond description. Never have I seen so varied a country, so suitable for cultivation. Everything was new and pleasing; the Indians frequently come to see us, and the chiefs of a tribe breakfasted at our tent this morning. All are so friendly that I can not help feeling sympathy and friendship for them. But on one sheet what can I say?

Since we have been on the Platte, we have had the river on one side and the ever varying mounds on the other, and have travelled through the bottom lands from one to two miles wide, with little or no timber. The soil is sandy, and last year, on account of the dry season, the emigrants found grass here scarce. Our cattle are in good order, and when proper care has been taken, none have been lost. Our milch cows have been of great service, indeed. They have been of more advantage than our meat. We have plenty of butter and milk.

We are commanded by Captain Russell, an amiable man. George Donner is himself yet. He crows in the morning and shouts out, "Chain up, boys! chain up!" with as much authority as though he was "something in particular." John Denton is still with us. We find him useful in the camp. Hiram Miller and Noah James are in good health and doing well. We have of the best people in our company, and some, too, that are not so good.

Buffaloes show themselves frequently.

We have found the wild tulip, the primrose, the lupine, the eardrop, the larkspur, and creeping hollyhock, and a beautiful flower resembling the blossom of the beech tree, but in bunches as large as a small sugar loaf, and of every variety of shade, to red and green.

I botanize and read some, but cook "heaps" more. There are four hundred and twenty wagons, as far as we have heard, on the road between here and Oregon and California.

Give our love to all inquiring friends. God bless them.

Yours truly,

Mrs. George Donner.

The following extract is part of a letter which appeared in *The Springfield Journal* of July 30, 1846 *:

* When Mr. Francis was appointed U. S. Consul by President Lincoln, he stored his files of *The Springfield, Illinois, Journal,* and upon his return from Victoria, B. C., found the files almost destroyed by attic

THE EXPEDITION OF THE DONNER PARTY

SOUTH FORK OF THE NEBRASKA,
TEN MILES FROM THE CROSSING,
Tuesday, June 16, 1846

DEAR FRIEND:

To-day, at nooning, there passed, going to the States, seven men from Oregon, who went out last year. One of them was well acquainted with Messrs. Ide and Cadden Keyes, the latter of whom, he says, went to California. They met the advance Oregon caravan about 150 miles west of Fort Laramie, and counted in all, for Oregon and California (excepting ours), 478 wagons. There are in our company over 40 wagons, making 518 in all; and there are said to be yet 20 behind. To-morrow we cross the river, and, by reckoning, will be over 200 miles from Fort Laramie, where we intend to stop and repair our wagon wheels. They are nearly all loose, and I am afraid we will have to stop sooner, if there can be found wood suitable to heat the tires. There is no wood here, and our women and children are out now gathering " buffalo chips " to burn, in order to do the cooking. These chips burn well.

MRS. GEORGE DONNER.

On the eighteenth of June, Captain Russell, who had been stricken with bilious fever, resigned his office of leader. My father and other subordinate officers also resigned their positions. The assembly tendered the retiring officials a vote of thanks for faithful service; and by common consent, ex-Governor Boggs moved at the head of the train and gave it his name.

We had expected to push on to Fort Laramie without stopping elsewhere, but when we reached Fort Bernard, a small fur-trading post ten miles east of Fort Laramie, we learned that the Sioux Indians were gathering on Laramie Plain, preparing for war with the Crows, and their allies, the Snakes; also that the

rodents, and my mother's earlier contributions in verse and prose, as well as her letters while *en route* to California were practically illegible.

[26]

FORT LARAMIE AS IT APPEARED WHEN VISITED BY THE DONNER PARTY

CHIMNEY ROCK

emigrants already encamped there found pasturage very short. Consequently, our train halted at this more advantageous point, where our cattle could be sent in charge of herders to browse along the Platte River, and where the necessary materials could be obtained to repair the great damage which had been done to our wagon wheels by the intense heat of the preceding weeks.

Meanwhile, Messrs. Russell and Bryant, with six young bachelor friends, found an opportunity to finish their journey with pack animals. They exchanged with traders from New Mexico their wagons and teams for the requisite number of saddle-horses, mules, pack-saddles, and other equipment, which would enable them to reach California a month earlier than by wagon route.

Both parties broke camp at the same hour on the last day of June, they taking the bridle trail to the right, and we turning to the left across the ridge to Fort Laramie.

Not an emigrant tent was to be seen as we approached the fort, but bands of horses were grazing on the plain, and Indians smeared with war-paint, and armed with hunting knives, tomahawks, bows and arrows, were moving about excitedly. They did not appear to notice us as we drove to the entrance of the strongly fortified walls, surrounding the buildings of the American Fur Company, yet by the time we were ready to depart, large crowds were standing close to our wagons to receive the presents which our people had to distribute among them. Many of the squaws and papooses were gorgeous in white doe skin suits, gaudily trimmed with beads, and bows of bright ribbons. They formed a striking contrast to us, travel-stained wayfarers in linsey dresses and sun-bonnets. Most of the white men connected with the fort had taken Indian wives and many little children played around their doors.

Mr. Bourdeau, the general manager at the fort, explained to us that the emigrants who had remained there up to the previous Saturday were on that day advised by several of the Sioux chiefs, for whom he acted as spokesman, " to resume their journey before the coming Tuesday, and to unite in strong companies, because their people were in large force in the hills, preparing to go out on the war-path in the country through which the travellers had yet to pass; that they were not pleased with the whites; that many of their warriors were cross and sulky in anticipation of the work before them; and that any white persons found outside the fort upon their arrival might be subject to robbery and other bad treatment." This advice of the chiefs had awakened such fear in the travellers that every camp-fire was deserted before sunrise the ensuing morning. We, in turn, were filled with apprehension, and immediately hurried onward in the ruts made by the fleeing wagons of the previous day.

Before we got out of the country of the Sioux, we were overtaken by about three hundred mounted warriors. They came in stately procession, two abreast; rode on in advance of our train; halted, and opened ranks; and as our wagons passed between their lines, the warriors took from between their teeth, green twigs, and tossed them toward us in pledge of friendship, then turned and as quietly and solemnly as they had come to us, rode toward the hills. A great sigh of relief expressed the company's satisfaction at being again alone; still no one could feel sure that we should escape a night attack. Our trail led up into the hills, and we travelled late into the night, and were again on the way by morning starlight. We heard wolf yelps and owl hoots in the distance, but were not approached by prowlers of any kind.

CHAPTER IV

FOURTH OF JULY IN AN EMIGRANT PARTY — OPEN LETTER
OF LANSFORD HASTINGS — GEORGE DONNER ELECTED
CAPTAIN OF PARTY BOUND FOR CALIFORNIA — ENTERING
THE GREAT DESERT — INSUFFICIENT SUPPLY OF FOOD —
VOLUNTEERS COMMISSIONED BY MY FATHER TO HASTEN
TO SUTTER'S FORT FOR RELIEF.

ON the second of July we met Mr. Bryant returning to prevail on some man of our company to
take the place of Mr. Kendall of the bridle party, who
had heard such evil reports of California from returning trappers that his courage had failed, and he had
deserted his companions and joined the Oregon company. Hiram Miller, who had driven one of my
father's wagons from Springfield, took advantage of
this opportunity for a faster method of travel and
left with Mr. Bryant.

The following evening we encamped near the re-
enforced bridle party, and on the morning of the
Fourth Messrs. Russell and Bryant came over to help
us to celebrate our national holiday. A salute was
fired at sunrise, and later a platform of boxes was arranged in a grove close by, and by half-past nine
o'clock every one in camp was in holiday attire, and
ready to join the procession which marched around

the camp and to the adjacent grove. There, patriotic songs were sung, the Declaration of Independence was read, and Colonel Russell delivered an address. After enjoying a feast prepared by the women of the company, and drinking to the health and happiness of friends and kindred in reverent silence, with faces toward the east, our guests bade us a final good-bye and godspeed.

We had on many occasions entertained eastward-bound rovers whose varied experiences on the Pacific coast made them interesting talkers. Those who favored California extolled its excellence, and had scant praise for Oregon. Those who loved Oregon described its marvellous advantages over California, and urged home-seekers to select it as the wiser choice; consequently, as we neared the parting of the ways, some of our people were in perplexity which to choose.

On the nineteenth of July we reached the Little Sandy River and there found four distinct companies encamped in neighborly groups, among them our friends, the Thorntons and Rev. Mr. Cornwall. Most of them were listed for Oregon, and were resting their cattle preparatory to entering upon the long, dry drive of forty miles, known as " Greenwood's Cut-off."

There my father and others deliberated over a new route to California.

They were led to do so by " An Open Letter," which had been delivered to our company on the seventeenth by special messenger on horseback. The letter was written by Lansford W. Hastings, author of

" Travel Among the Rocky Mountains, Through Oregon and California." It was dated and addressed, " At the Headwaters of the Sweetwater: To all California Emigrants now on the Road," and intimated that, on account of war between Mexico and the United States, the Government of California would probably oppose the entrance of American emigrants to its territory; and urged those on the way to California to concentrate their numbers and strength, and to take the new and better route which he had explored from Fort Bridger, by way of the south end of Salt Lake. It emphasized the statement that this new route was nearly two hundred miles shorter than the old one by way of Fort Hall and the headwaters of Ogden's River, and that he himself would remain at Fort Bridger to give further information, and to conduct the emigrants through to the settlement.

The proposition seemed so feasible, that after cool deliberation and discussion, a party was formed to take the new route.

My father was elected captain of this company, and from that time on it was known as the " Donner Party." It included our original Sangamon County folks (except Mrs. Keyes and Hiram Miller), and the following additional members: Patrick Breen, wife, and seven children; Lewis Keseberg, wife, and two children; Mrs. Lavina Murphy (a widow) and five children; William Eddy, wife, and two children; William Pike, wife, and two children; William Foster, wife, and child; William McCutchen, wife, and child;

Mr. Wolfinger and wife; Patrick Doland, Charles Stanton, Samuel Shoemaker, ——— Hardcoop, ——— Spitzer, Joseph Reinhart, James Smith, Walter Herron, and Luke Halloran.

While we were preparing to break camp, the last named had begged my father for a place in our wagon. He was a stranger to our family, afflicted with consumption, too ill to make the journey on horseback, and the family with whom he had travelled thus far could no longer accommodate him. His forlorn condition appealed to my parents and they granted his request.

All the companies broke camp and left the Little Sandy on the twentieth of July. The Oregon division with a section for California took the right-hand trail for Fort Hall; and the Donner Party, the left-hand trail to Fort Bridger.

After parting from us, Mr. Thornton made the following note in his journal:

July 20, 1846. The Californians were much elated and in fine spirits, with the prospect of better and nearer road to the country of their destination. Mrs. George Donner, however, was an exception. She was gloomy, sad, and dispirited in view of the fact that her husband and others could think of leaving the old road, and confide in the statement of a man of whom they knew nothing, but was probably some selfish adventurer.

Five days later the Donner Party reached Fort Bridger, and were informed by Hastings's agent that he had gone forward as pilot to a large emigrant train, but had left instructions that all later arrivals should follow his trail. Further, that they would find " an abundant supply of wood, water, and pasturage along the whole line of road, except one dry drive of thirty miles, or forty at most; that they would have no difficult cañons to pass; and that the road was generally smooth, level, and hard."

At Fort Bridger, my father took as driver for one of his wagons, John Baptiste Trubode, a sturdy young mountaineer, the offspring of a French father — a trapper — and a Mexican mother. John claimed to have a knowledge of the languages and customs of various Indian tribes through whose country we should have to pass, and urged that this knowledge might prove helpful to the company.

The trail from the fort was all that could be desired, and on the third of August, we reached the crossing of Webber River, where it breaks through the mountains into the cañon. There we found a letter from Hastings stuck in the cleft of a projecting stick near the roadside. It advised all parties to encamp and await his return for the purpose of showing them a better way than through the cañon of Webber River, stating that he had found the road over which he was then piloting a train very bad, and feared other parties might not be able to get their wagons through the cañon leading to the valley of the Great Salt Lake.

He referred, however, to another route which he declared to be much better, as it avoided the cañon altogether. To prevent unnecessary delays, Messrs. Reed, Pike, and Stanton volunteered to ride over the new route, and, if advisable, bring Hastings back to

JOHN BAPTISTE TRUBODE

GEORGIA ANN DONNER
(MRS. W. A. BABCOCK)

FRANCES DONNER
(MRS. WM. R. WILDER)

conduct us to the open valley. After eight days Mr. Reed returned alone, and reported that he and his companions overtook Hastings with his train near the south end of Salt Lake; that Hastings refused to leave his train, but was finally induced to go with them to the summit of a ridge of the Wahsatch Mountains and from there point out as best he could, the directions to be followed.

While exploring on the way back, Mr. Reed had become separated from Messrs. Pike and Stanton and now feared they might be lost. He himself had located landmarks and blazed trees and felt confident that, by making occasional short clearings, we could get our wagons over the new route as outlined by Hastings. Searchers were sent ahead to look up the missing men, and we immediately broke camp and resumed travel.

The following evening we were stopped by a thicket of quaking ash, through which it required a full day's hard work to open a passageway. Thence our course lay through a wilderness of rugged peaks and rock-bound cañons until a heavily obstructed gulch confronted us. Believing that it would lead out to the Utah River Valley, our men again took their tools and became roadmakers. They had toiled six days, when W. F. Graves, wife, and eight children; J. Fosdick, wife, and child, and John Snyder, with their teams and cattle, overtook and joined our train. With the assistance of these three fresh men, the road, eight miles in length, was completed two days later. It carried us out into a pretty mountain dell, not the opening we had expected.

Fortunately, we here met the searchers returning with Messrs. Pike and Stanton. The latter informed us that we must turn back over our newly made road and cross a farther range of peaks in order to strike the outlet to the valley. Sudden fear of being lost in the trackless mountains almost precipitated a panic, and it was with difficulty that my father and other cool-headed persons kept excited families from scattering rashly into greater dangers.

We retraced our way, and after five days of alternate travelling and road-making, ascended a mountain so steep that six and eight yoke of oxen were required to draw each vehicle up the grade, and most careful handling of the teams was necessary to keep the wagons from toppling over as the straining cattle zigzaged to the summit. Fortunately, the slope on the opposite side was gradual and the last wagon descended to camp before darkness obscured the way.

The following morning, we crossed the river which flows from Utah Lake to Great Salt Lake and found the trail of the Hastings party. We had been thirty days in reaching that point, which we had hoped to make in ten or twelve.

The tedious delays and high altitude wrought distressing changes in Mr. Halloran's condition, and my father and mother watched over him with increasing solicitude. But despite my mother's unwearying ministrations, death came on the fourth of September.

Suitable timber for a coffin could not be obtained, so his body was wrapped in sheets and carefully enclosed in a buffalo robe, then reverently laid to rest in a grave on the shore of Great Salt Lake, near that of a stranger, who had been buried bv the Hastings party a few weeks earlier.

Mr. Halloran had appreciated the tender care bestowed upon him by my parents, and had told members of our company that in the event of his death on the way, his trunk and its contents, and his horse and its equipments should belong to Captain Donner. When the trunk was opened, it was found to contain clothing, keepsakes, a Masonic emblem, and fifteen hundred dollars in coin.

A new inventory, taken about this time, disclosed the fact that the company's stock of supplies was insufficient to carry it through to California. A call was made for volunteers who should hasten on horseback to Sutter's Fort, procure supplies and, returning, meet the train *en route*. Mr. Stanton, who was without family, and Mr. McCutchen, whose wife and child were in the company, heroically responded. They were furnished with necessaries for their personal needs, and with letters to Captain Sutter, explaining the company's situation, and petitioning for supplies which would enable it to reach the settlement. As the two men rode away, many anxious eyes watched them pass out of sight, and many heartfelt prayers were offered for their personal safety, and the success of their mission.

In addressing this letter to Captain Sutter, my father followed the general example of emigrants to California in those days, for Sutter, great-hearted and generous, was the man to whom all turned in distress or emergencies. He himself had emigrated to the United States at an early age, and after a few years spent in St. Louis, Missouri, had pushed his way westward to California.

There he negotiated with the Russian Government for its holdings on the Pacific coast, and took them over when Russia evacuated the country. He then established himself on the vast estates so acquired, which, in memory of his parentage, he called New Helvetia. The Mexican Government, however, soon assumed his liabilities to the Russian Government, and exercised sovereignty over the territory. Sutter's position, nevertheless, was practically that of a potentate. He constructed the well-known fort near the present site of the city of Sacramento, as protection against Indian depredations, and it became a trading centre and rendezvous for incoming emigrants.

CHAPTER V

BEWILDERING GUIDE BOARD — SOUL-TRYING STRUGGLES — FIRST SNOW — REED-SNYDER TRAGEDY — HARDCOOP'S FATE.

OUR next memorable camp was in a fertile valley where we found twenty natural wells, some very deep and full to the brim of pure, cold water. "They varied from six inches to several feet in diameter, the soil around the edges was dry and hard, and as fast as water was dipped out, a new supply rose to the surface."* Grass was plentiful and wood easily obtained. Our people made much of a brief stay, for though the weather was a little sharp, the surroundings were restful. Then came a long, dreary pull over a low range of hills, which brought us to another beautiful valley where the pasturage was abundant, and more wells marked the site of good camping grounds.

Close by the largest well stood a rueful spectacle, — a bewildering guide board, flecked with bits of white paper, showing that the notice or message which had recently been pasted and tacked thereon had since been stripped off in irregular bits.

In surprise and consternation, the emigrants gazed

*Thornton.

at its blank face, then toward the dreary waste beyond. Presently, my mother knelt before it and began searching for fragments of paper, which she believed crows had wantonly pecked off and dropped to the ground.

Spurred by her zeal, others also were soon on their knees, scratching among the grasses and sifting the loose soil through their fingers. What they found, they brought to her, and after the search ended she took the guide board, laid it across her lap, and thoughtfully. began fitting the ragged edges of paper together and matching the scraps to marks on the board. The tedious process was watched with spellbound interest by the anxious group around her.

The writing was that of Hastings, and her patchwork brought out the following words:

" 2 days — 2 nights — hard driving — cross — desert — reach water."

This would be a heavy strain on our cattle, and to fit them for the ordeal they were granted thirty-six hours' indulgence near the bubbling waters, amid good pasturage. Meanwhile, grass was cut and stored, water casks were filled, and rations were prepared for desert use.

We left camp on the morning of September 9, following dimly marked wagon-tracks courageously, and entered upon the " dry drive," which Hastings and his agent at Fort Bridger had represented as being thirty-five miles, or forty at most. After two days and two nights of continuous travel, over a waste of alkali and sand, we were still surrounded as far as eye could see by a region of fearful desolation. The supply of feed for our cattle was gone, the water casks were empty, and a pitiless sun was turning its burning rays upon the glaring earth over which we still had to go.

Mr. Reed now rode ahead to prospect for water, while the rest followed with the teams. All who could walk did so, mothers carrying their babes in their arms, and fathers with weaklings across their shoulders moved slowly as they urged the famishing cattle forward. Suddenly an outcry of joy gave hope to those whose courage waned. A lake of shimmering water appeared before us in the near distance, we could see the wavy grasses and a caravan of people moving toward it.

" It may be Hastings! " was the eager shout. Alas, as we advanced, the scene vanished! A cruel mirage, in its mysterious way, had outlined the lake and cast our shadows near its shore.

Disappointment intensified our burning thirst, and my good mother gave her own and other suffering children wee lumps of sugar, moistened with a drop of peppermint, and later put a flattened bullet in each child's mouth to engage its attention and help keep the salivary glands in action.

Then followed soul-trying hours. Oxen, footsore and weary, stumbled under their yokes. Women, heartsick and exhausted, could walk no farther. As a last resort, the men hung the water pails on their arms, unhooked the oxen from the wagons, and by persuasion and force, drove them onward, leaving the women and children to await their return. Messrs. Eddy and Graves got their animals to water on the night of the twelfth, and the others later. As soon as the poor beasts were refreshed, they were brought back with water for the suffering, and also that they might draw the wagons on to camp. My father's wagons were the last taken out. They reached camp the morning of the fifteenth.

Thirty-six head of cattle were left on that desert, some dead, some lost. Among the lost were all Mr. Reed's herd, except an ox and a cow. His poor beasts had become frenzied in the night, as they were being driven toward water, and with the strength that comes with madness, had rushed away in the darkness. Meanwhile, Mr. Reed, unconscious of his misfortune, was returning to his family, which he found by his wagon, some distance in the rear. At daylight, he, with his wife and children, on foot, overtook my Uncle Jacob's wagons and were carried forward in them until their own were brought up.

After hurriedly making camp, all the men turned out to hunt the Reed cattle. In every direction they searched, but found no clue. Those who rode onward, however, discovered that we had reached only an oasis in the desert, and that six miles ahead of us lay another pitiless barren stretch.

Anguish and dismay now filled all hearts. Husbands bowed their heads, appalled at the situation of their families. Some cursed Hastings for the false statements in his open letter and for his broken pledge at Fort Bridger. They cursed him also for his misrepresentation of the distance across this cruel desert, traversing which had wrought such suffering and loss. Mothers in tearless agony clasped their children to their bosoms, with the old, old cry, " Father, Thy will, not mine, be done."

It was plain that, try as we might, we could not get back to Fort Bridger. We must proceed regardless of the fearful outlook.

After earnest consultation, it was deemed best to dig a trench and cache all Mr. Reed's effects, except such as could be packed into one wagon, and were essential for daily use. This accomplished, Messrs. Graves and Breen each loaned him an ox, and these in addition to his own ox and cow yoked together, formed his team. Upon examination, it was found that the woodwork of all the wagons had been shrunk and cracked by the dry atmosphere. One of Mr. Keseberg's and one of my father's were in such bad condition that they were abandoned, left standing near those of Mr. Reed, as we passed out of camp.

The first snow of the season fell as we were crossing the narrow strip of land upon which we had rested and when we encamped for the night on its boundary, the waste before us was as cheerless, cold, and white as the winding sheet which enfolds the dead.

At dawn we resumed our toilful march, and travelled until four o'clock the following morning, when we reached an extensive valley, where grass and water were plentiful. Several oxen had died during the night, and it was with a caress of pity that the surviving were relieved of their yokes for the day. The next sunrise saw us on our way over a range of hills sloping down to a valley luxuriant with grass and springs of delicious water, where antelope and mountain sheep were grazing, and where we saw Indians who seemed never to have met white men before. We were three days in crossing this magnificent stretch of country, which we called, "Valley of Fifty Springs." In it, several wagons and large cases of goods were cached by our company, and secret marks were put on trees near by, so that they could be recovered, should their owners return for them.

While on the desert, my father's wagons had travelled last in the train, in order that no one should stray, or be left to die alone. But as soon as we reached the mountainous country, he took the lead to open the way. Uncle Jacob's wagons were always close to ours, for the two brothers worked together, one responding when the other called for help; and with the assistance of their teamsters, they were able to free the trail of many obstructions and prevent unnecessary delays.

From the Valley of Fifty Springs, we pursued a southerly course over more hills, and through fertile valleys, where we saw Indians in a state of nudity, who looked at us from a distance, but never approached our wagons, nor molested any one. On the twenty-fourth of September, we turned due north and found the tracks of wagon wheels, which guided us to the valley of " Mary's River," or " Ogden's River," and on the thirtieth, put us on the old emigrant road leading from Fort Hall. This welcome landmark inspired us with renewed trust; and the energizing hope that Stanton and McCutchen would soon appear, strengthened our sorely tried courage. This day was also memorable, because it brought us a number of Indians who must have been Frémont's guides, for they could give information, and understand a little English. They went into camp with us, and by word and sign explained that we were still far from the sink of Mary's River, but on the right trail to it.

After another long day's drive, we stopped on a mountain-side close to a spring of cold, sweet water. While supper was being prepared, one of the fires crept beyond bounds, spread rapidly, and threatened destruction to part of our train. At the critical moment two strange Indians rushed upon the scene and rendered good service. After the fire was extinguished, the Indians were rewarded, and were also given a generous meal at the tent of Mr. Graves. Later, they settled themselves in friendly fashion beside his fire and were soon fast asleep. Next morning, the Indians were gone, and had taken with them a new shirt and a yoke of good oxen belonging to their host.

Within the week, Indians again sneaked up to camp, and stole one of Mr. Graves's saddle-horses. These were trials which made men swear vengeance, yet no one felt that it would be safe to follow the marauders. Who could know that the train was not being stealthily followed by cunning plunderers who would await their chance to get away with the wagons, if left weakly guarded?

Conditions now were such that it seemed best to divide the train into sections and put each section under a sub-leader. Our men were well equipped with side arms, rifles, and ammunition; nevertheless, anxious moments were common, as the wagons moved slowly and singly through dense thickets, narrow defiles, and rugged mountain gorges, one section often being out of sight of the others, and each man realizing that there could be no concerted action in the event of a general attack; that each must stay by his own wagon and defend as best he could the lives committed to his care. No one rode horseback now, except the leaders, and those in charge of the loose cattle. When darkness obscured the way, and after feeding-time, each section formed its wagons into a circle to serve as cattle corral, and night watches were keenly alert to give a still alarm if anything unusual came within sight or sound.

Day after day, from dawn to twilight, we moved onward, never stopping, except to give the oxen the necessary nooning, or to give them drink when water was available. Gradually, the distance between sections lengthened, and so it happened that the wagons of my father and my uncle were two days in advance of the others, on the eighth of October, when Mr. Reed, on horseback, overtook us. He was haggard and in great tribulation. His lips quivered as he gave substantially the following account of circumstances which had made him the slayer of his friend, and a lone wanderer in the wilderness.

On the morning of October 5, when Mr. Reed's section broke camp, he and Mr. Eddy ventured off to hunt antelope, and were shot at a number of times by Indians with bows and arrows. Empty-handed and disappointed, the two followed and overtook their companions about noon, at the foot of a steep hill near "Gravelly Ford," where the teams had to be doubled for the ascent. All the wagons, except Pike's and Reed's, and one of Graves's in charge of John Snyder, had already been taken to the top. Snyder was in the act of starting his team, when Milton Elliot, driving Reed's oxen, with Eddy's in the lead, also started. Suddenly, the Reed and Eddy cattle became unmanageable, and in some way got mixed up with Snyder's team. This provoked both drivers, and fierce words passed between them. Snyder declared that the Reed team ought to be made to drag its wagon up without help. Then he began to beat his own cattle about the head to get them out of the way.

Mr. Reed attempted to remonstrate with him for his cruelty, at which Snyder became more enraged, and threatened to strike both Reed and Elliot with his whip for interfering. Mr. Reed replied sharply that they would settle the matter later. This, Synder took as a threat, and retorted, "No, we'll settle it right here," and struck Reed over the head with the butt end of his whip, cutting an ugly scalp wound.

Mrs. Reed, who rushed between the two men for the purpose of separating them, caught the force of the second blow from Snyder's whip on her shoulder. While dodging the third blow, Reed drew his hunting knife and stabbed Snyder in the left breast. Fifteen minutes later, John Snyder, with his head resting on the arm of William Graves, died, and Mr. Reed stood beside the corpse, dazed and sorrowful.

Near-by sections were immediately called into camp, and gloom, consternation, and anger pervaded it. Mr. Reed and family were taken to their tent some distance from the others and guarded by their friends. Later, an assembly was convened to decide what should be done. The majority declared the deed murder, and demanded retribution. Mr. Eddy and others pleaded extenuating circumstances and proposed that the accused should leave the camp. After heated discussion this compromise was adopted, the assembly voting that Mr. Reed should be banished from the company.

Mr. Reed maintained that the deed was not prompted by malice, that he had acted in self-defence and in defence of his wife; and that he would not be driven from his helpless, dependent family. The assembly promised that the company would care for his family, and limited his stay in camp. His wife, fearing the consequence of noncompliance with the sentence, begged him to abide by it, and to push on to the settlement, procure food and assistance, and return for her and their children. The following morning, after participating in the funeral rites over the lamented dead, Mr. Reed took leave of his friends and sorrowing family and left the camp.

The group around my father's wagon were deeply touched by Mr. Reed's narrative. Its members were friends of the slain and of the slayer. Their sympathies clustered around the memory of the dead, and clung to the living. They deplored the death of a fellow traveller, who had manfully faced many hardships, and was young, genial, and full of promise. They regretted the act which took from the company a member who had been prominent in its organization, had helped to formulate its rules, and had, up to that unfortunate hour, been a co-worker with the other leading spirits for its best interests. It was plain that the hardships and misfortunes of the journey had sharpened the tempers of both men, and the vexations of the morning had been too much for the overstrained nerves.

Mr. Reed breakfasted at our tent, but did not continue his journey alone. Walter Herron, one of my father's helpers, decided to accompany him, and after hurried preparations, they went away together, bearing an urgent appeal from my father to Captain Sutter for necessary teams and provisions to carry the company through to California, also his personal pledge in writing that he would be responsible for the payment of the debt as soon as he should reach the settlement. My father believed the two men would reach their destination long before the slowly moving train.

Immediately after the departure of Messrs. Reed and Herron, our wagons moved onward. Night overtook us at a grewsome place where wood and feed were scarce and every drop of water was browned by alkali. There, hungry wolves howled, and there we found and buried the bleaching bones of Mr. Sallé, a member of the Hastings train, who had been shot by Indians. After his companions had left his grave, the savages had returned, dug up the body, robbed it of its clothing, and left it to the wolves.

At four o'clock the following morning, October 10, the rest of the company, having travelled all night, drove into camp. Many were in a state of great excitement, and some almost frenzied by the physical and mental suffering they had endured. Accounts of the Reed-Snyder tragedy differed somewhat from that we had already heard. The majority held that the assembly had been lenient with Mr. Reed and considerate for his family; that the action taken had been largely influenced by rules which Messrs. Reed, Donner, Thornton, and others had suggested for the government of Colonel Russell's train, and that there was no occasion for criticism, since the sentence was for the transgression, and not for the individual.

The loss of aged Mr. Hardcoop, whose fate was sealed soon after the death of John Synder, was the subject of bitter contention. The old man was travelling with the Keseberg family, and, in the heavy sand, when that family walked to lighten the load, he was required to do likewise. The first night after leaving Gravelly Ford, he did not come into camp with the rest. The company, fearing something amiss, sent a man on horseback to bring him in. He was found five miles from camp, completely exhausted and his feet in a terrible condition.

The following morning, he again started with Keseberg, and when the section had been under way only a short time, the old man approached Mr. Eddy and begged for a place in some other wagon, saying he was sick and exhausted, and that Keseberg had put him out to die. The road was still through deep, loose sand, and Mr. Eddy told him if he would only manage to go forward until the road should be easier on the oxen, he himself would take him in. Hardcoop promised to try, yet the roads became so heavy that progress was yet slower and even the small children were forced to walk, nor did any one see when Mr. Hardcoop dropped behind.

Mr. Eddy had the first watch that night, and kept a bright fire burning on the hillside in hopes that it would guide the belated into camp. Milton Elliot went on guard at midnight, and kept the fire till morning, yet neither sign nor sound of the missing came over that desolate trail.

In vain the watchers now besought Keseberg to return for Hardcoop. Next they applied to Messrs. Graves and Breen, who alone had saddle horses able to carry the helpless man, but neither of them would risk his animals again on that perilous road. In desperation, Messrs. William Pike, Milton Elliot, and William Eddy proposed to go out afoot and carry him in, if the wagons would wait. Messrs. Graves and Breen, however, in language so plain and homely that it seemed heartless, declared that it was neither the voice of common sense, nor of humanity that asked the wagons to wait there in the face of danger, while three foolhardy men rushed back to look for a helpless one, whom they had been unable to succor on the previous day, and for whom they could make no provision in the future, even if they should succeed then in snatching him from the jaws of death.

This exposition of undeniable facts defeated the plans of the would-be rescuers, yet did not quiet their consciences. When the section halted at noon, they again begged, though in vain, for horses which might enable them to do something for their deserted companion.

My father listened thoughtfully to the accounts of that harrowing incident, and although he realized that death must have ended the old man's sufferings within a few hours after he dropped by the wayside, he could not but feel deeply the bitterness of such a fate.

Who could peer into the near future and read between its lines the greater suffering which Mr. Hardcoop had escaped, or the trials in store for us?

We were in close range of ambushed savages, lying in wait for spoils. While the company were hurrying to get into marching order, Indians stole a milch cow and several horses belonging to Mr. Graves. Emboldened by success, they made a raid on our next camp and stampeded a bunch of eighteen horned cattle belonging to Mr. Wolfinger and my father and Uncle Jacob, and also flesh-wounded several poor beasts with arrows. These were more serious hindrances than we had yet experienced. Still, undaunted by the alarming prospects before us, we immediately resumed travel with cows under yoke in place of the freshly injured oxen.

CHAPTER VI

INDIAN DEPREDATIONS — WOLFINGER'S DISAPPEARANCE — STANTON RETURNS WITH SUPPLIES FURNISHED BY CAPTAIN SUTTER — DONNER WAGONS SEPARATED FROM TRAIN FOREVER — TERRIBLE PIECE OF NEWS — FORCED INTO SHELTER AT DONNER LAKE — DONNER CAMP ON PROSSER CREEK.

ALL who managed to get beyond the sink of Ogden's River before midnight of October 12, reached Geyser Springs without further molestation, but the belated, who encamped at the sink were surprised at daylight by the Indians, who, while the herders were hurriedly taking a cup of coffee, swooped down and killed twenty-one head of cattle. Among the number were all of Mr. Eddy's stock, except an ox and a cow that would not work together. Maddened by his appalling situation, Eddy called for vengeance on his despoilers, and would have rushed to certain death, if the breaking of the lock of his rifle at the start had not stopped him.

Sullen and dejected, he cached the contents of his wagons, and with a meagre supply of food in a pack on his back, he and his wife, each carrying a child, set forth to finish the journey on foot. To add to their discomfort, they saw Indians on adjacent hills dancing and gesticulating in savage delight. In relating the above occurrence after the journey was finished, Mr. Eddy declared that no language could portray the desolation and heartsick feeling, nor the physical and mental torture which he and his wife experienced while travelling between the sink of Ogden's River and the Geyser Springs.*

It was during that trying week that Mr. Wolfinger mysteriously disappeared. At the time, he and Keseberg, with their wagons, were at the rear of the train, and their wives were walking in advance with other members of the company. When camp was made, those two wagons were not in sight, and after dark the alarmed wives prevailed on friends to go in search of their missing husbands. The searchers shortly found Keseberg leisurely driving toward camp. He assured them that Wolfinger was not far behind him, so they returned without further search.

All night the frantic wife listened for the sound of the coming of her husband, and so poignant was her grief that at break of day, William Graves, Jr., and two companions went again in search of Mr. Wolfinger. Five or six miles from camp, they came upon his tenantless wagon, with the oxen unhooked and feeding on the trail near-by. Nothing in the wagon had been disturbed, nor did they find any sign of struggle, or of Indians. After a diligent search for the missing man, his wagon and team was brought to camp and restored to Mrs. Wolfinger, and she was permitted to believe that her husband had been murdered by Indians and his body carried off. Nevertheless, some suspected Keseberg of having had a hand in his dis-

*Thornton.

appearance, as he knew that Mr. Wolfinger carried a large sum of money on his person.

Three days later Reinhart and Spitzer, who had not been missed, came into camp, and Mrs. Wolfinger was startled to recognize her husband's gun in their possession. They explained that they were in the wagon with Mr. Wolfinger when the Indians rushed upon them, drove them off, killed Wolfinger and burned the wagon. My father made a note of this conflicting statement to help future investigation of the case.

At Geyser Springs, the company cached valuable goods, among them several large cases of books and other heavy articles belonging to my father. As will be seen later, the load in our family wagon thus lightened through pity for our oxen, also lessened the severity of an accident which otherwise might have been fatal to Georgia and me.

On the nineteenth of October, near the present site of Wadsworth, Nevada, we met Mr. Stanton returning from Sutter's Fort with two Indian herders driving seven mules, laden with flour and jerked beef. Their arrival was hailed with great joy, and after a brief consultation with my father, Stanton and his Indians continued toward the rear, in order to distribute first to those most in need of provisions, also that the pack animals might be the sooner set apart to the use of those whose teams had given out, or had been destroyed by Indians.

Mr. Stanton had left Mr. McCutchen sick at Sutter's Fort. He brought information also concerning

MARCH OF THE CARAVAN

UNITED STATES TROOPS CROSSING THE DESERT

Messrs. Reed and Herron, whom he had met in the Sacramento valley. At the time of meeting, they were quite a distance from the settlement, had been without food three days, and Mr. Reed's horse was completely worn out. Mr. Stanton had furnished Mr. Reed with a fresh mount, and provisions enough to carry both men to Sutter's Fort.

In camp that night, Mr. Stanton outlined our course to the settlement, and in compliance with my father's earnest wish, consented to lead the train across the Sierra Nevada Mountains. Frost in the air and snow on the distant peaks warned us against delays; yet, notwithstanding the need of haste, we were obliged to rest our jaded teams. Three yoke of oxen had died from exhaustion within a week, and several of those remaining were not in condition to ascend the heavy grades before them.

On the twentieth, Mr. Pike met death in his own tent by the accidental discharge of a six-shooter in the hands of Mr. Foster, his brother-in-law. He left a young wife, and two small children, Naomi, three years of age, and Catherine, a babe in arms. His loss was keenly felt by the company, for he was highly esteemed.

We broke camp on the twenty-second, and my father and uncle took our wagons to the rear of the train in order to favor our cattle, and also to be near families whose teams might need help in getting up the mountains. That day we crossed the Truckee River for the forty-ninth and last time in eighty miles, and encamped for the night at the top of a high hill, where we received our last experience of Indian cruelty. The perpetrator was concealed behind a willow, and with savage vim and well trained hand, sent nineteen arrows whizzing through the air, and each arrow struck a different ox. Mr. Eddy caught him in the act; and as he turned to flee, the white man's rifle ball struck him between the shoulders and pierced his body. With a spring into the air and an agonizing shriek, he dropped lifeless into the bushes below. Strange, but true, not an ox was seriously hurt!

The train took the trail early next morning, expecting to cross the summit of the Sierras and reach California in less than two weeks.

The following circumstances, which parted us forever from the train which father had led through so many difficulties, were told me by my sister, Mrs. Elitha C. Wilder, now of Bruceville, California:

Our five Donner wagons, and Mrs. Wolfinger's wagon, were a day or more behind the train, and between twelve and sixteen miles from the spot where we later made our winter camp, when an accident happened which nearly cost us your life, and indirectly prevented our rejoining the train. Your mother and Frances were walking on ahead; you and Georgia were asleep in the wagon; and father was walking beside it, down a steep hill. It had almost reached the base of the incline when the axle to the fore wheels broke, and the wagon tipped over on the side, tumbling its contents upon you two children. Father and uncle, in great alarm, rushed to your rescue. Georgia was soon hauled out safely through the opening in the back of the wagon sheets, but you were nowhere in sight, and father was sure you were smothering because you did not answer his call. They worked breathlessly getting things out, and finally uncle came to your limp form. You could not have lasted much longer, they said. How thankful we all were that our heaviest boxes had been cached at Geyser Springs!

Much as we felt the shock, there was little time for self-indulgence. Never were moments of greater importance; for while father and uncle were hewing a new axle, two men came from the head of the company to tell about the snow. It was a terrible piece of news!

Those men reported that on the twenty-eighth of that month the larger part of the train had reached a deserted cabin near Truckee Lake (the sheet of water now known as Donner Lake) at the foot of Frémont's Pass in the main chain of the Sierra Nevada Mountains. The following morning they had proceeded to within three miles of the summit; but finding snow there five feet in depth, the trail obliterated, and no place for making camp, they were obliged to return to the spot they had left early in the day. There, they said, the company had assembled to discuss the next move, and great confusion prevailed as the excited members gave voice to their bitterest fears. Some proposed to abandon the wagons and make the oxen carry out the children and provisions; some wanted to take the children and rations and start out on foot; and some sat brooding in dazed silence through the long night.

The messengers further stated that on the thirtieth, with Stanton as leader, and despite the falling sleet and snow, the forward section of the party united in another desperate effort to cross the summit, but encountered deeper drifts and greater difficulties. As darkness crept over the whitened waste, wagons became separated and lodged in the snow; and all had to cling to the mountain-side until break of day, when the train again returned to its twice abandoned camp, having been compelled, however, to leave several of the wagons where they had become stalled. The report concluded with the statement that the men at once began log-cutting for cabins in which the company might have to pass the winter.

After the messengers left, and as father and Uncle Jacob were hastening preparations for our own departure, new troubles beset us. Uncle was giving the finishing touches to the axle, when the chisel he was using slipped from his grasp, and its keen edge struck and made a serious wound across the back of father's right hand which was steadying the timber. The crippled hand was carefully dressed, and to quiet uncle's fears and discomfort, father made light of the accident, declaring that they had weightier matters for consideration than cuts and bruises. The consequences of that accident, however, were far more wide-reaching than could have been anticipated.

Up and up we toiled until we reached an altitude of six thousand feet, and were within about ten miles of our companions at the lake, when the intense cold drove us into camp on Prosser Creek in Alder Creek Valley, a picturesque and sheltered nook two and a half miles in length and three-quarters of a mile in width. But no one observed the picturesque grandeur of the forest-covered mountains which hem it in on the north and west; nor that eastward and southward it looks out across plateaus to the Washoe Mountains twenty miles away.

A piercing wind was driving storm-clouds toward us, and those who understood their threatening aspect realized that twenty-one persons, eight of them helpless children, were there at the mercy of the pitiless storm-king.

The teams were hurriedly unhooked, the tents pitched, and the men and the women began collecting material for more suitable quarters. Some felled trees, some lopped off the branches, and some, with oxen, dragged the logs into position. There was enough building material on the ground for a good sized foundation four logs deep, when night stopped the work. The moon and stars came out before we went to bed, yet the following morning the ground was covered with snow two or three feet in depth, which had to be shovelled from the exposed beds before their occupants could rise.

I remember well that new day. All plans for log cabins had to be abandoned. There was no sheltered nook for shivering children, so father lifted Georgia and me on to a log, and mother tucked a buffalo robe around us, saying, " Sit here until we have a better place for you." There we sat snug and dry, chatting and twisting our heads about, watching the hurrying, anxious workers. Those not busy at the wagons were helping the builders to construct a permanent camp.

They cleared a space under a tall pine tree and re-set the tent a few feet south of its trunk, facing the sunrise. Then, following the Indian method as described by John Baptiste, a rude semi-circular hut of poles was added to the tent, the tree-trunk forming part of its north wall, and its needled boughs, the rafters and cross-pieces to the roof. The structure was overlaid so far as possible with pieces of cloth, old quilts, and buffalo robes, then with boughs and branches of pine and tamarack. A hollow was scooped in the ground near the tree for a fireplace, and an opening in the top served as chimney and ventilator. One opening led into the tent and another served as an outer door.

To keep the beds off the wet earth, two rows of short posts were driven along the sides in the tent, and poles were laid across the tops, thus forming racks to support the pine boughs upon which the beds should be made. While this was being done, Elitha, Leanna, and Mrs. Wolfinger were bringing poles and brush with which to strengthen and sheath the tent walls against wind and weather. Even Sister Frances looked tall and helpful as she trudged by with her little loads.

The combination of tent and hut was designed for my father and family and Mrs. Wolfinger. The teamsters, Samuel Shoemaker, Joseph Reinhart, James Smith, and John Baptiste, built their hut in Indian wigwam fashion. Not far from us, across the stream, braced against a log, was reared a mixed structure of brush and tent for use of Uncle Jacob, Aunt Betsy, and William and Solomon Hook (Aunt Betsy's sons by a former husband), and their five small children, George, Mary, Isaac, Lewis, and Samuel Donner.

Before we two could leave our perch, the snow was falling faster and in larger flakes. It made pictures for Georgia and me upon the branches of big and little trees; it gathered in a ridge beside us upon the log; it nestled in piles upon our buffalo robe; and by the time our quarters were finished, it was veiling Uncle Jacob's from view. Everything within was cold, damp, and dreary, until our tired mother and elder sisters built the fire, prepared our supper, and sent us to bed, each with a lump of loaf sugar as comforter.

CHAPTER VII

WHEN we awoke the following morning, little heaps of snow lay here and there upon the floor. No threshold could be seen, only a snow-bank reaching up to the white plain beyond, where every sound was muffled, and every object was blurred by falling flakes.

Father's face was very grave. His morning caress had all its wonted tenderness, but the merry twinkle was gone from his eye, and the gladsome note from his voice. For eight consecutive days, the fatal snow fell with but few short intermissions. Eight days, in which there was nothing to break the monotony of torturing, inactive endurance, except the necessity of gathering wood, keeping the fires, and cutting anew the steps which led upward, as the snow increased in depth. Hope well-nigh died within us.

All in camp fared alike, and all were on short rations. Three of our men became dispirited, said that they were too weak and hungry to gather wood, and did not care how soon death should put an end to their miseries.

The out-of-door duties would have fallen wholly

upon my Aunt Betsy's two sons and on John Baptiste and on my crippled father, had the women lost their fortitude. They, however, hid their fears from their children, even from each other, and helped to gather fuel, hunt cattle, and keep camp.

Axes were dull, green wood was hard to cut, and harder to carry, whether through loose, dry snow, or over crusts made slippery by sleet and frost. Cattle tracks were covered over. Some of the poor creatures had perished under bushes where they sought shelter. A few had become bewildered and strayed; others were found under trees in snow pits, which they themselves had made by walking round and round the trunks to keep from being snowed under. These starvelings were shot to end their sufferings, and also with the hope that their hides and fleshless bones might save the lives of our snow-beleaguered party. Every part of the animals was saved for food. The locations of the carcasses were marked so that they could be brought piece by piece into camp; and even the green hides were spread against the huts to serve in case of need.

After the storm broke, John Baptiste was sent with a letter from my mother to the camp near the lake. He was absent a number of days, for upon his arrival there, he found a party of fourteen ready to start next morning, on foot, across the summit. He joined it, but after two days of vain effort, the party returned to camp, and he came back to us with an answer to the letter he had delivered.

We then learned that most of those at the lake were better housed than we. Some in huts, and the rest in three log structures, which came to be known respectively as the Murphy, Graves, and Breen cabins. The last mentioned was the relic of earlier travellers * and had been grizzled by the storms of several winters. Yet, despite their better accommodations, our companions at the lake were harassed by fears like ours. They too were short of supplies. The game had left the mountains, and the fish in the lake would not bite.

Different parties, both with and without children, had repeatedly endeavored to force their way out of that wilderness of snow, but each in turn had become confused, and unconsciously moved in a circle back to camp. Several persons had become snow-blind. Every landmark was lost, even to Stanton, who had twice crossed the range.

All now looked to the coming of McCutchen and Reed for deliverance. We had every reason to expect them soon, for each had left his family with the company, and had promised to return with succor. Moreover, Stanton had brought tidings that the timely assistance of himself and comrade had enabled Reed to reach Sutter's Fort in safety; and that McCutchen would have accompanied him back, had he not been detained by illness.

Well, indeed, was it that we could not know that at the very time we were so anxiously awaiting their arrival, those two men, after struggling desperately

*Built by Townsend party in 1844. See McGlashan's "History of the Donner Party."

to cross the snows, were finally compelled to abandon the attempt, bury the precious food they had striven to bring us, and return to the settlement.

It was also well that we were unaware of their baffling fears, when the vigorous efforts incited by the memorial presented by Reed to Commodore Stockton, the military Governor of California, were likewise frustrated by mountain storms.

CHAPTER VIII

ANOTHER STORM — FOUR DEATHS IN DONNER CAMP — FIELD
MICE USED FOR FOOD — CHANGED APPEARANCE OF THE
STARVING — SUNSHINE — DEPARTURE OF THE " FORLORN
HOPE"—WATCHING FOR RELIEF — IMPOSSIBLE TO DIS-
TURB THE BODIES OF THE DEAD IN DONNER CAMP — AR-
RIVAL AND DEPARTURE OF THE FIRST RELIEF PARTY.

MEANWHILE with us in the Sierras, November
ended with four days and nights of continuous
snow, and December rushed in with a wild, shrieking
storm of wind, sleet, and rain, which ceased on the
third. The weather remained clear and cold until the
ninth, when Milton Elliot and Noah James came on
snowshoes to Donner's camp, from the lake cabins, to
ascertain if their captain was still alive, and to report
the condition of the rest of the company.

Before morning, another terrific storm came swirl-
ing and whistling down our snowy stairway, making
fires unsafe, freezing every drop of water about the
camp, and shutting us in from the light of heaven.
Ten days later Milton Elliot alone fought his way
back to the lake camp with these tidings: " Jacob
Donner, Samuel Shoemaker, Joseph Rhinehart, and

James Smith are dead, and the others in a low condition." *

Uncle Jacob, the first to die, was older than my father, and had been in miserable health for years before we left Illinois. He had gained surprisingly on the journey, yet quickly felt the influence of impending fate, foreshadowed by the first storm at camp. His courage failed. Complete prostration followed.

My father and mother watched with him during the last night, and the following afternoon helped to lay his body in a cave dug in the mountain side, beneath the snow. That snow had scarcely resettled when Samuel Shoemaker's life ebbed away in happy delirium. He imagined himself a boy again in his father's house and thought his mother had built a fire and set before him the food of which he was fondest.

But when Joseph Rhinehart's end drew near, his mind wandered, and his whitening lips confessed a part in Mr. Wolfinger's death; and my father, listening, knew not how to comfort that troubled soul. He could not judge whether the self-condemning words were the promptings of a guilty conscience, or the ravings of an unbalanced mind.

Like a tired child falling asleep, was James Smith's death; and Milton Elliot, who helped to bury the four victims and then carried the distressing report to the lake camp, little knew that he would soon be among those later called to render a final accounting. Yet it was even so.

*Patrick Breen's Diary.

Our camp having been thus depleted by death, Noah James, who had been one of my father's drivers, from Springfield until we passed out of the desert, now cast his lot again with ours, and helped John Baptiste to dig for the carcasses of the cattle. It was weary work, for the snow was higher than the level of the guide marks, and at times they searched day after day and found no trace of hoof or horn. The little field mice that had crept into camp were caught then and used to ease the pangs of hunger. Also pieces of beef hide were cut into strips, singed, scraped, boiled to the consistency of glue, and swallowed with an effort; for no degree of hunger could make the saltless, sticky substance palatable. Marrowless bones which had already been boiled and scraped, were now burned and eaten, even the bark and twigs of pine were chewed in the vain effort to soothe the gnawings which made one cry for bread and meat.

During the bitterest weather we little ones were kept in bed, and my place was always in the middle where Frances and Georgia, snuggling up close, gave me of their warmth, and from them I learned many things which I could neither have understood nor remembered had they not made them plain.

Just one happy play is impressed upon my mind. It must have been after the first storm, for the snow bank in front of the cabin door was not high enough to keep out a little sunbeam that stole down the steps and made a bright spot upon our floor. I saw it, and sat down under it, held it on my lap, passed my hand

PASS IN THE SIERRA NEVADAS OF CALIFORNIA

From an old drawing made from description furnished by Wm. G. Murphy.

CAMP AT DONNER LAKE, NOVEMBER, 1846

up and down in its brightness, and found that I could break its ray in two. In fact, we had quite a frolic. I fancied that it moved when I did, for it warmed the top of my head, kissed first one cheek and then the other, and seemed to run up and down my arm. Finally I gathered up a piece of it in my apron and ran to my mother. Great was my surprise when I carefully opened the folds and found that I had nothing to show, and the sunbeam I had left seemed shorter. After mother explained its nature, I watched it creep back slowly up the steps and disappear.

Snowy Christmas brought us no "glad tidings," and New Year's Day no happiness. Yet, each bright day that followed a storm was one of thanksgiving, on which we all crept up the flight of snow steps and huddled about on the surface in the blessed sunshine, but with our eyes closed against its painful and blinding glare.

Once my mother took me to a hole where I saw smoke coming up, and she told me that its steps led down to Uncle Jacob's tent, and that we would go down there to see Aunt Betsy and my little cousins.

I stooped low and peered into the dark depths. Then I called to my cousins to come to me, because I was afraid to go where they were. I had not seen them since the day we encamped. At that time they were chubby and playful, carrying water from the creek to their tent in small tin pails. Now, they were so changed in looks that I scarcely knew them, and they stared at me as at a stranger. So I was glad when my mother came up and took me back to our own tent, which seemed less dreary because I knew the things that were in it, and the faces about me.

Father's hand became worse. The swelling and inflammation extending up the arm to the shoulder produced suffering which he could not conceal. Each day that we had a fire, I watched mother sitting by his side, with a basin of warm water upon her lap, laving the wounded and inflamed parts very tenderly, with a strip of frayed linen wrapped around a little stick. I remember well the look of comfort that swept over his worn features as she laid the soothed arm back into place.

By the middle of January the snow measured twelve and fourteen feet in depth. Nothing could be seen of our abode except the coils of smoke that found their way up through the opening. There was a dearth of water. Prosser Creek was frozen over and covered with snow. Icicles hung from the branches of every tree. The stock of pine cones that had been gathered for lights was almost consumed. Wood was so scarce that we could not have fire enough to cook our strips of rawhide, and Georgia heard mother say that we children had not had a dry garment on in more than a week, and that she did not know what to do about it. Then like a smile from God, came another sunny day which not only warmed and dried us thoroughly but furnished a supply of water from dripping snowbanks.

The twenty-first was also bright, and John Baptiste went on snowshoes with messages to the lake camp.

He found its inmates in a more pitiable condition than we were. Only one death had occurred there since our last communication, but he saw several of the starving who could not survive many days.

The number to consume the slender stock of food had been lessened, however, on the sixteenth of December, some six weeks previously, by the departure of William Eddy, Patrick Dolan, Lemuel Murphy, William Foster, Mrs. Sarah Foster, Jay Fosdick, Mrs. Sarah Fosdick, Mrs. William McCutchen, Mrs. Harriet Pike, Miss Mary Graves, Franklin Graves, Sr., C. T. Stanton, Antonio, Lewis, and Salvador.

This party, which called itself "The Forlorn Hope," had a most memorable experience, as will be shown later. In some instances husband had parted from wife, and father from children. Three young mothers had left their babes in the arms of grandmothers. It was a dire resort, a last desperate attempt, in face of death, to save those dependent upon them.

Staff in hand, they had set forth on snowshoes, each carrying a pack containing little save a quilt and light rations for six days' journeying. One had a rifle, ammunition, flint, and hatchet for camp use. William Murphy and Charles Burger, who had originally been of the number, gave out before the close of the first day, and crept back to camp. The others continued under the leadership of the intrepid Eddy and brave Stanton.

John Baptiste remained there a short time and returned to us, saying, " Those at the other camp believe the promised relief is close at hand! "

This rekindled hope in us, even as it had revived courage and prolonged lives in the lake cabins, and we prayed, as they were praying, that the relief might come before its coming should be too late.

Oh, how we watched, hour after hour, and how often each day John Baptiste climbed to the topmost bough of a tall pine tree and, with straining eyes, scanned the desolate expanse for one moving speck in the distance, for one ruffled track on the snow which should ease our awful suspense.

Days passed. No food in camp except an unsavory beef hide — pinching hunger called for more. Again John Baptiste and Noah James went forth in anxious search for marks of our buried cattle. They made excavations, then forced their hand-poles deep, deeper into the snow, but in vain their efforts — the nail and hook at the points brought up no sign of blood, hair, or hide. In dread unspeakable they returned, and said:

" We shall go mad; we shall die! It is useless to hunt for the cattle; but the *dead,* if they could be reached, their bodies might keep us alive."

" No," replied father and mother, speaking for themselves. " No, part of a hide still remains. When it is gone we will perish, if that be the alternative."

The fact was, our dead could not have been disturbed even had the attempt been made, for the many snowfalls of winter were banked about them firm as granite walls, and in that camp was neither implement nor arm strong enough to reach their resting-places.

It was a long, weary waiting, on starvation rations until the nineteenth of February. I did not see any one coming that morning; but I remember that, suddenly, there was an unusual stir and excitement in the camp. Three strangers were there, and one was talking with father. The others took packs from their backs and measured out small quantities of flour and jerked beef and two small biscuits for each of us. Then they went up to fell the sheltering pine tree over our tent for fuel; while Noah James, Mrs. Wolfinger, my two half-sisters, and mother kept moving about hunting for things.

Finally Elitha and Leanna came and kissed me, then father, " good-bye," and went up the steps, and out of sight. Mother stood on the snow where she could see all go forth. They moved in single file,— the leaders on snowshoes, the weak stepping in the tracks made by the strong. Leanna, the last in line, was scarcely able to keep up. It was not until after mother came back with Frances and Georgia that I was made to understand that this was the long-hoped-for relief party.

It had come and gone, and had taken Noah James, Mrs. Wolfinger, and my two half-sisters from us; then had stopped at Aunt Betsy's for William Hook, her eldest son, and my Cousin George, and all were now on the way to the lake cabins to join others who were able to walk over the snow without assistance.

The rescuers, seven in number, who had followed instructions given them at the settlement, professed to have no knowledge of the Forlorn Hope, except that this first relief expedition had been outfitted by Captain Sutter and Alcalde Sinclair in response to Mr. Eddy's appeal, and that other rescue parties were being organized in California, and would soon come prepared to carry out the remaining children and helpless grown folk. By this we knew that Mr. Eddy, at least, had succeeded in reaching the settlement.

CHAPTER IX

SUFFERINGS OF THE "FORLORN HOPE"— RESORT TO
HUMAN FLESH —"CAMP OF DEATH"— BOOTS CRISPED
AND EATEN — DEER KILLED — INDIAN *Rancheria* — THE
"WHITE MAN'S HOME" AT LAST.

ALTHOUGH we were so meagrely informed, it is
well that my readers should, at this point, become familiar with the experiences of the expedition
known as the Forlorn Hope,* and also the various
measures taken for our relief when our precarious
condition was made known to the good people of California. It will be remembered that the Forlorn Hope
was the party of fifteen which, as John Baptiste reported to us, made the last unaided attempt to cross
the mountains.

Words cannot picture, nor mind conceive, more torturing hardships and privations than were endured by
that little band on its way to the settlement. It left
the camp on the sixteenth of December, with scant rations for six days, hoping in that time to force its way
to Bear Valley and there find game. But the storms

*The experiences of the Donner Party, to which he refers in a foot-
note, suggested to Bret Harte the opening chapters of "Gabriel Con-
roy"; but he has followed the sensational accounts circulated by
the newspapers, and the survivors find his work a mere travesty of the
facts. The narrative, however, does not purport to set forth the truth,
but is confessedly imaginative.

which had been so pitiless at the mountain camps followed the unprotected refugees with seemingly fiendish fury. After the first day from camp, its members could no longer keep together on their marches. The stronger broke the trail, and the rest followed to night-camp as best they could.

On the third day, Stanton's sight failed, and he begged piteously to be led; but, soon realizing the heart-rending plight of his companions, he uncomplainingly submitted to his fate. Three successive nights, he staggered into camp long after the others had finished their stinted meal. Always he was shivering from cold, sometimes wet with sleet and rain.

It is recorded that at no time had the party allowed more than an ounce of food per meal to the individual, yet the rations gave out on the night of the twenty-second, while they were still in a wilderness of snow-peaks. Mr. Eddy only was better provided. In looking over his pack that morning for the purpose of throwing away any useless article, he unexpectedly found a small bag containing about a half-pound of dried bear-meat.* Fastened to the meat was a pen-cilled note from his wife, begging him to save the hidden treasure until his hour of direst need, since it might then be the means of saving his life. The note was signed, " Your own dear Elinor." With tender-est emotion, he slipped the food back, resolving to do the dear one's bidding, trusting that she and their children might live until he should return for them.

*Mr. Eddy had killed the bear and dried the meat early in the winter.

BEAR VALLEY, FROM EMIGRANT GAP

THE TRACKLESS MOUNTAINS

SEPARATION AND HUNGER

The following morning, while the others were preparing to leave camp, Stanton sat beside the smouldering fire smoking his pipe. When ready to go forth, they asked him if he was coming, and he replied, " Yes, I am coming soon." Those were his parting words to his friends, and his greeting to the Angel of Death.* He never left that fireside, and his companions were too feeble to return for him when they found he did not come into camp.

Twenty-four hours later, the members of that hapless little band threw themselves upon the desolate waste of snow to ponder the problems of life and death; to search each the other's face for answer to the question their lips durst not frame. Fathers who had left their families, and mothers who had left their babes, wanted to go back and die with them, if die they must; but Mr. Eddy and the Indians — those who had crossed the range with Stanton — declared that they would push on to the settlement. Then Mary Graves, in whose young heart were still whisperings of hope, courageously said:

" I, too, will go on, for to go back and hear the cries of hunger from my little brothers and sisters is more than I can stand. I shall go as far as I can, let the consequences be what they may."

W. F. Graves, her father, would not let his daughter proceed alone, and finally all decided to make a final, supreme effort. Yet — think of it — they were without one morsel of food!

*His body was found there later by the First Relief Party.

Even the wind seemed to hold its breath as the suggestion was made that, "were one to die, the rest might live." Then the suggestion was made that lots be cast, and whoever drew the longest slip should be the sacrifice. Mr. Eddy endorsed the plan. Despite opposition from Mr. Foster and others, the slips of paper were prepared, and great-hearted Patrick Dolan drew the fatal slip. Patrick Dolan, who had come away from camp that his famishing friends might prolong their lives by means of the small stock of food which he had to leave! Harm a hair of that good man's head? Not a soul of that starving band would do it.

Mr. Eddy then proposed that they resume their journey as best they could until death should claim a victim. All acquiesced. Slowly rising to their feet, they managed to stagger and to crawl forward about three miles to a tree which furnished fuel for their Christmas fire. It was kindled with great difficulty, for in cutting the boughs, the hatchet blade flew off the handle and for a time was lost in deep snow.

Meanwhile, every puff of wind was laden with killing frost, and in sight of that glowing fire, Antonio froze to death. Mr. Graves, who was also breathing heavily, when told by Mr. Eddy that he was dying, replied that he did not care. He, however, called his daughters, Mrs. Fosdick and Mary Graves, to him, and by his parting injunctions, showed that he was still able to realize keenly the dangers that beset them. Remembering how their faces had paled at the suggestion of using human flesh for food, he admonished them to put aside the natural repugnance which stood between them and the possibility of life. He commanded them to banish sentiment and instinctive loathing, and think only of their starving mother, brothers, and sisters whom they had left in camp, and avail themselves of every means in their power to rescue them. He begged that his body be used to sustain the famishing, and bidding each farewell, his spirit left its bruised and worn tenement before half the troubles of the night were passed.

About ten o'clock, pelting hail, followed by snow on the wings of a tornado, swept every spark of fire from those shivering mortals, whose voices now mingled with the shrieking wind, calling to heaven for relief. Mr. Eddy, knowing that all would freeze to death in the darkness if allowed to remain exposed, succeeded after many efforts in getting them close together between their blankets where the snow covered them.

With the early morning, Patrick Dolan became delirious and left camp. He was brought back with difficulty and forcibly kept under cover until late in the day, when he sank into a stupor, whence he passed quietly into that sleep which knows no waking.

The crucial hour had come. Food lay before the starving, yet every eye turned from it and every hand dropped irresolute.

Another night of agony passed, during which Lemuel Murphy became delirious and called long and loud for food; but the cold was so intense that it kept all under their blankets until four o'clock in the afternoon, when Mr. Eddy succeeded in getting a fire in the trunk of a large pine tree. Whereupon, his companions, instead of seeking food, crept forth and broke off low branches, put them down before the fire and laid their attenuated forms upon them. The flames leaped up the trunk, and burned off dead boughs so that they dropped on the snow about them, but the unfortunates were too weak and too indifferent to fear the burning brands.

Mr. Eddy now fed his waning strength on shreds of his concealed bear meat, hoping that he might survive to save the giver. The rest in camp could scarcely walk, by the twenty-eighth, and their sensations of hunger were deminishing. This condition forebode delirium and death, unless stayed by the only means at hand. It was in very truth a pitiful alternative offered to the sufferers.

With sickening anguish the first morsels were prepared and given to Lemuel Murphy, but for him they were too late. Not one touched flesh of kindred body. Nor was there need of restraining hand, or warning voice to gauge the small quantity which safety prescribed to break the fast of the starving. Death would have been preferable to that awful meal, had relentless fate not said: " Take, eat that ye may live. Eat, lest ye go mad and leave your work undone! "

All but the Indians obeyed the mandate, and were strengthened and reconciled to prepare the remaining flesh to sustain them a few days longer on their journey.

Hitherto, the wanderers had been guided partly by the fitful sun, partly by Lewis and Salvador, the Indians who had come with Stanton from Sutter's Fort. In the morning, however, when they were ready to leave that spot, which was thereafter known as the " Camp of Death," Salvador, who could speak a little English, insisted that he and Lewis were lost, and, therefore, unable to guide them farther.

Nevertheless, the party at once set out and travelled instinctively until evening. The following morning they wrapped pieces of blanket around their cracked and swollen feet and again struggled onward until late in the afternoon, when they encamped upon a high ridge. There they saw beyond, in the distance, a wide plain which they believed to be the Sacramento Valley.

This imaginary glimpse of distant lowland gave them a peaceful sleep. The entire day of December 31 was spent in crossing a cañon, and every footstep left its trace of blood in the snow.

When they next encamped, Mr. Eddy saw that poor Jay Fosdick was failing, and he begged him to summon up all his courage and energy in order to reach the promised land, now so near. They were again without food; and William Foster, whose mind had become unbalanced by the long fast, was ready to kill Mrs. McCutchen or Miss Graves. Mr. Eddy confronted and intimidated the crazed sufferer, who next threatened the Indian guides, and would have carried out his threat then, had Mr. Eddy not secretly warned them against danger and urged them to flee. But nothing could save the Indians from Foster's insane passion later, when he found them on the trail in an unconscious and dying condition.

January 1, 1847, was, to the little band of eight, a day of less distressing trials; its members resumed travel early, braced by unswerving will-power. They stopped at midday and revived strength by eating the toasted strings of their snowshoes. Mr. Eddy also ate his worn out moccasins, and all felt a renewal of hope upon seeing before them an easier grade which led to night-camp where the snow was only six feet in depth. Soothed by a milder temperature, they resumed their march earlier next morning and descended to where the snow was but three feet deep. There they built their camp-fire and slightly crisped the leather of a pair of old boots and a pair of shoes which constituted their evening meal, and was the last of their effects available as food.

An extraordinary effort on the third day of the new year brought them to bare ground between patches of snow. They were still astray among the western foot-hills of the Sierras, and sat by a fire under an oak tree all night, enduring hunger that was almost maddening.

Jay Fosdick was sinking rapidly, and Mr. Eddy resolved to take the gun and steal away from camp at dawn. But his conscience smote him, and he finally gave the others a hint of his intention of going in search of game, and of not returning unless successful. Not a moving creature nor a creeping thing had crossed the trail on their journey thither; but the open country before them, and minor marks well known to hunters, had caught Mr. Eddy's eye and strengthened his determination. Mrs. Pike, in dread and fear of the result, threw her arms about Mr. Eddy's neck and implored him not to leave them, and the others mingled their entreaties and protestations with hers. In silence he took his gun to go alone. Then Mary Graves declared that she would keep up with him, and without heeding further opposition the two set out. A short distance from camp they stopped at a place where a deer had recently lain.

With a thrill of emotion too intense for words, with a prayer in his heart too fervent for utterance, Mr. Eddy turned his tearful eyes toward Mary and saw her weeping like a child. A moment later, that man and that woman who had once said that they knew not how to pray, were kneeling beside that newly found track pleading in broken accents to the Giver of all life, for a manifestation of His power to save their starving band. Long restrained tears were still streaming down the cheeks of both, and soothing their anxious hearts as they arose to go in pursuit of the deer. J. Q. Thornton says:

They had not proceeded far before they saw a large buck about eighty yards distant. Mr. Eddy raised his rifle and for some time tried to bring it to bear upon the deer, but such was his extreme weakness that he could not. He breathed a little, changed his manner of holding the gun, and made another effort. Again his weakness prevented him from being able to hold upon it. He heard a low, suppressed sobbing behind him, and, turning around, saw Mary Graves weeping and in great agitation, her head bowed, and her hands upon her face. Alarmed lest she should cause the deer to run, Mr. Eddy begged her to be quiet, which she was, after exclaiming, "Oh, I am afraid you will not kill it."

He brought the gun to his face the third time, and elevated the muzzle above the deer, let it descend until he saw the animal through the sight, when the rifle cracked. Mary immediately wept aloud, exclaiming, "Oh, merciful God, you have missed it!" Mr. Eddy assured her that he had not; that the rifle was upon it the moment of firing; and that, in addition to this, the animal had dropped its tail between its legs, which this animal always does when wounded.

His belief was speedily confirmed. The deer ran a short distance, then fell, and the two eager watchers hastened to it as fast as their weakened condition would allow. Mr. Eddy cut the throat of the expiring beast with his pocket-knife, and he and his companion knelt down and drank the warm blood that flowed from the wound.

The excitement of getting that blessed food, and the strength it imparted, produced a helpful reaction, and enabled them to sit down in peace to rest a while, before attempting to roll their treasure to the tree near-by, where they built a fire and prepared the entrails.

Mr. Eddy fired several shots after dark, so that the others might know that he had not abandoned them. Meanwhile, Mr. and Mrs. Foster, Mrs. McCutchen, and Mrs. Pike had moved forward and made their camp half-way between Mr. Eddy's new one and that of the previous night. Mr. Fosdick, however, being too weak to rise, remained at the first camp. His devoted wife pillowed his head upon her lap, and prayed that death would call them away together. Mr. Thornton continues:

The sufferer had heard the crack of Mr. Eddy's rifle at the time he killed the deer, and said, feebly, " There! Eddy has killed a deer! Now, if I can only get to him I shall live! "

But in the stillness of that cold, dark night, Jay Fosdick's spirit fled alone. His wife wrapped their only blanket about his body, and lay down on the ground beside him, hoping to freeze to death. The morning dawned bright, the sun came out, and the lone widow rose, kissed the face of her dead, and, with a small bundle in her hand, started to join Mr. Eddy. She passed a hunger-crazed man on the way from the middle camp, going to hers, and her heart grew sick, for she knew that her loved one's body would not be spared for burial rites.

She found Mr. Eddy drying his deer meat before the fire, and later saw him divide it so that each of his companions in the camps should have an equal share.

The seven survivors, each with his portion of venison, resumed travel on the sixth and continued in the foothills a number of days, crawling up the ascents, sliding down the steeps; often harassed by fears of becoming lost near the goal, yet unaware that they were astray.

The venison had been consumed. Hope had almost died in the heart of the bravest, when at the close of day on the tenth of January, twenty-five days from the date of leaving Donner Lake, they saw an Indian village at the edge of a thicket they were approaching. As the sufferers staggered forward, the Indians were overwhelmed at sight of their misery. The warriors gazed in stolid silence. The squaws wrung their hands and wept aloud. The larger children hid themselves, and the little ones clung to their mothers in fear. The first sense of horror having passed, those dusky mothers fed the unfortunates. Some brought them unground acorns to eat, while others mixed the meal into cakes and offered them as fast as they could cook them on the heated stones. All except Mr. Eddy were strengthened by the food. It sickened him, and he resorted to green grass boiled in water.

The following morning the chief sent his runners to other *rancherias, en route* to the settlement, telling his people of the distress of the pale-faces who were coming toward them, and who would need food. When the Forlorn Hope was ready to move on, the chief led the way, and an Indian walked on either side of each sufferer supporting and helping the unsteady feet. At each *rancheria* the party was put in charge of a new leader and fresh supporters.

On the seventeenth, the chief with much difficulty procured, for Mr. Eddy, a gill of pine nuts which the latter found so nutritious that the following morning, on resuming travel, he was able to walk without support. They had proceeded less than a mile when his companions sank to the ground completely unnerved. They had suddenly given up and were willing to die.

DESPERATE STRUGGLE FOR LIFE

The Indians appeared greatly perplexed, and Mr. Eddy shook with sickening fear. Was his great effort to come to naught? Should his wife and babes die while he stood guard over those who would no longer help themselves? No, he would push ahead and see what he yet could do!

The old chief sent an Indian with him as a guide and support. Relieved of the sight and personal responsibility of his enfeebled companions, Mr. Eddy felt a renewal of strength and determination. He pressed onward, scarcely heeding his dusky guide. At the end of five miles they met another Indian, and Mr. Eddy, now conscious that his feet were giving out, promised the stranger tobacco, if he would go with them and help to lead him to the "white man's house."

And so that long, desperate struggle for life, and for the sake of loved ones, ended an hour before sunset, when Mr. Eddy, leaning heavily upon the Indians, halted before the door of Colonel M. D. Richey's home, thirty-five miles from Sutter's Fort.

The first to meet him was the daughter of the house, whom he asked for bread. Thornton says:

She looked at him, burst out crying, and took hold of him to assist him into the room. He was immediately placed in bed, in which he lay unable to turn his body during four days. In a very short time he had food brought to him by Mrs. Richey, who sobbed as she fed the miserable and frightful being before her. Shortly, Harriet, the daughter, had carried the news from house to house in the neighborhood, and horses were running at full speed from place to place until all preparations were made for taking relief to those whom Mr. Eddy had left in the morning.

William Johnson, John Howell, John Rhodes, Mr. Keiser, Mr. Sagur, Racine Tucker, and Joseph Varro assembled at Mr. Richey's immediately. The females collected the bread they had, with tea, sugar, and coffee, amounting to as much as four men could carry. Howell, Rhodes, Sagur, and Tucker started at once, on foot, with the Indians as guides, and arrived at camp, between fifteen and eighteen miles distant, at midnight.

Mr. Eddy had warned the outgoing party against giving the sufferers as much food as they might want, but, on seeing them, the tender-hearted men could not deny their tearful begging for "more." One of the relief was kept busy until dawn preparing food which the rest gave to the enfeebled emigrants. This overdose of kindness made its victims temporarily very ill, but caused no lasting harm.

Early on the morning of January 18, Messrs. Richey, Johnson, Varro, and Keiser, equipped with horses and other necessaries, hurried away to bring in the refugees, together with their comrades who had gone on before. By ten o'clock that night the whole of the Forlorn Hope were safe in the homes of their benefactors. Mr. Richey declared that he and his party had retraced Mr. Eddy's track six miles, by the blood from his feet; and that they could not have believed that he had travelled that eighteen miles, if they themselves had not passed over the ground in going to his discouraged companions.

CHAPTER X

RELIEF MEASURES INAUGURATED IN CALIFORNIA — DIS-
TURBED CONDITIONS BECAUSE OF MEXICAN WAR — GEN-
EROUS SUBSCRIPTIONS — THREE PARTIES ORGANIZE —
" FIRST RELIEF," UNDER RACINE TUCKER; " SECOND RE-
LIEF," UNDER REED AND GREENWOOD; AND RELAY CAMP
UNDER WOODWORTH—FIRST RELIEF PARTY CROSSES SNOW-
BELT AND REACHES DONNER LAKE.

THE kindness and sympathy shown Mr. Eddy by the good people in the neighborhood of the Richey and Johnson ranches encouraged his efforts in behalf of his fellow-sufferers in the mountains. While the early sunlight of January 19 was flooding his room with cheer and warmth, he dictated a letter to Mr. John Sinclair, Alcalde of the Upper District of California, living near Sutter's Fort, in which he stated as briefly as possible the conditions and perils surrounding the snow-bound travellers, and begged him to use every means in his power toward their immediate rescue.

Bear River was running high, and the plain between it and Sutter's Fort seemed a vast quagmire, but John Rhodes volunteered to deliver the letter. He was ferried over the river on a raft formed of two logs lashed together with strips of rawhide. Then he rolled his trousers above the knee and with his shoes in his hand, started on his mission. He saw no white faces until he reached Sinclair's, where the letter created a painful interest and won ready promises of help.

It was dark when he reached Sutter's Fort, nevertheless from house to house he spread the startling report: "Men, women, and little children are snowbound in the Sierras, and starving to death!"

Captain Kerns in charge at the Fort, pledged his aid, and influence to the cause of relief. Captain Sutter, who had already twice sent supplies, first by Stanton and again by McCutchen and Reed, in their unsuccessful attempt to cross the mountains, at once agreed to coöperate with Alcalde Sinclair.

While Captain Kerns at Sutter's Fort was sending messengers to different points, and Mrs. Sinclair was collecting clothing to replace the tattered garments of the members of the Forlorn Hope, her husband despatched an open letter to the people of San Francisco, describing the arrival of the survivors of the Forlorn Hope, and the heart-rending condition of those remaining in the mountains. He urged immediate action, and offered his services for individual work, or to coöperate with Government relief, or any parties that might be preparing to go out with Messrs. Reed and McCutchen, who were known to be endeavoring to raise a second expedition.

The letter was taken to the City Hotel in San Francisco, and read aloud in the dining-room. Its contents

SUTTER'S FORT

SAM BRANNAN'S STORE AT SUTTER'S FORT

aroused all the tender emotions known to human nature. Some of the listeners had parted from members of the Donner Party at the Little Sandy, when its prospects appeared so bright, and the misfortunes which had since befallen the party seemed incredible. Women left the room sobbing, and men called those passing, in from the street, to join the knots of earnest talkers. All were ready and willing to do; but, alas, the obstacles which had prevented Mr. Reed getting men for the mountain work still remained to be overcome.

Existing war between Mexico and the United States was keeping California in a disturbed condition. Most of the able-bodied male emigrants had enlisted under Captain Frémont as soon as they reached the country, and were still on duty in the southern part of the province; and the non-enlisted were deemed necessary for the protection of the colonies of American women and children encamped on the soil of the enemy. Moreover, all felt that each man who should attempt to cross the snow belt would do so at the peril of his life.

Mr. Reed, who in the late Autumn had sent petitions to the Military Governor and to Lieutenant Washington A. Bartlett of the United States Navy, Alcalde of the town and district of San Francisco, but as yet had obtained nothing, now appeared before each in person, and was promised assistance. Captain Mervine of the United States Navy, and Mr. Richardson, United States Collector, each subscribed fifty dollars to the cause on his own account.

As a result of these appeals, Alcalde Bartlett called a public meeting; and so intense was the feeling that Mr. Dunleary, "the first speaker, had scarcely taken his seat on the platform, when the people rushed to the chairman's table from all parts of the house with their hands full of silver dollars," and could hardly be induced to stay their generosity until the meeting was organized.

A treasurer and two committees were appointed; the one to solicit subscriptions, and the other to purchase supplies. The Alcalde was requested to act with both committees. Seven hundred dollars was subscribed before the meeting adjourned. Seven hundred dollars, in an isolated Spanish province, among newly arrived immigrants, was a princely sum to gather.

Messrs. Ward and Smith, in addition to a generous subscription, offered their launch *Dice mi Nana,* to transport the expedition to Feather River, and Mr. John Fuller volunteered to pilot the launch.

It was decided to fit out an expedition, under charge of Past Midshipman Woodworth, who had tendered his services for the purpose, he to act under instructions of the Military Governor and coöperate with the committee aiding Reed.

Soon thereafter "Old Trapper Greenwood" appeared in San Francisco, asking for assistance in fitting out a following to go to the mountains with himself and McCutchen, Mr. George Yount and others in and around Sonoma and Napa having recommended him as leader. Donations of horses, mules, beef, and flour had already been sent to his camp in Napa Valley. Furthermore, Lieut. William L. Maury, U. S. N., Commander at the port; Don Mariano G. Vallejo, Ex-Commandante-General of California; Mr. George Yount, and others subscribed the sum of five hundred dollars in specie toward outfitting Greenwood and the men he should select to cross the mountains.

Greenwood urged that he should have ten or twelve men on whom he could rely after reaching deep snow. These, he said, he could secure if he had the ready money to make advances and to procure the necessary warm clothing and blankets. He had crossed the Sierras before, when the snow lay deep on the summit, and now proposed to drive over horses and kill them at the camps as provisions for the sufferers. If this scheme should fail, he and his sons with others would get food to the camp on snowshoes. Thornton says:

The Governor-General of California, after due form, and trusting to the generosity and humanity of the Government which he represented, appropriated four hundred dollars on Government account toward outfitting this relief party. Furthermore, in compliance with an application from Alcalde Bartlett (for the committee), Captain Mervine, of the U. S. frigate *Savannah*, furnished from the ship's stores ten days' full rations for ten men. The crews of the *Savannah* and the sloop *Warren*, and the marines in garrison at San Francisco, increased the relief fund to thirteen hundred dollars. Messrs. Mellus and Howard tendered their launch to carry the party up the bay to Sonoma, and Captain Sutter proffered his launch *Sacramento* for river use.

It was now settled that the " Reed-Greenwood party " should go to Johnson's ranch by way of Sonoma and Napa, and Woodworth with his men and supplies, including clothing for the destitute, should go by boat to Sutter's Landing; there procure pack animals, buy beef cattle, and hurry on to the snow-belt; establish a relay camp, slaughter the cattle, and render all possible aid toward the immediate rescue of the snow-bound.

Meanwhile, before Alcalde Sinclair's letter had time to reach San Francisco, he and Captain Sutter began outfitting the men destined to become the "First Relief." Aguilla Glover and R. S. Moutrey volunteered their services, declaring their willingness to undertake the hazardous journey for the sake of the lives they might save.

To hasten recruits for service, Captain Sutter and Alcalde Sinclair promised that in case the Government should fail to grant the sum, they themselves would become responsible for the payment of three dollars per day to each man who would get food through to the snow-bound camps. Accordingly, Aguilla Glover and R. S. Moutrey, driving pack animals well laden with warm clothing, blankets, and food supplies, left the Fort at sunrise on the morning of February the first, and on the third reached Johnson's ranch, where they joined Messrs. Tucker, Johnson, Richey and others, who, being anxious to assist in the good work, had killed, and were fire-drying, beef to take up the mountains. Here two days were spent making pack-saddles, driving in horses, and getting supplies in shape. Indians were kept at the handmill grinding wheat. Part of the flour was sacked, and part converted into bread by the women in the vicinity.

On the morning of the fifth of February, Alcalde

" THE FIRST RELIEF PARTY "

Sinclair rode to Johnson's ranch, and all things being ready, he appointed Racine Tucker Captain of the company, and in touching words commended the heroic work of its members, and bade them godspeed on their errand of mercy. When ready to mount, he shook hands with each man, and recorded the names in a note-book as follows:

Racine Tucker, Aguilla Glover, R. S. Moutrey, John Rhodes, Daniel Rhodes, Edward Coffemeir, D. Richey, James Curtis, William Eddy,* William Coon, George Tucker, Adolph Brenheim, and John Foster.*

This party is generally known as the " First Relief." Their route to the snow-belt lay through sections of country which had become so soft and oozy that the horses often sank in mire, flank deep; and the streams were so swollen that progress was alarmingly slow. On the second day they were driven into camp early by heavy rains which drenched clothing, blankets, and even the provisions carefully stored under the saddles and leather saddle-covers. This caused a delay of thirty-six hours, for everything had to be sun or fire dried before the party could resume travel.

Upon reaching Mule Springs, the party found the snow from three to four feet deep, and, contrary to expectations, saw that it would be impossible to proceed farther with the horses. Mr. Eddy was now ill of fever, and unfit to continue the climb; whereupon his companions promised to bring out his loved ones if he would return with Joe Varro, whom Mr. Johnson

*Of the Forlorn Hope.

had sent along to bring the pack animals home after they should cease to be of use.

At Mule Springs, the party built a brush storehouse for the extra supplies and appointed George Tucker and William Coon camp-keepers. Then they prepared packs containing jerked beef, flour, and bread, each weighing between forty and seventy-five pounds, according to the temperament and strength of the respective carriers. The following morning ten men started on their toilsome march to Bear Valley, where they arrived on the thirteenth, and at once began searching for the abandoned wagon and provisions which Reed and McCutchen had cached the previous Autumn, after their fruitless attempt to scale the mountains. The wagon was found under snow ten feet in depth; but its supplies had been destroyed by wild beasts. Warned by this catastrophe, the First Relief decided to preserve its supplies for the return trip by hanging them in parcels from ropes tied to the boughs of trees.

The ten kept together courageously until the fifteenth; then Mr. M. D. Richey, James Curtis, and Adolph Brenheim gave up and turned back. Mr. Tucker, fearing that others might become disheartened and do likewise, guaranteed each man who would persevere to the end, five dollars per diem, dating from the time the party entered the snow. The remaining seven pushed ahead, and on the eighteenth, encamped on the summit overlooking the lake, where the snow was said to be forty feet in depth.

AFFECTED BY ALTITUDE

The following morning Aguilla Glover and Daniel Rhodes were so oppressed by the altitude that their companions had to relieve them of their packs and help them on to the cabins, which, as chronicled in a previous chapter, the party reached on the nineteenth of February, 1847.

CHAPTER XI

WATCHING FOR THE SECOND RELIEF PARTY — "OLD NAV-
AJO" — LAST FOOD IN CAMP.

AFTER the departure of the First Relief we who
were left in the mountains began to watch and
pray for the coming of the Second Relief, as we had
before watched and prayed for the coming of the
First.

Sixteen-year-old John Baptiste was disappointed
and in ill humor when Messrs. Tucker and Rhodes insisted that he, being the only able-bodied man in the
Donner camp, should stay and cut wood for the enfeebled, until the arrival of other rescuers. The little
half-breed was a sturdy fellow, but he was starving
too, and thought that he should be allowed to save
himself.

After he had had a talk with father, however, and
the first company of refugees had gone, he became
reconciled to his lot, and served us faithfully. He
would take us little ones up to exercise upon the snow,
saying that we should learn to keep our feet on the
slick, frozen surface, as well as to wade through slush
and loose drifts.

Frequently, when at work and lonesome, he would
call Georgia and me up to keep him company, and when

the weather was frosty, he would bring " Old Navajo," his long Indian blanket, and roll her in it from one end, and me from the other, until we would come together in the middle, like the folds of a paper of pins, with a face peeping above each fold. Then he would set us upon the stump of the pine tree while he chopped the trunk and boughs for fuel. He told us that he had promised father to stay until we children should be taken from camp, also that his home was to be with our family forever. One of his amusements was to rake the coals together nights, then cover them with ashes, and put the large camp kettle over the pile for a drum, so that we could spread our hands around it, " to get just a little warm before going to bed."

For the time, he lived at Aunt Betsy's tent, because Solomon Hook was snow-blind and demented, and at times restless and difficult to control. The poor boy, some weeks earlier, had set out alone to reach the settlement, and after an absence of forty-eight hours was found close to camp, blind, and with his mind unbalanced. He, like other wanderers on that desolate waste, had become bewildered, and, unconsciously, circled back near to the starting-point.

Aunt Betsy came often to our tent, and mother frequently went to hers, and they knelt together and asked for strength to bear their burdens. Once, when mother came back, she reported to father that she had discovered bear tracks quite close to camp, and was solicitous that the beast be secured, as its flesh might sustain us until rescued.

As father grew weaker, we children spent more time upon the snow above camp. Often, after his wound was dressed and he fell into a quiet slumber, our ever-busy, thoughtful mother would come to us and sit on the tree trunk. Sometimes she brought paper and wrote; sometimes she sketched the mountains and the tall tree-tops, which now looked like small trees growing up through the snow. And often, while knitting or sewing, she held us spell-bound with wondrous tales of " Joseph in Egypt," of " Daniel in the den of lions," of " Elijah healing the widow's son," of dear little Samuel, who said, " Speak Lord, for Thy servant heareth," and of the tender, loving Master, who took young children in his arms and blessed them.

With me sitting on her lap, and Frances and Georgia at either side, she referred to father's illness and lonely condition, and said that when the next " Relief " came, we little ones might be taken to the settlement, without either parent, but, God willing, both would follow later. Who could be braver or tenderer than she, as she prepared us to go forth with strangers and live without her? While she, without medicine, without lights, would remain and care for our suffering father, in hunger and in cold, and without her little girls to kiss good-morning and good-night. She taught us how to gain friends among those whom we should meet, and what to answer when asked whose children we were.

Often her eyes gazed wistfully to westward, where sky and mountains seemed to meet, and she told us that beyond those snowy peaks lay California, our land of food and safety, our promised land of happiness, where God would care for us. Oh, it was painfully quiet some days in those great mountains, and lonesome upon the snow. The pines had a whispering homesick murmur, and we children had lost all inclination to play.

The last food which I remember seeing in our camp before the arrival of the Second Relief was a thin mould of tallow, which mother had tried out of the trimmings of the jerked beef brought us by the First Relief. She had let it harden in a pan, and after all other rations had given out, she cut daily from it three small white squares for each of us, and we nibbled off the four corners very slowly, and then around and around the edges of the precious pieces until they became too small for us to hold between our fingers.

CHAPTER XII

ARRIVAL OF SECOND RELIEF, OR REED-GREENWOOD PARTY —
FEW SURVIVORS STRONG ENOUGH TO TRAVEL — WIFE'S
CHOICE — PARTINGS AT DONNER CAMP — MY TWO SIS-
TERS AND I DESERTED — DEPARTURE OF SECOND RELIEF
PARTY.

IT was the first of March, about ten days after the arrival of the First Relief, before James Reed and William McCutchen succeeded in reaching the party they had left long months before. They, together with Brit Greenwood, Hiram Miller, Joseph Jondro, Charles Stone, John Turner, Matthew Dofar, Charles Cady, and Nicholas Clark constituted the Second Relief.

They reported having met the First Relief with eighteen refugees at the head of Bear Valley, three having died *en route* from the cabins. Among the survivors Mr. Reed found his wife, his daughter Virginia, and his son James F. Reed, Jr. He learned there from his anxious wife that their two younger children, Martha J. and Thomas K. Reed, had also left the cabin with her, but had soon given out and been carried back and left at the mountain camp by Messrs. Glover and Moutrey, who then retraced their steps and rejoined the party.

Consequently this Reed-Greenwood party, realizing that this was no time for tarrying, had hurried on to the lake cabins, where Mr. Reed had the happiness of finding his children still alive. There he and five companions encamped upon the snow and fed and soothed the unfortunates. Two members continued on to Aunt Betsy's abode, and Messrs. Cady and Clark came to ours.

This Relief had followed the example of its predecessor in leaving supplies at marked caches along the trail for the return trip. Therefore, it reached camp with a frugal amount for distribution. The first rations were doled out with careful hand, lest harm should come to the famishing through overeating, still, the rescuers administered sufficient to satisfy the fiercest cravings and to give strength for the prospective journey.

While crossing Alder Creek Valley to our tent that first afternoon, Messrs. Cady and Clark had seen fresh tracks of a bear and cubs, and in the evening the latter took one of our guns and went in pursuit of the game which would have been a godsend to us. It was dark when he returned and told my mother that he had wounded the old bear near the camp, but that she had escaped with her young through the pines into a clump of tamarack, and that he would be able to follow her in the morning by the blood-stains on the snow.

Meanwhile, the two men who had come to Aunt Betsy's with food thought it best not to tell her that her son William had died *en route* to the settlement with the First Relief. They selected from among her children in camp, Solomon, Mary, and Isaac, as able to follow a leader to the lake cabins, and thence to go with the outgoing Second Relief, across the mountains. Hopefully, that mother kissed her three children good-bye, and then wistfully watched them depart with their rescuers on snowshoes. She herself was strong enough to make the journey, but remained because there was no one to help to carry out her two youngest children.

Thirty-one of the company were still in the camps when this party arrived, nearly all of them children, unable to travel without assistance, and the adults were too feeble to give much aid to the little ones upon the snow. Consequently, when my father learned that the Second Relief comprised only ten men, he felt that he himself would never reach the settlement. He was willing to be left alone, and entreated mother to leave him and try to save herself and us children. He reminded her that his life was almost spent, that she could do little for him were she to remain, and that in caring for us children she would be carrying on his work.

She who had to choose between the sacred duties of wife and mother, thought not of self. She looked first at her helpless little children, then into the face of her suffering and helpless husband, and tenderly, unhesitatingly, announced her determination to remain and care for him until both should be rescued, or death should part them.

From an old drawing made from description furnished by Wm. G. Murphy.

ARRIVAL OF RELIEF PARTY, FEBRUARY 18, 1847

Photograph by Lynwood Abbott.

DONNER LAKE

PREPARATION FOR JOURNEY

Perplexities and heartaches multiplied with the morning hours of the following day. Mr. Clark, being anxious to provide more food, started early to hunt the wounded bear. He had not been gone long, when Mr. Stone arrived from the lake cabins and told Mr. Cady that the other members of the Relief had become alarmed at gathering storm clouds, and had resolved to select at once the ablest among the emigrants and hasten with them across the summit, and to leave Clark, Cady, and himself to cut the necessary fuel for the camps, and otherwise assist the sufferers until the Third Relief should reach them.

Cady and Stone, without waiting to inform Clark, promptly decided upon their course of action. They knew the scarcity of provisions in camp, the condition of the trail over the mountains, the probability of long, fierce March storms, and other obstacles which might delay future promised relief, and, terror-stricken, determined to rejoin their party, regardless of opposition, and return to the settlement.

Mother, fearing that we children might not survive another storm in camp, begged Messrs. Cady and Stone to take us with them, offering them five hundred dollars in coin, to deliver us to Elitha and Leanna at Sutter's Fort. The agreement was made, and she collected a few keepsakes and other light articles, which she wished us to have, and which the men seemed more than willing to carry out of the mountains. Then, lovingly, she combed our hair and helped us to dress quickly for the journey. When we were ready, except cloak and hood, she led us to the bedside, and we took leave of father. The men helped us up the steps and stood us up on the snow. She came, put on our cloaks and hoods, saying, as if talking to herself, " I may never see you again, but God will take care of you."

Frances was six years and eight months old and could trudge along quite bravely, but Georgia, who was little more than five, and I, lacking a week of four years, could not do well on the heavy trail, and we were soon taken up and carried. After travelling some distance, the men left us sitting on a blanket upon the snow, and went ahead a short distance where they stopped and talked earnestly with many gesticulations. We watched them, trembling lest they leave us there to freeze. Then Frances said,

" Don't feel afraid. If they go off and leave us, I can lead you back to mother by our foot tracks on the snow."

After a seemingly long time, they returned, picked us up and took us on to one of the lake cabins, where without a parting word, they left us.

The Second Relief Party, of which these men were members, left camp on the third of March. They took with them seventeen refugees — the Breen and Graves families, Solomon Hook, Isaac and Mary Donner, and Martha and Thomas, Mr. Reed's two youngest children.

CHAPTER XIII

A FATEFUL CABIN — MRS. MURPHY GIVES MOTHERLY COM-
FORT — THE GREAT STORM — HALF A BISCUIT — ARRIVAL
OF THIRD RELIEF — " WHERE IS MY BOY? "

HOW can I describe that fateful cabin, which was dark as night to us who had come in from the glare of day? We heard no word of greeting and met no sign of welcome, but were given a dreary resting-place near the foot of the steps, just inside the open doorway, with a bed of branches to lie upon, and a blanket to cover us. After we had been there a short time, we could distinguish persons on other beds of branches, and a man with bushy hair reclining beside a smouldering fire.

Soon a child began to cry, " Give me some bread. Oh, give me some meat! "

Then another took up the same pitiful wail. It continued so long that I wept in sympathy, and fastened my arms tightly around my sister Frances' neck and hid my eyes against her shoulder. Still I heard that hungry cry, until a husky voice shouted,

" Be quiet, you crying children, or I 'll shoot you."

But the silence was again and again broken by that heart-rending plea, and again and again were the voices hushed by the same terrifying threat. And we three, fresh from our loving mother's embrace, believed the awful menace no vain threat.

We were cold, and too frightened to feel hungry, nor were we offered food that night, but next morning Mr. Reed's little daughter Mattie appeared carrying in her apron a number of newly baked biscuits which her father had just taken from the hot ashes of his camp fire. Joyfully she handed one to each inmate of the cabin, then departed to join those ready to set forth on the journey to the settlement. Few can know how delicious those biscuits tasted, and how carefully we caught each dropping crumb. The place seemed drearier after their giver left us, yet we were glad that her father was taking her to her mother in California.

Soon the great storm which had been lowering broke upon us. We were not exposed to its fury as were those who had just gone from us, but we knew when it came, for snow drifted down upon our bed and had to be scraped off before we could rise. We were not allowed near the fire and spent most of our time on our bed of branches.

Dear, kind Mrs. Murphy, who for months had taken care of her own son Simon, and her grandson George Foster, and little James Eddy, gave us a share of her motherly attention, and tried to feed and comfort us. Affliction and famine, however, had well nigh sapped her strength and by the time those plaintive voices ceased to cry for bread and meat, her willing hands were too weakened to do much for us.

FRIGHTENED CHILDREN

I remember being awakened while there by two little arms clasped suddenly and tightly about me, and I heard Frances say,

" No, she shall not go with you. You want to kill her! "

Near us stood Keseberg, the man with the bushy hair. In limping past our sleeping place, he had stopped and said something about taking me away with him, which so frightened my sisters that they believed my life in danger, and would not let me move beyond their reach while we remained in that dungeon. We spoke in whispers, suffered as much as the starving children in Joseph's time, and were more afraid than Daniel in the den of lions.

How long the storm had lasted, we did not know, nor how many days we had been there. We were forlorn as children can possibly be, when Simon Murphy, who was older than Frances, climbed to his usual " look out " on the snow above the cabin to see if any help were coming. He returned to us, stammering in his eagerness:

" I seen — a woman — on snow shoes — coming from the other camp! She 's a little woman — like Mrs. Donner. She is not looking this way — and may pass! "

Hardly had he spoken her name, before we had gathered around him and were imploring him to hurry back and call our mother. We were too excited to follow him up the steps.

She came to us quickly, with all the tenderness and

courage needed to lessen our troubles and soften our fears. Oh, how glad we were to see her, and how thankful she appeared to be with us once more! We heard it in her voice and saw it in her face; and when we begged her not to leave us, she could not answer, but clasped us closer to her bosom, kissed us anew for father's sake, then told how the storm had distressed them. Often had they hoped that we had reached the cabins too late to join the Relief — then in grieving anguish felt that we had, and might not live to cross the summit.

She had watched the fall of snow, and measured its depth; had seen it drift between the two camps making the way so treacherous that no one had dared to cross it until the day before her own coming; then she induced Mr. Clark to try to ascertain if Messrs. Cady and Stone had really got us to the cabins in time to go with the Second Relief.

We did not see Mr. Clark, but he had peered in, taken observations, and returned by nightfall and described to her our condition.

John Baptiste had promised to care for father in her absence. She left our tent in the morning as early as she could see the way. She must have stayed with us over night, for I went to sleep in her arms, and they were still around me when I awoke; and it seemed like a new day, for we had time for many cherished talks. She veiled from us the ghastliness of death, telling us Aunt Betsy and both our little cousins had gone to heaven. She said Lewis had been first to go, and his mother had soon followed; that she herself had carried little Sammie from his sick mother's tent to ours the very day we three were taken away; and in order to keep him warm while the storm raged, she had laid him close to father's side, and that he had stayed with them until " day before yesterday."

I asked her if Sammie had cried for bread. She replied, " No, he was not hungry, for your mother saved two of those little biscuits which the relief party brought, and every day she soaked a tiny piece in water and fed him all he would eat, and there is still half a biscuit left."

How big that half-biscuit seemed to me! I wondered why she had not brought at least a part of it to us. While she was talking with Mrs. Murphy, I could not get it out of my mind. I could see that broken half-biscuit, with its ragged edges, and knew that if I had a piece, I would nibble off the rough points first. The longer I waited, the more I wanted it. Finally, I slipped my arm around mother's neck, drew her face close to mine and whispered,

" What are you going to do with the half-biscuit you saved? "

" I am keeping it for your sick father," she answered, drawing me closer to her side, laying her comforting cheek against mine, letting my arm keep its place, and my fingers stroke her hair.

The two women were still talking in subdued tones, pouring the oil of sympathy into each others' gaping wounds. Neither heard the sound of feet on the snow above; neither knew that the Third Relief Party was at hand, until Mr. Eddy and Mr. Foster came down the steps, and each asked anxiously of Mrs. Murphy, " Where is my boy? "

Each received the same sorrowful answer — " Dead."

CHAPTER XIV

THE QUEST OF TWO FATHERS — SECOND RELIEF IN DISTRESS
— THIRD RELIEF ORGANIZED AT WOODWORTH'S RELAY
CAMP — DIVIDES AND ONE HALF GOES TO SUCCOR SECOND
RELIEF AND ITS REFUGEES; AND THE OTHER HALF PRO-
CEEDS TO DONNER LAKE — A LAST FAREWELL — A WOM-
AN'S SACRIFICE.

IT will be remembered that Mr. Eddy, being ill, was
dropped out of the First Relief at Mule Springs
in February, and sent back to Johnson's Ranch to
await the return of this party, which had promised to
bring out his family. Who can realize his distress
when it returned with eighteen refugees, and informed
him that his wife and little Maggie had perished before it reached the camps, and that it had been obliged
to leave his baby there in care of Mrs. Murphy?

Disappointed and aggrieved, the afflicted father immediately set out on horseback, hoping that he would
meet his child on the trail in charge of the Second Relief, which it seemed reasonable to expect would follow
closely in the footsteps of the first. He was accompanied by Mr. Foster, of the Forlorn Hope, who had
been forced to leave his own little son at the camp in
charge of Mrs. Murphy, its grandmother.

On the evening of the second day, the two reached

Woodworth's camp, established as a relay station pursuant to the general plan of rescue originally adopted. They found the midshipman in snug quarters with several men to do his bidding. He explained that the lack of competent guides had prevented his venturing among the snow peaks. Whereupon, Mr. Eddy earnestly assured him that the trail of those who had already gone up outlined the way.

After much deliberation, Woodworth and his men agreed to start out next morning for the mountain camps, but tried to dissuade Mr. Eddy from accompanying them on account of his apparent depleted condition. Nevertheless both he and Mr. Foster remained firm, and with the party, left the relay camp, crossed the low foothills and encamped for the night on the Yuba River.

At dusk, Woodworth was surprised by the arrival of two forlorn-looking individuals, whom he recognized as members of the Reed-Greenwood Relief, which had gone up the mountain late in February and was overdue. The two implored food for themselves, also for their seven companions and three refugees, a mile back on the trail, unable to come farther.

When somewhat refreshed, they were able to go more into detail, and the following explanation of their plight was elicited:

" One of our men, Clark, is at Donner's Camp, and the other nine of us left the cabins near the lake on the third of March, with seventeen of the starving emigrants. The storm caught us as we crossed the summit, and ten miles below, drove us into camp. It got so bad and lasted so long that our provisions gave out, and we almost froze to death cutting wood. We all worked at keeping the fires until we were completely exhausted, then seeing no prospects of help coming to us, we left, and made our way down here, bringing Reed's two children and Solomon Hook, who said he could and would walk. The other fourteen that we brought over the summit are up there at what we call Starved Camp. Some are dead, the rest without food."

Woodworth and two followers went at once with provisions to the near-by sufferers, and later brought them down to camp.

Messrs. Reed and Greenwood stated that every available means had been tried by them to get the seventeen unfortunates well over the summit before the great storm reached its height. They said the physical condition of the refugees was such, from the very start, that no persuasion, nor warnings, nor threats could quicken their feeble steps. All but three of the number were children, with their hands and feet more or less frozen. Worse still, the caches on which the party had relied for sustenance had been robbed by wild animals, and the severity of the storm had forced all into camp, with nothing more than a breastwork of brush to shelter them. Mrs. Elisabeth Graves died the first night, leaving to the party the hopeless task of caring for her emaciated babe in arms, and her three other children between the ages of nine and five years. Soon, however, the five-year-old followed his mother, and the number of starving was again lessened on the third night when Isaac Donner went to sleep beside his sister and did not waken. The storm had continued so furiously that it was impossible to bury the dead. Days and nights were spent in steadfast struggling against the threatening inevitable, before the party gave up; and Greenwood and Reed, taking the two Reed children and also Solomon Hook, who walked, started down the mountain, hoping to save their own lives and perhaps get fresh men to complete the pitiful work which they had been forced to abandon.

When Messrs. Reed and Greenwood closed their account of the terrible physical and mental strain their party had undergone, "Mr. Woodworth asked his own men of the relay camp, if they would go with him to rescue those unfortunates at ' Starved Camp,' and received an answer in the negative." *

The following morning there was an earnest consultation, and so hazardous seemed the trail and the work to be done that for a time all except Eddy and Foster refused to go farther. Finally, John Stark stepped forward, saying,

" Gentlemen, I am ready to go and do what I can for those sufferers, without promise of pay."

By guaranteeing three dollars per day to any man who would get supplies to the mountain camps, and fifty dollars in addition to each man who should carry

*Extract from Thornton's work.

ARRIVAL OF THE CARAVAN AT SANTA FE

ON THE BANKS OF THE SACRAMENTO RIVER

a helpless child, not his own, back to the settlement, Mr. Eddy * secured the services of Hiram Miller, who had just come down with the Second Relief; and Mr. Foster hired, on the same terms, Mr. Thompson from the relay camp. Mr. Woodworth offered like inducements, on Government account, to the rest of his men, and before the morning was far advanced, with William H. Eddy acting as leader, William Foster, Hiram Miller, Mr. Thompson, John Stark, Howard Oakley, and Charles Stone (who had left us little ones at the lake camp) shouldered their packs and began the ascent.

Meanwhile how fared it at Starved Camp? Mr. and Mrs. Breen being left there with their own five suffering children and the four other poor, moaning little waifs, were tortured by situations too heart-rending for description, too pitiful to seem true. Suffice it to relate that Mrs. Breen shared with baby Graves the last lump of loaf sugar and the last drops of tea, of that which she had denied herself and had hoarded for her own babe. When this was gone, with quivering lips she and her husband repeated the litany and prayed for strength to meet the ordeal,— then, turning to the unburied dead, they resorted to the only means left to save the nine helpless little ones.

When Mr. Eddy and party reached them, they found much suffering from cold and crying for "something to eat," but not the wail which precedes delirium and death.

This Third Relief Party settled for the night upon

*Thornton saw Eddy pay Hiram Miller the promised fifty dollars after the Third Relief reached the settlement.

the snow near these refugees, who had twice been in the shadow of doom; and after giving them food and fire, Mr. Eddy divided his force into two sections. Messrs. Stark, Oakley, and Stone were to remain there and nurture the refugees a few hours longer, then carry the small children, and conduct those able to walk to Mule Springs, while Eddy and three companions should hasten on to the cabins across the summit.*

Section Two, spurred on by paternal solicitude, resumed travel at four o'clock the following morning, and crossed the summit soon after sunrise. The nearer they approached camp, the more anxious Messrs. Eddy and Foster became to reach the children they hoped to find alive. Finally, they rushed ahead, as we have seen, to the Murphy cabin. Alas! only disappointment met them there.

Even after Mrs. Murphy had repeated her pitiful answer, "Dead," the afflicted fathers stood dazed and silent, as if waiting for the loved ones to return.

Mr. Eddy was the first to recover sufficiently for action. Presently Simon Murphy and we three little girls were standing on the snow under a clear blue sky, and saw Hiram Miller and Mr. Thompson coming toward camp.

The change was so sudden it was difficult to understand what had happened. How could we realize that we had passed out of that loathsome cabin, never to return; or that Mrs. Murphy, too ill to leave her bed, and Keseberg, too lame to walk, by reason of a deep

*See McGlashan's "History of the Donner Party."

cleft in his heel, made by an axe, would have to stay alone in that abode of wretchedness?

Nor could we know our mother's anguish, as she stepped aside to arrange with Mr. Eddy for our departure. She had told us at our own camp why she would remain. She had parted from us there and put us in charge of men who had risked much and come far to do a heroic deed. Later she had found us, abandoned by them, in time of direst need, and in danger of an awful death, and had warmed and cheered us back to hope and confidence. Now, she was about to confide us to the care of a party whose leader swore either to save us or die with us on the trail. We listened to the sound of her voice, felt her good-bye kisses, and watched her hasten away to father, over the snow, through the pines, and out of sight, and knew that we must not follow. But the influence of her last caress, last yearning look of love and abiding faith will go with us through life.

The ordeal through which she passed is thus told by Colonel Thornton, after a personal interview with Mr. Eddy:

Mrs. George Donner was able to travel. But her husband was in a helpless condition, and she would not consent to leave him while he survived. She expressed her solemn and unalterable purpose, which no danger or peril could change, to remain and perform for him the last sad office of duty and affection. She manifested, however, the greatest solicitude for her children, and informed Mr. Eddy that she had fifteen hundred dollars in silver, all of which she would give him, if he would save the lives of the children.

He informed her that he would not carry out one hundred dollars of all she had, but that he would save her children or die in the effort. The party had no provisions to leave for the sustenance of these unhappy, unfortunate beings.

After remaining about two hours, Mr. Eddy informed Mrs. Donner that he was constrained by force of circumstances to depart. It was certain that George Donner would never rise from the miserable bed upon which he had lain down, worn by toil and wasted by famine.

A woman was probably never before placed in circumstances of greater or more peculiar trial; but her duty and affection as a wife triumphed over all her instincts of reason.

The parting scene between parent and children is represented as being one that will never be forgotten, so long as life remains or memory performs its functions.

My own emotions will not permit me to attempt a description which language, indeed, has not power to delineate. It is sufficient to say that it was affecting beyond measure; and that the last words uttered by Mrs. Donner in tears and sobs to Mr. Eddy were, " Oh, save, save my children! "

CHAPTER XV

SIMON MURPHY, FRANCES, GEORGIA, AND I TAKEN FROM THE LAKE CABINS BY THE THIRD RELIEF — NO FOOD TO LEAVE — CROSSING THE SNOW — REMNANT OF THE SECOND RELIEF OVERTAKEN — OUT OF THE SNOW — INCIDENTS OF THE JOURNEY — JOHNSON'S RANCH — THE SINCLAIR HOME — SUTTER'S FORT.

WHEN we left the lake cabin, we still wore the clothing we had on when we came from our tent with Messrs. Cady and Stone. Georgia and I were clad in quilted petticoats, linsey dresses, woollen stockings, and well-worn shoes. Our cloaks were of a twilled material, garnet, with a white thread interwoven, and we had knitted hoods to match. Frances' clothing was as warm; instead of cloak, however, she wore a shawl, and her hood was blue. Her shoes had been eaten by our starving dog before he disappeared, and as all others were buried out of reach, mother had substituted a pair of her own in their stead.

Mr. Foster took charge of Simon Murphy, his wife's brother, and Messrs. Eddy and Miller carried Georgia and me. Mr. Eddy always called Georgia " my girl," and she found great favor in his eyes, because in size and looks she reminded him of his little daughter who had perished in that storm-bound camp.

Our first stop was on the mountain-side overlooking the lake, where we were given a light meal of bread and meat and a drink of water. When we reached the head of the lake, we overtook Nicholas Clark and John Baptiste who had deserted father in his tent and were hurrying toward the settlement. Our coming was a surprise to them, yet they were glad to join our party.

After our evening allowance of food we were stowed snugly between blankets in a snow trench near the summit of the Sierras, but were so hungry that we could hardly get to sleep, even after being told that more food would do us harm.

Early next morning we were again on the trail. I could not walk at all, and Georgia only a short distance at a time. So treacherous was the way that our rescuers often stumbled into unseen pits, struggled among snow drifts, and climbed icy ridges where to slip or fall might mean death in the yawning depth below.

Near the close of this most trying day, Hiram M. Miller put me down, saying wearily, " I am tired of carrying you. If you will walk to that dark thing on the mountain-side ahead of us, you shall have a nice lump of loaf sugar with your supper."

My position in the blanket had been so cramped that my limbs were stiff and the jostling of the march had made my body ache. I looked toward the object to which he pointed. It seemed a long way off; yet I wanted the sugar so much that I agreed to walk. The wind was sharp. I shivered, and at times could hardly lift my feet; often I stumbled and would have fallen had he not held my hand tightly, as he half led, half drew me onward. I did my part, however, in glad expectation of the promised bit of sweetness. The sun had set before we reached our landmark, which was a felled and blackened tree, selected to furnish fuel for our night fire. When we children were given our evening allowance of food, I asked for my lump of sugar, and cried bitterly on being harshly told there was none for me. Too disappointed and fretted to care for anything else, I sobbed myself to sleep.

Nor did I waken happy next morning. I had not forgotten the broken promise, and was lonesome for mother. When Mr. Miller told me that I should walk that day as far as Frances and Georgia did, I refused to go forward, and cried to go back. The result was that he used rough means before I promised to be good and do as he commanded. His act made my sister Frances rush to my defence, and also, touched a chord in the fatherly natures of the other two men, who summarily brought about a more comfortable state of affairs.

When we proceeded on our journey, I was again carried by Mr. Miller in a blanket on his back as young children are carried by Indians on long journeys. My head above the blanket folds bobbed uncomfortably at every lurch. The trail led up and down and around snow peaks, and under overhanging banks that seemed ready to give way and crush us.

At one turn our rescuers stopped, picked up a bundle, and carefully noted the fresh human foot prints in the snow which indicated that a number of persons were moving in advance. By our fire that night, Mr. Eddy opened the bundle that we had found upon the snow, and to the surprise of all, Frances at once recognized in it the three silk dresses, silver spoons, small keepsakes, and articles of children's clothing which mother had intrusted to the care of Messrs. Cady and Stone.

The spoons and smaller articles were now stowed away in the pockets of our rescuers for safekeeping on the journey; and while we little girls dressed ourselves in the fresh underwear, and watched our discarded garments disappear in the fire, the dresses, which mother had planned should come to us later in life, were remodelled for immediate use.

Mr. Thompson pulled out the same sharp pocket-knife, coarse black thread, and big-eyed needle, which he had used the previous evening, while making Frances a pair of moccasins out of his own gauntlet gloves. With the help of Mr. Eddy, he then ripped out the sleeves, cut off the waists about an inch above the skirt gathers, cut slits in the skirts for arm-holes, and tacked in the sleeves. Then, with mother's wish in mind, they put the dove-colored silk on Frances, the light brown on Georgia, and the dark coffee-brown on me. Pleats and laps in the skirt bands were necessary to fit them to our necks. Strings were tied around our waists, and the skirts tacked up until they were of walking length. These ample robes served for cloaks as well as dresses for we could easily draw our hands back through the sleeves and keep our arms warm beneath the folds. Thus comfortably clad, we began another day's journey.

Before noon we overtook and passed Messrs. Oakley, Stone, and Stark, having in charge the following refugees from Starved Camp: Mr. and Mrs. Patrick Breen and their five children; Mary Donner, Jonathan Graves, Nancy Graves, and baby Graves. Messrs. Oakley and Stone were in advance, the former carrying Mary Donner over his shoulder; and the latter baby Graves in his arms. Great-hearted John Stark had the care of all the rest. He was broad-shouldered and powerful, and would stride ahead with two weaklings at a time, deposit them on the trail and go back for others who could not keep up. These were the remnant of the hopeful seventeen who had started out on the third of March with the Second Relief, and with whom mother had hoped we children would cross the mountains.

It was after dark when our own little party encamped at the crossing of the Yuba River. The following morning Lieutenant Woodworth and attendants were found near-by. He commended the work done by the Third Relief; yet, to Mr. Eddy's dismay, he declared that he would not go to the rescue of those who were still in the mountains, because the warmer weather was melting the snow so rapidly that the lives of his men would be endangered should he attempt to lead them up the trail which we had just followed down. He gave our party rations, and said that he would at once proceed to Johnson's Ranch and from there send to Mule Springs the requisite number of horses to carry to the settlement the persons now on the trail.

Our party did not resume travel until ten o'clock that morning; nevertheless, we crossed the snow line and made our next camp at Mule Springs. There we caught the first breath of springtide, touched the warm, dry earth, and saw green fields far beyond the foot of that cold, cruel mountain range. Our rescuers exclaimed joyfully, " Thank God, we are at last out of the snow, and you shall soon see Elitha and Leanna, and have all you want to eat."

Our allowance of food had been gradually increased and our improved condition bore evidence of the good care and kind treatment we had received. We remained several days at Mule Springs, and were comparatively happy until the arrival of the unfortunates from Starved Camp, who stretched forth their gaunt hands and piteously begged for food which would have caused death had it been given to them in sufficient quantities to satisfy their cravings.

When I went among them I found my little cousin Mary sitting on a blanket near Mr. Oakley, who had carried her thither, and who was gently trying to engage her thoughts. Her wan face was wet with tears, and her hands were clasped around her knee as she rocked from side to side in great pain. A large woollen stocking covered her swollen leg and frozen foot which had become numb and fallen into the fire one night at

Starved Camp and been badly maimed before she awakened to feel the pain. I wanted to speak to her, but when I saw how lonesome and ill she looked, something like pain choked off my words.

Her brother Isaac had died at that awful camp and she herself would not have lived had Mr. Oakley not been so good to her. He was now comforting her with the assurance that he would have the foot cared for by a doctor as soon as they should reach the settlement; and she, believing him, was trying to be brave and patient.

We all resumed travel on horseback and reached Johnson's Ranch about the same hour in the day. As we approached, the little colony of emigrants which had settled in the neighborhood the previous Autumn crowded in and about the two-roomed adobe house which Mr. Johnson had kindly set apart as a stopping place for the several relief parties on their way to and from the mountains. All were anxious to see the sufferers for whose rescue they had helped to provide.

Survivors of the Forlorn Hope and of the First Relief were also there awaiting the arrival of expected loved ones. There Simon Murphy, who came with us, met his sisters and brother; Mary Graves took from the arms of Charles Stone, her slowly dying baby sister; she received from the hands of John Stark her brother Jonathan and her sister Nancy, and heard of the death of her mother and of her brother Franklin at Starved Camp. That house of welcome became a house of mourning when Messrs. Eddy and Foster repeated the names of those who had perished in the snows. The scenes were so heart-rending that I slipped out of doors and sat in the sunshine waiting for Frances and Georgia, and thinking of her who had intrusted us to the care of God.

Before our short stay at the Johnson Ranch ended, we little girls had a peculiar experience. While standing in a doorway, the door closed with a bang upon two of my fingers. My piercing cry brought several persons to the spot, and one among them sat down and soothed me in a motherly way. After I was myself again, she examined the dress into which Messrs. Thompson and Eddy had stitched so much good-will, and she said:

" Let me take off this clumsy thing, and give you a little blue dress with white flowers on it." She made the change, and after she had fastened it in the back she got a needle and white thread and bade me stand closer to her so that she might sew up the tear which exposed my knees. She asked why I looked so hard at her sewing, and I replied,

" My mother always makes little stitches when she sews my dresses."

No amount of pulling down of the sleeves or straightening out of the skirt could conceal the fact that I was too large for the garment. As I was leaving her, I heard her say to a companion, " That is just as good for her, and this will make two for my little girl." Later in the day Frances and Georgia parted with their silks and looked as forlorn as I in calico substitutes.

Oh, the balm and beauty of that early morning when Messrs. Eddy, Thompson, and Miller took us on horse-back down the Sacramento Valley. Under the leafy trees and over the budding blossoms we rode. Not rapidly, but steadily, we neared our journey's end. Toward night, when the birds had stopped their sing-ing and were hiding themselves among bush and bough, we reached the home of Mr. and Mrs. John Sinclair on the American River, thirty-five miles from Johnson's Ranch and only two and a half from Sutter's Fort.

That hospitable house was over-crowded with earlier arrivals, but as it was too late for us to cross the river, sympathetic Mrs. Sinclair said that she would find a place for us. Having no bed to offer, she loosened the rag-carpet from one corner of the room, had fresh straw put on the floor, and after supper, tucked us away on it, drawing the carpet over us in place of quilts.

We had bread and milk for supper that night, and the same good food next day. In the afternoon we were taken across the river in an Indian canoe. Then we followed the winding path through the tules to Sut-ter's Fort, where we were given over to our half-sisters by those heroic men who had kept their pledge to our mother and saved our lives.

CHAPTER XVI

ELITHA AND LEANNA — LIFE AT THE FORT — WATCHING THE COW PATH — RETURN OF THE FALLON PARTY — KESEBERG BROUGHT IN BY THEM — FATHER AND MOTHER DID NOT COME.

THE room in which Elitha and Leanna were staying when we arrived at Sutter's Fort was part of a long, low, single-story adobe building outside the fortification walls, and like others that were occupied by belated travellers, was the barest and crudest structure imaginable. It had an earthen floor, a thatched roof, a batten door, and an opening in the rear wall to serve as window.

We little ones were oblivious of discomfort, however. The tenderness with which we were received, and the bewildering sense of safety that we felt, blinded us even to the anguish and fear which crept over our two sisters, when they saw us come to them alone. How they suffered I learned many years later from Elitha, who said, in referring to those pitiful experiences:

After Sister Leanna and I reached the Fort with the First Relief, we were put in different families to await our parents; but as soon as the Second Relief was expected, we

went to housekeeping, gathered wood, and had everything
ready. No one came. Then we waited and watched anxiously
for the Third Relief, and it was a sad sight to see you
three and no more.

I went in, kindled the fire, and gave you supper. I had
a bed of shavings hemmed in with poles for father and
mother. They did not come. We five lay down upon it,
and Sister Leanna and I talked long after you three were
asleep, wondering what we should do. You had no clothes,
except those you wore, so the next day I got a little cotton
stuff and commenced making you some. Sister Leanna did
the cooking and looked after you, which took all her time.

The United States Army officer at the Fort had left orders
at Captain Sutter's store, that we should be furnished with
the necessaries of life, and that was how we were able to get
the food and few things we had when you arrived.

Messrs. Eddy and Thompson did not tell my sisters
that they had no expectation of father's getting
through, and considered mother's chance very slight,
but went directly to the Fort to report to Colonel
McKinstry and to Mr. Kerns what their party had accomplished, and to inform them that Lieutenant Woodworth was about to break camp and return to the
settlement instead of trying to get relief to the four
unfortunates still at the mountain camp.

Very soon thereafter, a messenger on horseback
from the Fort delivered a letter to Lieutenant Woodworth, and a fourth party was organized, " consisting
of John Stark, John Rhodes, E Coffeymier, John Del,
Daniel Tucker, Wm. Foster, and Wm. Graves. But
this party proceeded no farther than Bear Valley on
account of the rapidly melting snows." *

The return of the party after its fruitless efforts

*Thornton.

[133]

was not made known to Elitha and Leanna; nor were they aware that Thomas Fallon, with six companions, had set out for the mountain camps on the tenth of April.

Neither fear nor misgivings troubled us little ones the morning we started out, hand in hand, to explore our new surroundings. We had rested, been washed, combed, and fed, and we believed that father and mother would soon come to us. Everything was beautiful to our eyes. We did not care if " the houses did look as if they were made of dry dirt and had n't anything but holes for windows." We watched the mothers sitting on the door sills or on chairs near them laughing as they talked and sewed, and it seemed good to see the little children at play and hear them singing their dolls to sleep.

The big gate to the adobe wall around Captain Sutter's home was open, and we could look in and see many white-washed huts built against the back and side walls, and a flag waving from a pole in front of the large house, which stood in the middle of the ground. Cannons like those we had seen at Fort Laramie were also peeping out of holes in these walls, and an Indian soldier and a white soldier were marching to and fro, each holding a gun against his shoulder, and it pointing straight up in the air.

Often we looked at each other and exclaimed, " How good to be here instead of up in the snow." It was hard to go back to the house when sisters called us.

ELITHA DONNER
(MRS. BENJAMIN WILDER)

LEANNA DONNER
(MRS. JOHN APP)

GEORGE DONNER, NEPHEW OF
CAPT. DONNER

MARY DONNER

DEEDS OF KINDNESS

I do not remember the looks or the taste of anything they gave us to eat. We were so eager to stay out in the sunshine. Before long, we went to that dreary, bare room only to sleep. Many of the women at the Fort were kind to us; gave us bread from their scant loaves not only because we were destitute, but because they had grateful recollection of those whose name we bore.

Once a tall, freckle-faced boy, with very red hair, edged up to where I was watching others at play, and whispered:

" See here, little gal, you run get that little tin cup of yourn, and when you see me come out of Mrs. Wimmer's house with the milk pail on my arm, you go round yonder to the tother side of the cow-pen, where you 'll find a hole big enough to put the cup through. Then you can watch me milk it full of the nicest milk you ever tasted. You needn't say nothing to nobody about it. I give your little sister some last time, and I want to do the same for you. I hain't got no mother neither, and I know how it is."

When I got there he took the cup and, as he sat down under old Bossy, smilingly asked if I liked lots of foam. I told him I did. He milked a faster, stronger stream, then handed me the cup, full as he could carry it, and a white cap of foam stood above its rim. I tasted it and told him it was too good to drink fast, but he watched me until it was all gone. Then, saying he didn't want thanks, he hurried me back to the children. I never saw that boy again, but have ever been grateful for his act of pure kindness.

Every day or two a horse all white with lather and dripping with sweat would rush by, and the Indian or white man on his back would guide him straight to Captain Kerns' quarters, where he would hand out papers and letters. The women and children would flock thither to see if it meant news for them. Often they were disappointed and talked a great deal about the tediousness of the Mexican War and the delays of Captain Frémont's company. They wanted the war to end, and their men folk back so that they could move and get to farming before it should be too late to grow garden truck for family use.

While they thus anxiously awaited the return of their soldiers, we kept watch of the cow-path by which we had reached the Fort; for Elitha had told us that we might " pretty soon see the relief coming." She did not say, " with father and mother " ; but we did, and she replied, " I hope so."

We were very proud of the new clothes she had made us; but the first time she washed and hung them out to dry, they were stolen, and we were again destitute. Sister Elitha thought perhaps strange Indians took them.

In May, the Fallon party arrived with horses laden with many packs of goods, but their only refugee was Lewis Keseberg, from the cabin near the lake.

It was evening, and some one came to our door,

spoke to Elitha and Leanna in low tones and went away. My sisters turned, put their arms about us and wept bitterly. Then, gently, compassionately, the cruel, desolating truth was told. Ah, how could we believe it? No anxious watching, no weary waiting would ever bring father and mother to us again!

CHAPTER XVII

ORPHANS — KESEBERG AND HIS ACCUSERS — SENSATIONAL ACCOUNTS OF THE TRAGEDY AT DONNER LAKE — PROPERTY SOLD AND GUARDIAN APPOINTED — KINDLY INDIANS — " GRANDPA " — MARRIAGE OF ELITHA.

THE report of our affliction spread rapidly, and the well-meaning, tender-hearted women at the Fort came to condole and weep with us, and made their children weep also by urging, " Now, do say something comforting to these poor little girls, who were frozen and starved up in the mountains, and are now orphans in a strange land, without any home or any one to care for them."

Such ordeals were too overwhelming. I would rush off alone among the wild flowers to get away from the torturing sympathy. Even there, I met those who would look at me with great serious eyes, shake their heads, and mournfully say, " You poor little mite, how much better it would be if you had died in the mountains with your dear mother, instead of being left alone to struggle in this wicked world! "

This would but increase my distress, for I did not want to be dead and buried up there under the cold, deep snow, and I knew that mother did not want me to be there either. Had she not sent me away to save me, and asked God, our Heavenly Father, to take care of me?

Intense excitement and indignation prevailed at the Fort after Captain Fallon and other members of his party gave their account of the conditions found at the mountain camps, and of interviews had with Keseberg, whom they now called, "cannibal, robber, and murderer." The wretched man was accused by this party, not only of having needlessly partaken of human flesh, and of having appropriated coin and other property which should have come to us orphaned children, but also of having wantonly taken the life of Mrs. Murphy and of my mother.

Some declared him crazy, others called him a monster. Keseberg denied these charges and repeatedly accused Fallon and his party of making false statements. He sadly acknowledged that he had used human flesh to keep himself from starving, but swore that he was guiltless of taking human life. He stated that Mrs. Murphy had died of starvation soon after the departure of the "Third Relief," and that my mother had watched by father's bedside until he died. After preparing his body for burial, she had started out on the trail to go to her children. In attempting to cross the distance from her camp to his, she had strayed and wandered about far into the night, and finally reached his cabin wet, shivering, and grief-stricken, yet determined to push onward. She had brought nothing with her, but told him where to find money to take to her children in the event of her not reaching them.

He stated that he offered her food, which she refused. He then attempted to persuade her to wait until morning, and while they were talking, she sank upon the floor completely exhausted, and he covered her with blankets and made a fire to warm her. In the morning he found her cold in death.

Keseberg's vehement and steadfast denial of the crimes of which he stood accused saved him from personal violence, but not from suspicion and ill-will. Women shunned him, and children stoned him as he walked about the fort. *The California Star* printed in full the account of the Fallon party, and blood-curdling editorials increased public sentiment against Keseberg, stamping him with the mark of Cain, and closing the door of every home against him.*

Elitha and Leanna tried to keep us little ones in ignorance of the report that our father's body was mutilated, also of what was said about the alleged murder of our mother. Still we did hear fragments of conversations which greatly disturbed us, and our sisters found it difficult to answer some of our questions.

Meanwhile, more disappointments for us were brewing at the fort. Fallon's party demanded an immediate settlement of its claim. It had gone up the mountains under promise that its members should have not only a *per diem* as rescuers, but also one half of all the property that they might bring to the settlement, and they had brought valuable packs from

---

*See Appendix for account of the Fallon party, quoted from Thornton's work.

the camps of the Donners. Captain Fallon also had two hundred and twenty-five dollars in gold coin taken from concealment on Keseberg's person, and two hundred and seventy-five dollars additional taken from a cache that Keseberg had disclosed after the Captain had partially strangled him, and otherwise brutally treated him, to extort information of hidden treasure.

Keseberg did not deny that this money belonged to the Donners, but asserted that it was his intention and desire to take it to the Donner children himself as he had promised their mother.

Eventually, it was agreed that the Donner properties should be sold at auction, and that " one half of the proceeds should be handed over to Captain Fallon to satisfy the claims of his party, and the other half should be put into the hands of a guardian for the support of the Donner children." Hiram Miller was appointed guardian by Alcalde Sinclair.

Notwithstanding these plans for our well-being, unaccountable delays followed, making our situation daily more trying.

Elitha was not yet fifteen years of age, and Leanna was two years younger. They had not fully recovered from the effects of their long privations and physical sufferings in the mountains; and the loss of parents and means of support placed upon them responsibilities greater than they could carry, no matter how bravely they strove to meet the situation. " How can we provide for ourselves and these little sisters? "

was a question which haunted them by night and perplexed them by day.

They had no way of communicating with our friends in Eastern States, and the women at the Fort could ill afford to provide longer for us, since their bread winners were still with Frémont, and their own supplies were limited. Finally, my two eldest sisters were given employment by different families in exchange for food, which they shared with us; but it was often insufficient, and we little ones drifted along forlornly. Sometimes home was where night overtook us.

Often, we trudged to the *rancheria* beyond the pond, made by the adobe-moulders who had built the houses and wall surrounding the fort. There the Indian mothers were good to us. They gave us shreds of smoked fish and dried acorns to eat; lowered from their backs the queer little baby-beds, called "bickooses," and made the chubby faces in them laugh for our amusement. They also let us pet the dogs that perked up their ears and wagged their tails as our own Uno used to do when he wanted to frolic. Sometimes they stroked our hair and rubbed the locks between their fingers, then felt their own as if to note the difference. They seemed sorry because we could not understand their speech.

The pond also, with its banks of flowers, winding path, and dimpling waters, had charms for us until one day's experience drove us from it forever. We three were playing near it when a joyous Indian girl with a bundle of clothes on her head ran down the bank to the water's edge. We, following, watched her drop her bundle near a board that sloped from a rock into nature's tub, then kneel upon the upper end and souse the clothes merrily up and down in the clear water. She lathered them with a freshly gathered soap-root and cleansed them according to the ways of the Spanish mission teachers. As she tied the wet garments in a bundle and turned to carry them to the drying ground, Frances espied some loose yellow poppies floating near the end of the board and lay down upon it for the purpose of catching them.

Georgia and I saw her lean over and stretch out her hand as far as she could reach; saw the poppies drift just beyond her finger tips; saw her lean a little farther, then slip, head first, into the deep water. Such shrieks as terrified children give, brought the Indian girl quickly to our aid. Like a flash, she tossed the bundle from her head, sprang into the water, snatched Frances as she rose to the surface, and restored her to us without a word. Before we had recovered sufficiently to speak, she was gone.

Not a soul was in sight when we started toward the Fort, all unconscious of what the inevitable " is to be " was weaving into our lives.

We were too young to keep track of time by calendar, but counted it by happenings. Some were marked with tears, some with smiles, and some stole unawares upon us, just as on that bright June evening, when we did not find our sisters, and aimlessly followed others to the little shop where a friendly-appearing elderly man was cutting slices of meat and handing them to customers. We did not know his name, nor did we realize that he was selling the meat he handed out, only that we wanted some. So, after all the others had gone, we addressed him, asking,

"Grandpa, please give us a little piece of meat."

He looked at us, and inquired whose children we were, and where we lived. Upon learning, he turned about, lifted a liver from a wooden peg and cut for each, a generous slice.

On our way out, a neighbor intercepted us and said that we should sleep at her house that night and see our sisters in the morning. She also gave us permission to cook our pieces of liver over her bed of live coals. Frances offered to cook them all on her stick, but Georgia and I insisted that it would be fun for each to broil her own. I, being the smallest child, was given the shortest stick, and allowed to stand nearest the fire. Soon the three slices were sizzling and browning from the ends of three willow rods, and smelled so good that we could hardly wait for them to be done. Presently, however, the heat began to burn my cheeks and also the hand that held the stick. The more I wiggled about, the hotter the fire seemed, and it ended in Frances having to fish my piece of liver from among the coals, burned in patches, curled over bits of dying embers, and pretty well covered with ashes, but she knew how to scrape them away, and my supper was not spoiled.

Our neighbor gave us breakfast next morning and

spruced us up a bit, then led us to the house where a number of persons had gathered, most of them sitting at table laughing and talking, and among them, Elitha and Leanna. Upon our entrance, the merriment ceased and all eyes were turned inquiringly toward us. Some one pointed to him who sat beside our eldest sister and gayly said, " Look at your new brother." Another asked, " How do you like him? " We gazed around in silent amazement until a third continued teasingly, " She is no longer Elitha Donner, but Mrs. Perry McCoon. You have lost your sister, for her husband will take her away with him." " Lost your sister! " Those harrowing words stirred our pent feelings to anguish so keen that he who had uttered them in sport was touched with pity by the pain they caused.

Tears came also to the child-wife's eyes as she clasped her arms about us soothingly, assuring us that she was still our sister, and would care for us. Nevertheless, she and her husband slipped away soon on horseback, and we were told that we were to stay at our neighbor's until they returned for us.

This marriage, which was solemnized by Alcalde John Sinclair on the fourth of June, 1847, was approved by the people at the Fort. Children were anxious to play with us because we had " a married sister and a new brother." Women hurried through noon chores to meet outside, and some in their eagerness forgot to roll down their sleeves before they began to talk. One triumphantly repeated to each newcomer the motherly advice which she gave the young couple when she " first noticed his affection for that sorrowing girl, who is too pretty to be in this new country without a protector." They also recalled how Perry McCoon's launch had brought supplies up the river for the Second Relief to take over the mountains; and how finally, he himself had carried to the bereaved daughter the last accounts from Donner Camp.

Then the speakers wondered how soon Elitha would be back. Would she take us three to live with her on that cattle ranch twenty-five miles by bridle trail from the Fort? And would peace and happiness come to us there?

CHAPTER XVIII

WE were still without Elitha, when up the road and toward the Fort came a stout little old woman in brown. On one arm she carried a basket, and from the hand of the other hung a small covered tin pail. Her apron was almost as long as her dress skirt, which reached below her ankles, yet was short enough to show brown stockings above her low shoes. Two ends of the bright kerchief which covered her neck and crossed her bosom were pinned on opposite sides at the waist-line. A brown quilted hood of the same shade and material as her dress and apron concealed all but the white lace frill of a " grandma cap," which fastened under her chin with a bow. Her dark hair drawn down plain to each temple was coiled there into tiny wheels, and a brass pin stuck through crosswise to hold each coil in place. Her bright, speaking eyes, more brown than gray, gave charm to a face which might have been pretty had disease not marred it in youth.

As she drew near, her wonderful eyes looked into our faces and won from our lips a timid " Good morning, grandma."

That title, which we had been taught to use when

speaking to the aged, was new and sweet to her, who had never been blessed with child. She set the basket on the ground, put the pail beside it, and caressed us in a cheery way, then let us peep in and see what she had brought especially for us. How did it happen? That is something we were to learn later. Such luxuries,— eggs, bread, butter, cheese, and milk in the dear little tin pail!

Seeing how thin and hungry we looked she gave each a piece of buttered bread before going with us to our neighbor's house, where she left the food, with instructions, in broken English, that it was for us three little girls who had called her " grandma," and that we must not be given too much at a time.

When next grandma came she took puny Georgia home with her, and left me hugging the promise that I also should have a visit, if I would await my turn patiently.

Who can picture my delight when Georgia got back and told me of all she had seen? Cows, horses, pigs, and chickens, but most thrilling of all was about the cross old sheep, which would not let her pass if she did not carry a big stick in sight. Still, I should not have been so eager to go, nor so gleeful on the way, had I known that the " good-bye " kiss I gave my sister Frances at parting that day, would be the last kiss in five long years.

Grandma was as happy as I. She could understand English better than she could speak it, and in answering my questions, explained largely by signs. " Courage," her gray poodle, left deep footprints in the dust, as he trotted ahead over the well-known road, and I felt an increasing affection for him upon learning that he, too, had crossed the plains in an emigrant wagon and had reached the Fort at about the same time I had reached the snow. He was so small that I imagined he must have been a wee baby dog when he started, and that he was not yet half grown. My surprise and admiration quickened beyond expression when grandma assured me that he could do many tricks, understood French and German, and was learning English.

Then she laughed, and explained that he was thus accomplished because she and Christian Brunner, her husband, and Jacob, her brother-in-law, had come from a place far away across lands and big waters where most of the people spoke both French and German and that they had always talked to Courage in one or the other of these languages.

As soon as we got into the house she opened the back door and called "Jacob!" Then turning, she took a small cup of rennet clabber from the shelf, poured a little cream over it, put a spoon in it, and set it on the table before me. While I was eating, a pleasant elderly man came in and by nods, motions, and words, partly English and partly something else, convinced me that he liked little girls, and was glad to see me. Then of a sudden, he clasped his hands about my waist and tossed me in the air as father did before his hand was hurt, and when he wanted to startle me, and then hear me laugh. This act, which brought back loving memories, made Jacob seem nearer to me; nearer still when he told me I must not call him anything but Jakie.

Everything about the house was as Georgia had described. Even the big stick she had used to keep the old sheep from butting her over was behind the door where she had left it.

When Christian Brunner got home from the Fort, grandma had supper nearly ready, and he and I were friends the instant we looked into each other's face; for he was " grandpa " who had given us the liver the evening we did not find our sisters. He had gone home that night and said: " Mary, at the Fort are three hungry little orphan girls. Take them something as soon as you can. One child is fair, two are dark. You will know them by the way they speak to you."

Grandpa had now hastened home to hold me on his lap and to hear me say that I was glad to be at his house and intended to help grandma all I could for being so good as to bring me there. After I told how we had cooked the liver and how good it tasted, he wiped his eyes and said: " Mine child, when you little ones thanked me for that liver, it made me not so much your friend as when you called me 'grandpa.' "

As time went on, grandma declared that I helped her a great deal because I kept her chip-box full, shooed the hens out of the house, brought in the eggs, and drove the little chicks to bed, nights. I don't recollect that I was ever tired or sleepy, yet I know that

the night must have sped, between the time of my last
nod at the funny shadow picture of a rabbit which
Jakie made hop across the wall behind the lighted
candle, and Courage's barking near my pillow, which
grandma said meant, " Good-morning, little girl! "

It was after one of these reminders of a new day
that I saw Leanna. I don't know when or how she
came, but I missed Frances and Georgia the more because I wanted them to share our comforts. Nevertheless a strange feeling of uneasiness crept over me
as I noticed, later, that grandpa lingered and that the
three spoke long in their own tongue, and glanced
often toward me.

Finally grandpa and Jakie went off in the wagon
and grandma also disappeared, but soon returned,
dressed for a trip to the Fort, and explained that she
had heard that Georgia was sick and she would take
me back and bring her in my place. I had known from
the beginning that I was to stay only a little while, yet
I was woefully disturbed at having my enjoyment so
abruptly terminated. My first impulse was to cry,
but somehow, the influence of her who under the sough-
ing pines of the Sierras had told me that " friends do
not come quickly to a cry-baby child " gave me courage, and I looked up into the dear old face before me
and with the earnestness of an anxious child asked,
" Grandma, why can't you keep two of us? "

She looked at me, hesitated, then replied, " I will
see." She kissed away my fears and rode off on old
Lisa. I did not know that she would ride farther than

the fort and imagined she had gone on horseback so that she might the easier bring back my little sister.

Leanna washed the dishes and did the other work before she joined me in watching for grandma's return. At last she came in sight and I ran up the road craning my neck to see if Georgia were really behind on old Lisa's back, and when I saw her pinched face aglow with smiles that were all for me, I had but one wish, and that was to get my arms around her.

One chair was large enough to hold us both when we got into the house, and the big clock on the wall with long weights reaching almost to the floor and red roses painted around its white face, did not tick long before we were deaf to its sound, telling each other about the doings of the day.

She knew more than I, who listened intently as she excitedly went on:

" Me and Frances started to find you this morning, but we was n't far when we met Jacob in the wagon, and he stopped and asked us where we was going. We told him. Then he told us to get in by him. But he did n't come this way, just drove down to the river and some men lifted us out and set us in a boat and commenced to paddle across the water. I knew that was n't the way, and I cried and cried as loud as I could cry, and told them I wanted to go to my little sister Eliza, and that I 'd tip the boat over if they did not take me back; and one man said, ' It 's too bad! It ain't right to part the two littlest ones.' And they told me if I 'd sit still and stop crying they would bring me back with them by and by, and that I should come to you. And I minded.

" Then they taked us to that house where we sleeped under the carpet the night we did n't get to the Fort. Don't you remember? Well, lots of people was there and talked about us and about father and mother, and waited for grandma to come. Pretty soon grandma come, and everybody talked, and talked. And grandma told them she was sorry for us, and would take you and me if she could keep Leanna to help her do the work. When I was coming away with grandma, Frances cried like everything. She said she wanted to see you, and told the people mother said we should always stay together. But they would n't let her come. They 've gived her to somebody else, and now she is their little girl."

We both felt sorry for Frances, and wished we could know where she was and what she was doing.

While we were talking, grandma kept busily at work, and sometimes she wiped her face with the corner of her apron, yet we did not think of her as listening, nor of watching us, nor would we ever have known it, had we not learned it later from her own lips, as she told others the circumstances which had brought us into her life.

Some days later Georgia and I were playing in the back yard when Leanna appeared at the door and called out in quick, jubilant tones: " Children, run around to the front and see who has come! "

True enough, hitched to a stake near the front door

was a bay horse with white spots on his body and a white stripe down his face, and tied to the pommel of his saddle was another horse with a side saddle on its back. It did not take us long to get into the house where we found Elitha and our new brother, who had come to arrange about taking us away with them. While Elitha was talking to grandma and Leanna, Georgia stood listening, but I sat on my new brother's knee and heard all about his beautiful spotted horse and a colt of the same colors.

Elitha could not persuade Leanna or Georgia to go with her, nor was I inclined to do so when she and grandma first urged me. But I began to yield as the former told me she was lonesome; wanted at least one little sister to live with her, and that if I would be that one, I should have a new dress and a doll with a face. Then my new brother settled the matter by saying: "Listen to me. If you'll go, you shall have the pinto colt that I told you about, a little side saddle of your own, and whenever you feel like it, you can get on it and ride down to see all the folks." The prospects were so alluring that I went at once with Leanna, who was to get me ready for the journey.

Leanna did not share my enthusiasm. She said I was a foolish little thing, and declared I would get lonesome on such a big place so far away; that the colt would kick me if I tried to go near it, and that no one ever made saddles for colts. She was not so gentle as usual when she combed my hair and gave my face a right hard scrubbing with a cloth and whey, which grandma bade her use, " because it makes the skin so nice and soft."

Notwithstanding these discouragements, I took my clothes, which were tied up in a colored handkerchief, kissed them all good-bye, and rode away sitting behind my new brother on the spotted horse, really believing that I should be back in a few days on a visit.

CHAPTER XIX

WE left the Fort and grandma's house far behind, and still rode on and on. The day was warm, the wild flowers were gone, and the plain was yellow with ripening oats which rustled noisily as we passed through, crowding and bumping their neighborly heads together. Yet it was not a lonesome way, for we passed elk, antelope, and deer feeding, with pretty little fawns standing close to their mothers' sides. There were also sleek fat cattle resting under the shade of live oak trees, and great birds that soared around overhead casting their shadows on the ground. As we neared the river, smaller birds of brighter colors could be heard and seen in the trees along the banks where the water flowed between, clear and cold.

All these things my sister pointed out to me as we passed onward. It was almost dark before we came in sight of the adobe ranch house. We were met on the road by a pack of Indian dogs, whose fierce looks and savage yelping made me tremble, until I got into the house where they could not follow.

The first weeks of my stay on the ranch passed quickly. Elitha and I were together most of the time.

She made my new dress and a doll which was perfection in my eyes, though its face was crooked, and its pencilled hair was more like pothooks than curls. I did not see much of her husband, because in the mornings he rode away early to direct his Indian cattle-herders at the *rodeos,* or to oversee other ranch work, and I was often asleep when he returned nights.

The pinto colt he had promised me was, as Leanna had said, " big enough to kick, but too small to ride," and I at once realized that my anticipated visits could not be made as planned.

Occasionally, men came on horseback to stay a day or two, and before the summer was over, a young couple with a small baby moved into one part of our house. We called them Mr. and Mrs. Packwood and Baby Packwood. The mother and child were company for my sister, while the husbands talked continually of ranches, cattle, hides, and tallow, so I was free to roam around by myself.

In one of my wanderings I met a sprightly little Indian lad, whose face was almost as white as my own. He was clad in a blue and white shirt that reached below his knees. Several strings of beads were around his neck, and a small bow and arrow in his hand. We stopped and looked at each other; were pleased, yet shy about moving onward or speaking. I, being the larger, finally asked,

" What 's your name? "

To my great delight, he answered, " Name, Billy."

While we were slowly getting accustomed to each

other, a good-natured elderly squaw passed. She wore a tattered petticoat, and buttons, pieces of shell, and beads of bird bones dangled from a string around her neck. A band of buckskin covered her forehead and was attached to strips of rawhide, which held in place the water-tight basket hanging down her back. Billy now left me for her, and I followed the two to that part of our yard where the tall ash-hopper stood, which ever after was like a story book to me.

The squaw set the basket on the ground, reached up, and carefully lifted from a board laid across the top of the hopper, several pans of clabbered milk, which she poured into the basket. Instead of putting the pans back, she tilted them up against the hopper, squatted down in front and with her slim forefinger, scraped down the sides and bottom of each pan so that she and Billy could scoop up and convey to their mouths, by means of their three crooked fingers, all that had not gone into the basket. Then she licked her improvised spoon clean and dry; turned her back to her burden; replaced the band on her forehead; and with the help of her stick, slowly raised herself to her feet and quietly walked away, Billy after her.

Next day I was on watch early. My kind friend, the choreman, let me go with him when he carried the lye from the hopper to the soap fat barrel. Then he put more ashes on the hopper and set the pans of milk in place for the evening call of Billy and his companion.

He pointed out the *rancheria* by the river where the Indian herders lived with others of their tribe, among

PAPOOSES IN BICKOOSES

SUTTER'S MILL, WHERE MARSHALL DISCOVERED GOLD,
JANUARY 19, 1848

them, Billy and his mother. He also informed me that the squaws took turns in coming for the milk, and that Billy came as often as he got the chance; that he was a nice little fellow, who had learned a few English words from his white papa, who had gone off and left him.

Billy and I might never have played together as we did, if my brother-in-law had not taken his wife to San Francisco and left me in the care of Mr. and Mrs. Packwood. Their chief aim in life was to please their baby. She was a dear little thing when awake, but the house had to be kept very still while she slept, and they would raise a hand and say, " Hu-sh! " as they left me, and together tip-toed to the cradle to watch her smile in her sleep. I had their assurance that they would like to let me hold her if her little bones were not so soft that I might break them.

They were never unkind or cross to me. I had plenty to eat, and clean clothes to wear, but they did not seem to realize how I yearned for some one to love. So I went to Mr. Choreman. He told me about the antelope that raced across the ranch before I was up; of the elk, deer, bear, and buffalo he had shot in his day; and of beaver, otter, and other animals that he had trapped along the rivers. Entranced with his tales I became as excited as he, while listening to the dangers he had escaped.

One day he showed me a little chair which I declared was the cunningest thing I had ever seen. It had a high, straight back, just like those in the house, only that it was smaller. The seat was made of strips of rawhide woven in and out so that it looked like patchwork squares. He let me sit on it and say how beautiful it was, before telling me that he had made it all for me. I was so delighted that I jumped up, clasped it in my arms and looked at him in silent admiration. I do not believe that he could understand how rich and grateful I felt, although he shook his head saying, " You are not a bit happier than I was while making it for you, nor can you know how much good it does me to have you around."

Gradually, Billy spent more time near the ranch house, and learned many of my kind of words, and I picked up some of his. Before long, he discovered that he could climb up on the hopper, and then he helped me up. But I could not crook my fingers into as good a spoon as he did his, and he got more milk out of the pan than I.

We did not think any one saw us, yet the next time we climbed up, we found two old spoons stuck in a crack, in plain sight. After we got through using them, I wiped them on my dress skirt and put them back. Later, I met Mr. Choreman, who told me that he had put the spoons there because I was too nice a little girl to eat as Billy did, or to dip out of the same pan. I was ashamed and promised not to do so again, nor to climb up there with him.

As time passed, I watched wistfully for my sister's return, and thought a great deal about the folks at grandma's. I tried to remember all that had hap-

pened while I was there, and felt sure they were
waiting for me to pay the promised visit. A great
longing often made me rush out behind a large tree
near the river, where no one could see or hear me feel
sorry for myself, and where I would wonder if God
was taking care of the others and did not know where
I lived.

I still feel the wondrous thrill, and bid my throb-
bing heart beat slower, when I recall the joy that
tingled through every part of my being on that evening
when, unexpectedly, Leanna and Georgia came to the
door. Yet, so short-lived was that joy that the event
has always seemed more like a disquieting dream than
a reality; for they came at night and were gone in the
morning, and left me sorrowing.

A few months ago, I wrote to Georgia (now Mrs.
Babcock), who lives in the State of Washington, for
her recollections of that brief reunion, and she replied:

Before we went to Sonoma with Grandma Brunner in the
Fall of 1847, Leanna and I paid you a visit. We reached
your home at dusk. Mr. McCoon and Elitha were not there.
We were so glad to meet, but our visit was too short. You
and I were given a cup of bread and milk and sent to bed.
Leanna ate with the grown folks, who, upon learning that
we had only come to say good-bye, told her we must for your
sake get away before you awoke next morning. We arose
and got started early, but had only gone a short distance
when we heard your pitiful cry, begging us to take you with
us. Leanna hid her face in her apron, while a man caught
you and carried you back. I think she cried all the way
home. It was so hard to part from you.

Mr. Packwood carried me into the house, and both
he and his wife felt sorry for me. My head ached and

the tears would come as often as any one looked at me. Mrs. Packwood wet a piece of brown paper, laid it on my forehead, and bade me lie on my bed until I should feel better. I could not eat or play, and even Mr. Choreman's bright stories had lost their charm.

"Come look, see squaw, papoose! Me go, you go?" exclaimed Billy excitedly one soft gray morning after I had regained my spirits. I turned in the direction he pointed and saw quite a number of squaws trudging across an open flat with babies in bickooses, and larger children scampering along at various paces, most of them carrying baskets.

With Mrs. Packwood's permission, Billy and I sped away to join the line. I had never been granted such a privilege before, and had no idea what it all meant.

As we approached the edge of the marsh, the squaws walked more slowly, with their eyes fixed upon the ground. Every other moment some of them would be down, digging in the earth with forefinger or a little stick, and I soon learned they were gathering bulbs about a quarter of an inch in thickness and as large around as the smaller end of a woman's thimble. I had seen the plants growing near the pond at the fort, but now the bulbs were ripe, and were being gathered for winter use. In accordance with the tribal custom, not a bulb was eaten during harvest time. They grew so far apart and were so small that it took a long while to make a fair showing in the baskets.

When no more bulbs could be found, the baskets were put on the ground in groups, and the mothers carefully leaned their bickooses against them in such positions that the wide awake papooses could look out from under their shades and smile and sputter at each other in quaint Indian baby-talk; and the sleeping could sleep on undisturbed.

That done, the squaws built a roaring fire, and one of them untied a bundle of hardwood sticks which she had brought for the purpose, and stuck them around under the fuel in touch with the hottest parts of the burning mass. When the ends glowed like long-lasting coals, the waiting crowd snatched them from their bed and rushed into the low thicket which grew in the marsh. I followed with my fire-brand, but, not knowing what to do with it, simply watched the Indians stick theirs into the bushes, sometimes high up, sometimes low down. I saw them dodge about, and heard their shouts of warning and their peals of laughter. Then myriads of hornets came buzzing and swarming about. This frightened me so that I ran back to where the brown babies were cooing in safety.

Empty-handed, but happy, they at length returned, and though I could not understand anything they were saying, their looks and actions betokened what a good time they had had.

Years later, I described the scene to Elitha, who assured me that I had been highly favored by those Indians for they had permitted me to witness their annual " Grub Feast." The Piutes always use burning fagots to drive hornets and other stinging insects from their nests, and they also use heat in opening the comb cells so that they can easily remove the larvæ, which they eat without further preparation.

With the first cold snaps of winter, my feet felt the effect of former frost bites, and I was obliged to spend most of my time within doors. Fortunately Baby Packwood had grown to be quite a frolicsome child. She was fond of me, and her bones had hardened so that there was no longer danger of my breaking them when I lifted her or held her on my lap. Her mother had also discovered that I was anxious to be helpful, pleased when given something to do, and proud when my work was praised.

I was quite satisfied with my surroundings, when, unexpectedly, Mr. McCoon brought my sister back, and once more we had happy times together.

CHAPTER XX

I RETURN TO GRANDMA — WAR RUMORS AT THE FORT —
LINGERING HOPE THAT MY MOTHER MIGHT BE LIVING —
AN INDIAN CONVOY — THE BRUNNERS AND THEIR HOME.

THE Spring of 1848 was at hand when my brother-in-law said to me, " Grandma Brunner wants you to come back to her; and if, you would like to go, I'll take you to the Fort, as soon as the weather changes, and leave you with the people who are getting ready to move north and are willing to take you with them to Sonoma, where grandma now lives."

The storm was not over, but the day was promising, when my bundle of clothes was again on the pommel of the saddle, and I ready to begin my journey. I was so excited that I could hardly get around to say good-bye to those who had gathered to see me off. We returned by the same route that we had followed out on that warm June day, but everything seemed different. The catkins on the willows were forming and the plain was green with young grass.

As we neared the Fort we passed a large camp of fine-looking Indians who, I was told, were the friendly Walla-Wallas, that came every spring to trade ponies, and otter, and beaver-skins with Captain Sutter for provisions, blankets, beads, gun caps, shot, and powder.

A large emigrant wagon stood near the adobe house where my new brother-in-law drew rein. Before dismounting, he reached back, took me by the arm and carefully supported me as I slid from the horse to the ground. I was so stiff that I could hardly stand, but he led me to the door where we were welcomed by a good-natured woman, to whom he said,

"Well, Mrs. Lennox, you see I 've brought the little girl. I don't think she 'll be much trouble, unless she talks you to death."

Then he told her that I had, during the ride, asked him more questions than a man six times his size could answer. But she laughed, and "'lowed" that I could n't match either of her three boys in asking questions, and then informed him that she did not "calculate on making the move until the roads be dryer and the weather settled." She promised, however, that I should have good care until I could be handed over to the Brunners. After a few words with her in private Perry McCoon bade me good-bye, and passed out of my life forever.

I was now again with emigrants who had crossed the plains in 1846, but who had followed the Fort Hall route and so escaped the misfortunes that befell the Donner Party.

Supper over, Mrs. Lennox made me a bed on the floor in the far corner of the room. I must have fallen asleep as soon as my head touched the pillow, for I remember nothing more until I was awakened by voices, and saw the candle still burning and Mrs. Lennox and two men and a woman sitting near the table. The man speaking had a shrill voice, and his words were so terrifying that I shook all over; my hair felt as though it were trying to pull itself out by its roots; a cold sweat dampened my clothes. I was afraid to move or to turn my eyes. Listening, I tried to remember how many Indians he was talking about. I knew it must be a great many, for it was such a long word. After they went away and the house was dark, I still seemed to see his excited manner and to hear him say:

"Mrs. Lennox, we 've got to get out of here right away, for I heard tell at the store before I come up that there 's bound to be an Injun outbreak. Them savages from Sonora are already on their way up, and they 'll kill and scalp every man, woman, and child they can ketch, and there 's nothing to keep them from ketching us, if we stay at this here little fort any longer."

I lay awake a long while. I did not dare call out because I imagined some of those Indians might have got ahead of the rest and be sneaking up to our house at that very moment. I wondered where I could hide if they should climb through the window, and I felt that Georgia would never know what had become of me, if they should kill and scalp me.

As soon as Mrs. Lennox stirred in the morning, I ran to her and had a good cry. She threatened all sorts of things for the man who had caused me such torture, and declared that he believed everything he heard. He did not seem to remember how many hundred miles away Sonora was, nor how many loaded cannon there were at the Fort. I felt better satisfied, however, when she told me that she had made up her mind to start for Sonoma the next day.

After breakfast her younger boys wanted to see the Walla-Wallas, and took me along. A cold breath from the Sierra Nevadas made me look up and shiver. Soon Captains Sutter and Kern passed us, the former on his favorite white horse, and the latter on a dark bay. I was delighted to catch a glimpse of those two good friends, but they did not know it. They had been to see the Indian ponies, and before we got to the big gate, they had gone in and the Walla-Wallas were forming in line on both sides of the road between the gate and the front of the store.

Only two Indians at a time were allowed to enter the building, and as they were slow in making their trades, we had a good chance to see them all. The men, the boys, and most of the women were dressed in fringed buckskin suits and their hands and faces were painted red, as the Sioux warriors of Fort Laramie painted their cheeks.

The Lennox boys took greatest interest in the little fellows with the bows and arrows, but I could not keep my eyes from the young princess, who stood beside her father, the chief. She was all shimmering with beads. They formed flowers on her moccasins; fringed the outer seams of her doeskin trousers and the hem of her tunic; formed a stripe around her arm holes and her belt; glittered on a band which held in place the eagle plume in her hair; dangled from her ears; and encircled her neck and arms. Yet she did not seem to wear one too many. She looked so winsome and picturesque that I have never forgotten the laughing, pretty picture.

We started back over ground where my little sisters and I had wandered the previous Spring. The people whom I remembered had since gone to other settlements, and strangers lived in the old huts. I could not help looking in as we passed, for I still felt that mother might not be dead. She might have come down the mountain alone and perhaps I could find her. The boys, not knowing why I lagged behind, tried to hurry me along; and finally left me to go home by myself. This, not from unkindness, but rather love of teasing, and also oblivion of the vain hope I cherished.

Mrs. Lennox let me dry the dishes for her after the noon meal, then sent me to visit the neighbor in the next house, while she should stow her things in the wagon and get ready for the journey. I loved this lady * in the next house as soon as she spoke to me, and I was delighted with her baby, who reached out his little arms to have me take him, and raised his head for me to kiss his lips. While he slept, his mother sewed and talked with me. She had known my parents on the plains, and now let me sit at her feet, giving me her workbox, that I might look at its bobbins of different-colored thread and the pretty needle-book. When I told her that the things looked a little like

*Mrs. Andrew J. Grayson, wife of the well-known ornithologist, frequently referred to as the " Audubon of the West."

mother's and that sometimes mother let me take the tiniest bit of her wax, she gave me permission to take a tiny taste of that which I held in my hand to see if it was like that which I remembered.

Only she, the baby, and I sat down to tea, yet she said that she was glad she had company, for baby's papa was away with Captain Frémont, and she was lonesome.

After I learned that she would have to stay until he came back, I was troubled, and told what I had heard in the night. She assured me that those in charge of the Fort heard every day all that was going on for miles and miles around, and that if they should learn that fighting Indians were coming, they would take all the white people and the good Indians into the fort, and then shoot the bad ones with the cannon that peeped through its embrasures.

The dainty meal and her motherly talk kept me a happy child until I heard the footsteps of the Lennox boys. I knew they were coming for me, and that I should have to sleep in that dark room where I had been so afraid. Quickly slipping from my chair, under the table, and hiding behind my new friend's dress skirt, I begged her not to let them know where I was, and please, to let me stay with her all night. I listened as she sent the boys back to tell their mother that she would keep me until morning, adding that she would step in and explain matters after she put her baby to bed. Before I went to sleep she heard me say my prayers and kissed me good-night.

ENCAMPED BY THE RIVER

When I awoke next morning, I was not in her house, but in Mrs. Lennox's wagon, on the way to Sonoma.

The distance between the Fort and Sonoma was only about eighty miles, yet the heavy roads and the frequent showers kept us on the journey more than a week. It was still drizzling when we reached the town and Mrs. Lennox learned where the Brunners lived. I had been told that they would be looking for me, and I expected to go to them at once.

As we approached the west bank of the creek, which winds south past the town, we could see the branches on the trees in grandma's dooryard swaying. Yet we could not reach there, because a heavy mountain storm had turned a torrent into the creek channel, washed away the foot bridge, and overflowed the low land. Disappointed, we encamped on high ground to wait for the waters to recede.

Toward evening, Jakie gathering his cows on the opposite side, noticed our emigrant wagon, and oxen, and as he drew nearer recognized Mrs. Lennox. Both signalled from where they stood, and soon he descried me, anxious to go to him. He, also, was disappointed at the enforced delay, and returned often to cheer us, and to note the height of the water. It seemed to me that we had been there days and days, when a Mission Indian on a gray pony happened to come our way, and upon learning what was wanted, signalled that he would carry me over for a Mexican silver dollar. Jakie immediately drew the coin from his pocket and held it between thumb and forefinger, high above his head in the sunshine, to show the native that his price would be paid.

Quickly the Indian dismounted, looked his pony over carefully, cinched the blanket on tighter, led him to the water's edge, and turned to me. I shuddered, and when all was ready, drew near the deep flowing current tremblingly, yet did not hesitate; for my loved ones were beyond, and to reach them I was willing to venture.

The Indian mounted and I was placed behind him. By sign, he warned me not to loosen my hold, lest I, like the passing branches, should become the water's prey. With my arms clasped tightly about his dusky form, and his elbows clamped over them, we entered the stream. I saw the water surge up around us, felt it splash over me! Oh, how cold it was! I held my breath as we reached the deepest part, and in dread clung closer to the form before me. We were going down stream, drifting past where Jakie stood! How could I know that we were heading for the safe slope up the bank where we landed?

The Indian took his dollar with a grunt of satisfaction, and Jakie bade me wave to the friends I had left behind, as he put me on old Lisa's back and hurried off to grandma, Leanna, and Georgia, waiting at the gate to welcome me home.

Georgia had a number of patches of calico and other trinkets which she had collected for me, and offered them as soon as we had exchanged greetings, then eagerly conducted me about the place.

THE BRUNNER FAMILY

Grandma was more energetic and busier than at the Fort, and I could only talk with her as she worked, but there was so much to see and hear that before nightfall my feet were heavy and my brain was weary. However, a good sleep under the roof of those whom I loved was all the tonic I needed to prepare me for a fair start in the new career, and grandma's assurance, " This be your home so long as you be good," filled me with such gladness that, childlike, I promised to be good always and to do everything that should be required of me.

Most of the emigrants in and around the Pueblo of Sonoma were Americans from the western frontiers of the United States. They had reached the province in the Summer or early Autumn of 1846, and for safety had settled near this United States Army post. Here they had bought land and made homes within neighboring distance of each other and begun life anew in simple, happy, pioneer fashion. The Brunners were a different type. They had immigrated from Switzerland and settled in New Orleans, Louisiana, when young, and by toil and economy had saved the snug sum of money which they brought to invest in California enterprises.

They could speak and read French and German, and had some knowledge of figures. Being skilled in the preparation of all the delicacies of the meat market, and the products of the dairy, they had brought across the plains the necessary equipment for both branches of business, and had already established a butcher shop in the town and a dairy on the farm, less than a mile from it.

Jakie was busy and useful at both places, but grandpa was owner of the shop, and grandma of the dairy. Her hand had the cunning of the Swiss cheese-maker, and the deftness of the artist in butter mould-ing. She was also an experienced cook, and had many household commodities usually unknown to pioneer homes. They were thus eminently fitted for life in a crude new settlement, and occupied an important place in the community.

A public road cut their land into two unequal parts. The cattle corrals and sheds were grouped on one side of the road, and the family accommodations on the other. Three magnificent oaks and a weird, blackened tree-trunk added picturesqueness to the ground upon which the log cabin and outbuildings stood. The trim live oak shaded the adobe milk-room and smoke-house, while the grand old white oak spread its far-reaching boughs over the curbed well and front dooryard.

The log cabin was a substantial three-roomed struc-ture. Its two outer doors opened with latch strings and were sawed across just above the middle, so that the lower sections might be kept closed against the straying pigs and fowls, while the upper part remained open to help the windows opposite give light and ven-tilation. The east end formed the ample store-room with shelves for many stages of ripening cheese. The west end served as sleeping apartment for all except Jakie. The large middle room was set apart as kitchen

PLAZA AND BARRACKS OF SONOMA

ONE OF THE OLDEST BUILDINGS IN SONOMA

and general living room. Against its wall were braced the dear old clock and conveniences for holding dishes, and the few keepsakes which had shared the wanderings of their owners on two continents.

The adobe chimney, which formed part of the partition between the living and the sleeping apartment, gave a huge fireplace to each. From the side of the one that cheered the living room, swung a crane worthy of the great copper cheese kettle that hung on its arm. In tidy rows on the chimney shelf stood bottles and boxes of medicine, two small brass kettles, and six bright candlesticks with hoods, trays, and snuffers to match. On the wide hearth beneath were ranged the old-fashioned three-legged iron pots, dominated by the large round one, used as a bake oven. Hovering over the fire sat the iron tea-kettle, with its slender throat and pointed lips, now warmed to song by the blazing logs, now rattling its lid with increasing fervor.

A long table with rough redwood benches around it, a few straight-backed chairs against the wall, and Jakie's half-concealed bed, in the far corner, constituted the visible furnishings of this memorable room, which was so spick and span in German order and cleanliness, that even its clay floor had to be sprinkled in regular spots and rings before being swept.

It was under the great oaks that most of the morning work was done. There the pails and pans were washed and sunned, the meats chopped, the sausage made, head-cheese moulded, ham and bacon salted, and the lard tried out over the out-door fires. Among those busy scenes, Georgia and I spent many happy hours, and learned some of our hardest lessons; for to us were assigned regular tasks, and we were also expected to do the countless little errands which save steps to grown people, and are supposed not to tire the feet of children.

Grandma, stimulated by the success of her mixing and moulding, and elated by the profit she saw in it, was often too happy and bustling to remember how young we were, or that we got tired, or had worries of our own to bear.

Our small troubles, however, were soon forgotten, when we could slip away for a while to the lovely playhouse which Leanna had secretly made for us in an excavation in the back yard. There we forgot work, used our own language, and played we were like other children; for we owned the beautiful cupboard dug in the wall, and the pieces of Delft and broken glass set in rows upon the shelves, also the furniture, made of stumps and blocks of wood, and the two bottles standing behind the brush barricade to act as sentries in case of danger during our absence.

One stolen visit to that playhouse led me into such disgrace, that grandma did not speak to me the rest of the day, and told Jakie all about it.

In the evening, when no one else was near, he called me to him. I obeyed with downcast head. Putting his hand under my chin, and turning my face up, he made me look straight into his eyes, as he asked,

" Who broke dat glass cup vat grandma left on die

dinner table full of milk, and told you watch it bis Hendrik come to his dinner, or bis she be done mit her nap?"

I tried to turn my eyes down, but he would not let me, and I faltered, " The chicken knocked it off,— but he left the door open so it could get in."

Then, he raised his other hand, shook his finger, and in awe-inspiring tone continued: " Yes, I be sure die chicken do dat, but vot for you tell grandma dat Heinrick do dat? Der debil makes peoples tell lies, and den he ketch sie for his fire, und he vill ketch you, if you do dat some more. Gott, who you mutter telled you 'bout, will not love you. I will not love you, if you do dat some more. I be sorry for you, because I tought you vas His little girl, and mine little girl."

Jakie must have spent much time in collecting so many English words, and they were effective, for before he got through repeating them to me, I was as heart-sore and penitent as a child could be.

After he had forgiven me, he sent me to grandma, later to acknowledge my wrong to Hendrik, and before I slept, I had to tell God what a bad child I had been, and ask Him to make me good.

I had promised to be very careful and to try never to tell another lie, and I had been unhappy enough to want to keep the promise. But, alas, my sympathy for Jakie led me into more trouble, and it must have been on Sunday too, for he was not working, but sitting reverently under the tree with his elbows upon a table, and his cheeks resting in the hollows of his hands. Before him lay the Holy Scriptures from which he was slowly reading aloud in solemn tones.

Georgia and I standing a short distance from him, listened very intently. Not hearing a single English word, and not understanding many of the German, I became deeply concerned and turning to her asked,

" Are n't you awful sorry for poor Jakie? There he is, reading to God in German, and God can't understand him. I 'm afraid Jakie won't go to heaven when he dies."

My wise little sister turned upon me indignantly, assuring me that " God sees everybody and understands everybody's talk." To prove the truth of her statement, she rushed to the kitchen and appealed to grandma, who not only confirmed Georgia's words, but asked me what right I had to believe that God was American only, and could not understand good German people when they read and spoke to Him? She wanted to know if I was not ashamed to think that they, who had loved me, and been kind to me would not go to Heaven as well as I who had come to them a beggar? Then she sent me away by myself to think of my many sins; and I, weeping, accepted banishment from Georgia, lest she should learn wickedness from me.

Georgia was greatly disturbed on my account, because she believed I had wilfully misrepresented God, and that He might not forgive me. When Jakie learned what had happened, he declared that I had spoken like a child, and needed instruction more than punishment. So for the purpose of broadening my religious views, and keeping before me the fact that "God can do all things and knows all languages," grandma taught me the Lord's Prayer in French and German, and heard me repeat it each night in both languages, after I had said it as taught me by my mother.

It was about this time, that Leanna confided to me that she was homesick for Elitha, and she would go to her very soon. She said that I must not object when the time came, for she loved her own sister just as much as I did mine, and was as anxious to go to Elitha as I had been to come to Georgia. She had been planning several weeks, and knew of a family with which she could travel to Sutter's Fort. Later, when she collected her things to go away, she left with us a pair of beautifully knit black silk stockings, marked near the top in fine cross-stitch in white, "D," and under that "5." The stockings had been our mother's. She had knit them herself and worn them. Georgia gave one to me and kept the other. We both felt that they were almost too sacred to handle. They were our only keepsakes.

Later, Georgia found a small tin box in which mother had kept important papers. Recently, when referring to that circumstance, Georgia said: "Grandma for a long time had used it for a white-sugar box, and kept it on a shelf so high that we could see it only when she lifted it down; and I don't think we took our eyes from it until it was put back. We felt that it was too valuable for us ever to own. One day, I found it thrown away. One side had become unsoldered from the ends and the bottom also was hanging loose. With a full heart, I grasped the treasure and put it where we could often see it. Long afterwards, Harry Huff kindly offered to repair it; and the solder that still holds it together is also regarded as a keepsake from a dear friend.''

CHAPTER XXI

MORAL DISCIPLINE — THE HISTORICAL PUEBLO OF SONOMA — SUGAR PLUMS.

GRANDMA often declared that she loved me, and did not want to be too severe; but, for fear that I had learned much wickedness from the little Indians with whom I had played after I left her at the Fort, she should watch me very closely herself, and also have Georgia tell her whenever she should see me do wrong. Consequently, for a while after I reached Sonoma, I was frequently on the penitential bench, and was as often punished for fancied misdoings as for real ones. Yet, I grant that grandma was warranted in being severe the day that she got back from town before I was ready for her.

She had left us with the promise that she would bring us something nice if we would be good children and do certain work that she had planned. After we had finished the task, we both became restless, wondered how soon she would come back, and what we could do next to keep from being lonesome. Then I espied on the upper shelf the cream-colored sugar bowl, with the old-fashioned red roses and black foliage on its cover and sides. Grandma had occasionally given us lumps of sugar out of it; and I now asked Georgia if I had n't better get it down, so that we could each have a lump of sugar. Hesitatingly, she said, " No, I am afraid you will break it." I assured her that I would be very careful, and at once set a chair in place and climbed up. It was quite a strain to reach the bowl, so I lifted it down and rested it on the lower shelf, expecting to turn and put it into Georgia's hands. But, somehow, before I could do this, the lid slipped off and lay in two pieces upon the floor. Georgia cried out reproachfully,

" There, you know I did n't want you to do it, and now you will get a good whipping for breaking grandma's best sugar bowl! "

I replied loftily that I was not afraid, because I would ask God to mend it for me. She did not think He would do it, but I did. So I matched the broken edges and put it on the chair, knelt down before it and said " Please " when I made my request. I touched the pieces very carefully, and pleaded more earnestly each time that I found them unchanged. Finally, Georgia, watching at the door, said excitedly, " Here comes grandma! "

I arose, so disappointed and chagrined that I scarcely heard her as she entered and spoke to me. I fully believed that He would have mended that cover if she had remained away a little longer; nevertheless, I was so indignant at Him for being so slow about it, that I stood unabashed while Georgia told all that had happened. The whipping I got did not make much im-

pression, but the after talks and the banishment from
" good company " were terrible.

Later, when I was called from my hiding-place,
grandma saw that I had been very miserable, and she
insisted upon knowing what I had been thinking about.
Then I told her, reluctantly, that I had talked to God
and told Him I did not think that He was a very good
Heavenly Father, or He would not let me get into so
much trouble; that I was mad at Him, and did n't believe He knew how to mend dishes. She covered her
face with her apron and told me, sobbingly, that she
had expected me to be sorry for getting down her sugar
bowl and for breaking its cover; that I was so bad that
I would " surely put poor old grandma's gray hair in
her grave, who had got one foot there already and the
other on the brink."

This increased my wretchedness, and I begged her to
live just a little longer so that I might show her that I
would be good. She agreed to give me another trial
and ended by telling me about the " beautiful, wicked
angel who had been driven out of paradise, and spends
his time coaxing people to be bad, and then remembers
them, and after they die, takes them on his fork and
pitches them back and forth in his fire." Jakie had
told me his name and also the name of his home.

Toward evening, my head ached, and I felt so ill that
I crept close to grandma and asked sorrowfully if she
thought the devil meant to have me die that night, and
then take me to his hell. At a glance, she saw that I
suffered, and drew me to her, pillowed my head against

her bosom and soothingly assured me that I would be forgiven if I would make friends with God and remember the lesson that I had learned that day. She told me, later, I must never say " devil," or " hell," because it was not nice in little girls, but that, instead, I might use the words, "blackman," and "blackman's fires." At first, I did not like to say it that way, because I was afraid that the beautiful devil might think that I was calling him nicknames and get angry with me.

Notwithstanding my shortcomings, the Brunners were very willing to keep me, and strove to make a " Schweitzer child " of me, dressed me in clothes modelled after those which grandma wore when she was small, and by verse and legend filled my thoughts with pictures of their Alpine country. I liked the German language, learned it rapidly and soon could help to translate orders. Those which pleased grandma best were from the homes of Mr. Jacob Leese, Captain Fitch, Major Prudon, and General Vallejo; for their patronage influenced other distinguished Spanish families at a distance to send for her excellent cheese and fancy pats of butter. Yet, with equal nicety, she filled the orders that came from the messroom of the officers of our own brave boys in blue, and always tried to have a better kerchief and apron on the evenings that officers and orderly rode out to pay the bills.

Visitors felt more than a passing interest in us two little ones, for accounts of the sufferings of the Donner Party had been carried to all the settlements on the Pacific coast and had been sent in print or writings to all parts of the United States as a warning against further emigration to California by way of Hastings Cut-Off. Thus the name we bore awakened sympathy for us, and in the huts of the lowly natives as well as in the homes of the rulers of the province, we found welcome and were greeted with words of tenderness, which were often followed by prayers for the repose of the souls of our precious dead.

Marked attentions were also shown us by officers and soldiers from the post. The latter gathered in the evenings at the Brunner home for social intercourse. Some played cards, checkers, and dominoes, or talked and sang about *"des Deutschen Vaterland."* Others reviewed happenings in our own country, recalled battles fought and victories won. And we, sitting between our foster grandparents, or beside Jakie, listening to their thrilling tales, were, unwittingly, crammed with crumbs of truth and fiction that made lasting impressions upon our minds.

Nor were these odd bits of knowledge all we gained from those soldier friends. They taught us the alphabet, how to spell easy words, and then to form letters with pencil. They explained the meaning of fife and drum calls which we heard during the day, and in mischievous earnestness, declared that they, the best fighters of Colonel Stephenson's famous regiment of New York Volunteers, had pledged their arms and legs to our defence, and had only come to see if we were worth the price they might have to pay. Yet they made grim faces when, all too soon, the retreat call from the barracks sounded, and away they would have to go on the double quick, to be at post by the time of roll call, and in bed at sound of taps.

On those evenings when grandma visited the sick, or went from home on errands, we children were tucked away early in our trundle bed. There, and by ourselves, we spoke of mother and the mountains. Not infrequently, however, our thoughts would be recalled to the present by loud, wailing squeak-squawk, squeak-squawks. As the sound drew nearer and became shriller, we would put our fingers in our ears to muffle the dismal tones, which we knew were only the creakings of the two wooden wheels of some Mexican *carreta,* laboriously bringing passengers to town, or perhaps a cruder one carrying hides to the *embarcadero,* or possibly supplies to adjacent *ranchos.* We wondered how old people and mothers with sick children could travel in such uncomfortable vehicles and not become distracted by their nerve-piercing noises. Then, like a bird-song, pleasanter scenes would steal in upon our musings, of gay horseback parties on their way to church feasts, or fandangos, preceded or followed by servants in charge of pack animals laden with luggage.

We rarely stayed awake long enough to say all we wished about the Spanish people. Their methods of travel, modes of dress, and fascinating manners were sources of never-ending discussion and interest.

OLD MEXICAN CARRETA

RESIDENCE OF JUDGE A. L. RHODES, A TYPICAL CALIFORNIA HOUSE OF
THE BETTER CLASS IN 1849

PUEBLO OF SONOMA

We had seen princely dons of many leagues ride by in state; dashing *caballeros* resplendent in costumes of satin and velvet, on their way to sing beneath the windows of dark-eyed *señoritas;* and had stood close enough to the wearers of embroidered and lace-bedecked small clothes, to count the scallops which closed the seams of their outer garments, and to hear the faint tinkle of the tiny silver bells which dangled from them. We had feasted our eyes on magnificently robed *señoras* and *señoritas;* caught the scent of the roses twined in their hair, and the flash of jewels on their persons.

Such frequent object-lessons made the names and surroundings of those grandees easy to remember. Some lived leagues distant, some were near neighbors in that typical Mexican Pueblo of Sonoma, whose adobe walls and red-tiled roofs nestled close to the foot of the dimpled hills overlooking the valley from the north, and whose historic and romantic associations were connected with distinguished families who still called it home.

Foremost among the men was General Mariano Guadalupe Vallejo, by whom Sonoma was founded in 1834, upon ground which had twice been consecrated to Mission use. First by Padre Altemera, who had, in 1823, established there the church and mission building of San Francisco Solano. And four years later, after hostile Indians had destroyed the sacred structures, Padre Fortune, under protection of Presidio Golden Gate, blessed the ashes and rebuilt the church and the parochial houses named last on the list of the historic Missions of California.

The Vallejo home covered the largest plot of ground on the north side of the plaza, and its great house had a hospitable air, despite its lofty watchtower, begrimed by sentry holes, overlooking every part of the valley.

During the period that its owner was *commandante* of the northern frontier, the Vallejo home was headquarters for high officials of the province. But after Commodore Sloat raised the Stars and Stripes at Monterey, General Vallejo espoused the cause of the United States, put aside much of his Spanish exclusiveness, and opened his doors to Americans as graciously as to friends of his own nationality.

A historic souvenir greatly prized by Americans in town and valley was the flag pole, which in Sonoma's infancy had been hewn from the distant mountain forest, and brought down on pack animals by mission Indians under General Vallejo's direction. It originally stood in the centre of the plaza, where it was planted with sacred ceremonials, and where amid ringing cheers of " *Viva Mexico!* " it first flung to the breeze that country's symbolical banner of green, white, and red. Through ten fitful years it loyally waved those colors; then followed its brief humiliation by the Bear Flag episode, and early redemption by order of Commodore Sloat, who sent thither an American flag-bearer to invest it with the Stars and Stripes. Thereafter, a patriotic impulse suggested its removal to the parade ground of the United States Army post, and as Spanish residents looked upon it as a thornful reminder of lost power they felt no regret when Uncle Sam's boys transplanted it to new environments and made it an American feature by adoption.

But the Mexican landmark which appealed to me most pathetically was the quaint rustic belfry which stood solitary in the open space in front of the Mission buildings. Its strong columns were the trunks of trees that looked as though they might have grown there for the purpose of shouldering the heavy cross-beams from which the chimes hung. Its smooth timbers had been laboriously hewn by hand, as must be the case in a land where there are no saw mills. The parts that were not bound together with thongs of rawhide, were held in place by wooden pegs. The strips of rawhide attached to the clappers dropped low enough for me to reach, and often tempted me to make the bells speak.

Mission padres no longer dwelt in the buildings, but shepherds from distant folds came monthly to administer to the needs of this consecrated flock. Then the many bells would call the faithful to mass, and to vespers, or chime for the wedding of favored sons and daughters. Part of them would jingle merrily for notable christenings; but one only would toll when death whitened the lips of some distinguished victim; and again, while the blessed body was being borne to its last resting-place.

During one of my first trips to town, Jakie and I

were standing by grandpa's shop on the east side of the plaza, when suddenly those bells rang out clear and sweet, and we saw the believing glide out of their homes in every direction and wend their way to the church. The high-born ladies had put aside their jewels, their gorgeous silks and satins, and donned the simpler garb prescribed for the season of fasts and prayer. Those to the manor born wore the picturesque *rebosa* of fine lace or gauzy silk, draped over the head and about the shoulders; while those of humbler station made the shawl serve in place of the *rebosa*. The Indian servants, who with mats and kneeling cushions followed their mistresses, wore white chemises, bright-colored petticoats, and handkerchiefs folded three-cornerwise over the head and knotted under the chin. The costumes of the young girls were modelled after those of their mothers; and the little ladies appeared as demure and walked as stately as their elders. The gentlemen also were garbed in plainer costumes than their wont, and, for custom's sake, rode on horseback even the short distances which little children walked.

The town seemed deserted, and the church filled, as we started homeward, I skipping ahead until we reached a shop window where I waited for Jakie and asked him if he knew what those pretty little things were that I saw on a shelf, in big short-necked glass jars. Some were round and had little " stickers " all over them, and others looked like birds' eggs, pink, yellow, white, and violet.

He told me the round ones were sugar plums, and the egg-shaped had each an almond nut under its bright crust; that they were candies that had come from France in the ships that had brought the Spanish people their fine clothes; and that they were only for the rich, and would make poor little girls' teeth ache, if they should eat them.

Yet, after I confided to him how mother had given me a lump of loaf sugar each night as long as it lasted, and how sorry we both felt when there was no more, he led me into the shop and let me choose two of each kind and color from the jars. We walked faster as I carried them home. Jakie and grandma would not take any, but she gave Georgia and me each a sugar plum and an egg, and saved the rest for other days when we should be good children.

CHAPTER XXII

IN the year 1848, while the settlers and their families were contentedly at work developing the resources of the country, the astounding cry, "Gold discovered!" came through the valley like a blight, stopping every industry in its wake.

Excited men, women, and children rushed to town in quest of information. It was furnished by Alcalde Boggs and General Vallejo, who had been called away privately two weeks earlier, and had just returned in a state of great enthusiasm, declaring that gold, "in dust, grains, and chunks had been discovered at Coloma, not more than a day's journey from Sutter's Fort."

"How soon can we get there?" became the all-absorbing problem of eager listeners. The only hotel-keeper in the town sold his kettles and pans, closed his house, and departed. Shopkeepers packed most of their supplies for immediate shipment, and raised the price of those left for home trade. Men and half-grown boys hardly took time to collect a meagre outfit before they were off with shovel and pan and " something big to hold the gold." A few families packed their effects into emigrant wagons and deserted house and lands for the luring gold fields.

Crowds from San Francisco came hurrying through, some stopping barely long enough to repeat the maddening tales that had started them off to the diggings with pick and shovel. Each new rumor increased the exodus of gold-seekers; and by the end of the first week in August, when the messenger arrived with the long-hoped-for report of the ratification of the treaty of peace, and General Mason's proclamation officially announcing it, there were not enough men left in the valley, outside of the barracks, to give a decent round of cheers for the blessing of peace.

Grandpa brought the news home, " California is ours. There will be no more war, no more trouble, and no more need of soldiers."

Yet the women felt that their battles and trials had just begun, since they had suddenly become the sole home-keepers, with limited ways and means to provide for the children and care for the stock and farms. Discouragement would have rendered the burdens of many too heavy to carry, had not " work together," and " help your neighbor," become the watchwords of the day. No one was allowed to suffer through lack of practical sympathy. From house to house, by turns, went the strong to help the weak to bridge their troubles. They went, not with cheering words only, but with something in store for the empty cupboards and with ready hands to help to milk, wash, cook, or sew.

Grandma was in such demand that she had little time to rest; for there was not a doctor nor a " medicine shop " in the valley, and her parcels of herbs and knowledge of their uses had to serve for both. Nights, she set her shoes handy, so that she could dress quickly when summoned to the sick; and dawn of day often marked her home-coming.

Georgia and I were led into her work early, for we were sent with broths and appetizers to the sick on clearings within walking distances; and she would bid us stay a while at different houses where we could be helpful, but to be sure and bring careful reports from each home we entered. Under such training, we learned much about diseases and the care of the suffering. Anon, we would find in the plain wooden cradle, a dainty bundle of sweetness, all done up in white, which its happy owner declared grandma had brought her, and we felt quite repaid for our tiresome walk if permitted to hold it a wee while and learn its name.

We were sent together on these missions, in order that we might help each other to remember all that was told us; yet grandma had us take turns, and the one whom she commissioned to make the inquiries was expected to bring the fuller answers. Sometimes, we played on the way and made mistakes. Then she would mete out to us that hardest of punishments, namely, that we were not to speak with each other until she

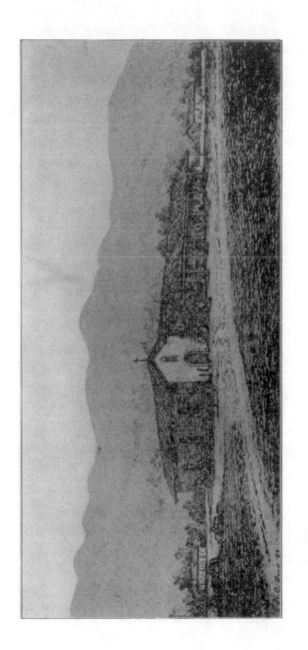

MISSION SAN FRANCISCO SOLANO, LAST OF THE HISTORIC
MISSIONS OF CALIFORNIA

RUINS OF THE MISSION AT SONOMA

should forgive our offence. Forgiveness usually came before time to drive up the cows, for she knew that we were nimbler-footed when she started us off in happy mood.

Each cow wore a bell of different tone and knew her own name; yet it was not an easy task, even in pleasant weather, to collect the various strings and get them home on time. They mixed, and fed with neighbors' cattle on the range, and hid themselves behind clumps of trees and other convenient obstructions. Often grandma would get her string in by the main trail and have them milked before we could bring up the laggards that provokingly dawdled along, nibbling stray bunches of grass. When late on the road, we saw coyotes sneaking out for their evening meal and heard the far-away cry of the panther. But we were not much afraid when it was light enough, so that imagination could not picture them creeping stealthily behind us.

Our gallant Company C, officered by Captain Bartlett and Lieutenants Stoneman and Stone, was ordered to another post early in August; and its departure caused such universal regret that no one supposed Company H, under Captain Frisbie, could fill its place. Nevertheless, that handsome young officer soon found his way to the good-will of the people, and when Captain Joe Hooker brought him out to visit grandma's dairy, she, too, was greatly pleased by his soldierly bearing. After he mentioned that he had heard of her interest in the company which had been called away, and that he believed she would find Company H equally deserving of her consideration, she readily extended to the new men the homelike privileges which the others had enjoyed. Thus more friends came among us.

Notable among mine was the old darkey cook at headquarters, from whom Georgia and I tried to hide, the first time she waddled out to our house. She searched us out, saying:

"Now, honeys, don't yo be so scared of dis ole Aunt Lucy, 'cos she's done heared Captain Hooker tell lots 'bout yos, and has come to see yos."

Her face was one great smile, and her voice was so coaxing that she had little difficulty in gaining our favor, the more so, as upon leaving, she called back, "I's surely g'wine ter make dat little pie and cake I's promised yos, so yos must n't forgit to come git it."

On one occasion, when I was sent to the post on an errand, she had no pie or cake; but she brought out a primer and said thoughtfully, "I's g'wine ter give yo dis A-B-C book, 'cos I want yo should grow up like quality folks."

Its worn leaves showed that its owner had studied its first few pages only; and when I replied, "Grandma says that I must not take everything that is offered me," she chuckled and continued:

"Lawd, honey, yo need n't have no 'punctions 'bout takin' dis yer book, 'cos I could n't learn to read nohow when I was a gal, and I's too ole to now. Now, I wants yo to be nice; and yo can't, lessen yo can read and talk like de Captain done tole me yo mudder done.''

I was delighted with the book, and told her so, and hugged it all the way home; for it had a beautiful picture near the back, showing a little girl with a sprinkling pot, watering her garden of stocks, sweet-williams, and hollyhocks. Her hair was in four long curls, and she had trimming on her dress, apron, and long pantalets. I was also impressed by the new words which I had heard Aunt Lucy use, '' 'punctions,'' and '' quality folks.'' I repeated them over and over to myself, so that I should be able to tell them to Georgia.

Our last visit to Aunt Lucy must have been prearranged, for as she admitted us, she said, '' I's mighty glad yos done come so soon, 'cos I been 'specting yos, and mus' take yos right in to de General.''

I had never seen a general, and was shy about meeting one, until after she assured me that only cowards and bad men feared him.

We walked down the corridor and entered a large room, where an elderly gentleman in uniform sat writing at a table. Aunt Lucy stopped beside him, and still holding each by the hand, bowed low, saying, '' General Smith, I's brung der two little Donner gals in to see yo, sah ''; then she slipped out.

He was as courteous to us as though we were grown ladies, shook hands, asked how we felt, begged us to be seated, and then stepped to a door and called, '' Susan! Susan! '' I liked the name. A sweet voice answered, '' Coming! ''

Presently, a pretty dark-eyed Southern lady appeared, who called us " honeys," and " dear little girls." She sat between us, joining with her husband in earnest inquiries about our stay in the mountains and our home with grandma. Georgia did most of the talking. I was satisfied just to look at them and hear them speak. At the close of our visit, with a knowing look, she took us to see what Aunt Lucy had baked.

The General and she had recently come to pay a last visit to a sick officer, who had been sent from San Francisco with the hope that our milder climate would prolong his life. They themselves stayed only a short time, and their friend never left our valley. The day he died, the flag swung lower on the staff. Soldiers dug his grave on the hillside north of town, and word came from army headquarters that he would be buried on the morrow at midday, with military honors. Georgia and I wanted to know what military honors were, and as it came time for the funeral, we gathered with others on the plaza, where the procession formed. We were deeply impressed.

The emigrants uncovered and bowed their heads reverently, but the soldiers in line, with guns reversed, stood erect and motionless as figures in stone, while the bier of the dead was being carried through open ranks to the waiting caisson. The coffin was covered with a flag, and upon it lay his chapeau, gauntlets, sash, and sword. His boots, with their toes reversed, hung over the saddle of a riderless horse, led behind the caisson. The solemn tones of fife and muffled drum led the way through the town, past the old Mission bells and up the hillside. Only soldiers stood close around the grave and heard what was read by the officer who stood at its head, with an open book in one hand and a drawn sword in the other. Three times the file of soldiers fired a volley over the grave, then the muffled drum sounded its farewell taps, and the officers, with their men and the funeral caisson, returned to their quarters in silent order.

CHAPTER XXIII

REAPING AND THRESHING — A PIONEER FUNERAL — THE HOMELESS AND WAYFARING APPEAL TO MRS. BRUNNER — RETURN OF THE MINERS — SOCIAL GATHERINGS — OUR DAILY ROUTINE — STOLEN PLEASURES — A LITTLE DAIRY-MAID — MY DOGSKIN SHOES.

REAPING and threshing were interesting events to us that summer. Mission Indians, scantily clothed, came and cut the grain with long knives and sickles, bound it in small sheaves, and stacked it in the back yard opposite grandma's lookout window, then encircled it with a rustic fence, leaving a wide bare space between the stack and the fence, which they swept clean with green branches from live oak trees.

After many days, Mexican drivers brought a band of wild mares to help with the work. A thick layer of unthreshed grain was pitched on to the bare space surrounding the stack and the mares were driven around and around upon it. From time to time, fresh material was supplied to meet the needs of the threshers. And, at given signals from the men on the stack, the mares were turned out for a short rest, also in order to allow the Indians a chance to throw out the waste straw and to heap the loose grain on the winnowing ground. So they did again and again, until the last sheaf had been trodden under foot.

When the threshing was finished, the Indians rested; then prepared their fires, and feasted on the head, feet, and offal of a bullock which grandpa had slaughtered.

Like buzzards came the squaws and papooses to take what was left of the food, and to claim a share from the pile of worn-out clothes which grandma brought out for distribution. Amid shouts of pleasure, gesticulations, and all manner of begging, the distribution began, and when it ended, our front yard looked as though it were stocked with prize scarecrows.

One big fellow was resplendent in a battered silk hat and a tattered army coat; another was well dressed in a pair of cast-off boots and one of grandma's ragged aprons. Georgia and I tried to help to sort the things as they should be worn, but our efforts were in vain. Wrong hands would reach around and get the articles, and both sexes interchanged suits with apparent satisfaction. Grandma got quite out of patience with one great fellow who was trying to put on a petticoat that his squaw needed, and rushed up to him, jerked it off, gave him a vigorous push, and had the garment on his squaw, before he could do more than grunt. In the end they went away caring more for the clothes that had been given them than for the money they had earned.

Before the summer waned, death claimed one of our own brave women, and immigrants from far and near gathered to do her honor. I do not recollect her name, but know that she was tall and fair, and that grandma, who had watched with her through her last hours, told Georgia and me that when we saw the procession leave the house, we might creep through our back fence and reach the grave before those who should walk around by the road. We were glad to go, for we had watched the growth of the fresh ridge under a large oak tree, not far from our house, and had heard a friend say that it would be " a heavenly resting place for the freed sufferer."

Her family and nearest neighbors left the house afoot, behind the wagon which carried the plain red-wood coffin. At the cross-road several fell in line, and at the grave was quite a gathering. A number came in their ox wagons, others on horseback; among them, a father afoot, leading a horse upon whose back sat his wife with an infant in arms and a child behind clinging to her waist; and several old nags, freighted with children, were led by one parent, while the other walked alongside to see that none should lose their balance and fall off.

No minister of the Gospel was within call, so, after the coffin was placed upon the bars above the open grave, and the lid removed, a friend who had crossed the plains with the dead, offered a prayer, and all the listeners said, " Amen."

I might not have remembered all these things, if Georgia and I had not watched over that grave, when all others seemed to have forgotten it. As we brought brush to cover it, in order to keep the cattle from dusting themselves in the loose earth, we talked matters over, and felt as though that mother's grave had been bequeathed to us. Grandma had instructed us that the graveyard is "God's acre," and that it is a sin to live near and not tend it. Still, no matter how often we chased the cattle away, they would return. We could not make them understand that their old resting-place had become sacred ground.

About the middle of October, 1848, the last of the volunteers were mustered out of service, and shortly thereafter the excess of army stores were condemned and sold. Ex-soldiers had preference over settlers, and could buy the goods at Government rates, plus a small cost of transportation to the Pacific coast. Grandma profited by the good-will of those whom she had befriended. They stocked her store-room with salt pork, flour, rice, coffee, sugar, ship-bread, dried fruit, and camp condiments at a nominal figure above what they themselves paid for them.

This was fortunate, for the hotel was still closed, and the homeless and wayfaring appealing to grandma, easily persuaded her to make room for them at her table. The greater the number, the harder she worked, and the more she expected of us. Although we rose at dawn, and rolled our sleeves high as she rolled hers, and like her, turned up our dress skirts and pinned them behind under our long belt aprons, we could not keep pace with her work.

Nevertheless, we were pleasing reminders of little

girls whom she had known in her native village, and she was proud of us, and had two little white dresses fashioned to be worn on very special occasions. After they were finished, we also were proud, and made many trips into the room to see how beautiful they looked hanging against the wall under the curtain.

Marvellous accounts of the extent and richness of the gold-diggings were now brought to town by traffickers in provisions for mining-camps. This good news inspired our home-keepers with renewed courage. They worked faster while planning the comfort they should enjoy after the return of the absent.

The first to come were the unfortunate, who sought to shake off rheumatism, lung trouble, or the stubborn low-grade fever brought on by working in the water, sleeping on damp ground, eating poorly cooked food, or wearing clothing insufficient to guard against the morning and evening chill. Few had much to show for their toil and privation; yet, not disheartened, even in delirium, they clamored to hasten back for the precious treasure which seemed ever beckoning them onward.

When wind and weather drove them home, the robust came with bags of gold rolled in their snug packs. They called each other "lucky dogs," yet looked like grimy beggars, with faces so bewhiskered, and clothing so ragged, or so wonderfully patched, that little children cried when they drew near, and wives threw up their hands, exclaiming, "For the land's sake! can it be?" Yet each home-comer found glad welcome, and messengers were quick to spread the news, and friends gathered to rejoice with the returned.

Now each home-cooked dish was a feast for the camp-fed to contrast with their fare at Coloma, Wood's Camp,* and sundry other places, where flour, rice, ship-bread, and coffee were three dollars a pound; salt pork and white beans, two dollars a pound; jerked beef, eight dollars a pound; saleratus, sixteen dollars an ounce; and salt, sugar, and raisins were put on the scales to balance their weight in gold dust; where liquor was fifty cents a tablespoonful, and candles five dollars each. It was not the prices at which they complained, but at the dearth of these staples, which had forced them home to wait until spring should again open the road to supply-trains.

The homeless, who in the evenings found comfort and cheer around grandma's table, would take out their treasure bags and boxes and pour their dust and grains of gold in separate piles, to show the quality and quantity, then pass the nuggets around that all might see what strange figures nature had moulded in secret up among the rocks and ravines of the Sierras.

One Roman Catholic claimed as his choicest prize a perfectly shaped cross of free gold, which he had cradled from the sands in the bed of a creek. Another had an image of the Virgin and Child. A slight stretch of the imagination turned many of the beautifully fretted pieces into miniature birds and other admirable designs for sweetheart brooches.

*Now Jamestown.

The exhibition over, each would scrape his hoard back into its receptacle, blow the remaining yellow particles on to the floor so that the table should not show stain, and then settle himself to take his part in relating amusing and thrilling incidents of life in the mining camps. Not a window was closed, nor a door locked, nor a wink of sleep lost in those days, guarding bags of gold. " Hands off " was the miners' law, and all knew that death awaited him who should venture to break it.

Heavy purses made willing spenders, and generous impulses were untrammelled. Nothing could be more gratifying or touching than the respect shown by those homeless men to the pioneer women and children. They would walk long distances and suffer delays and inconveniences for the privilege of passing a few hours under home influences, and were ever ready to contribute toward pleasures in which all might participate.

There were so few young girls in the community, and their presence was so greatly desired, that in the early winter, Georgia and I attended as welcome guests some of the social gatherings which began at early candle-light, and we wore the little white dresses that were so precious in our eyes.

Before the season was half over, heavy rain was followed by such bitter cold that all the ground and still waters were frozen stiff. Although we were well muffled, and grandma warmed us up with a drink of hot water and sweetened cream before starting us out after the cows, the frost nipped at our feet until the

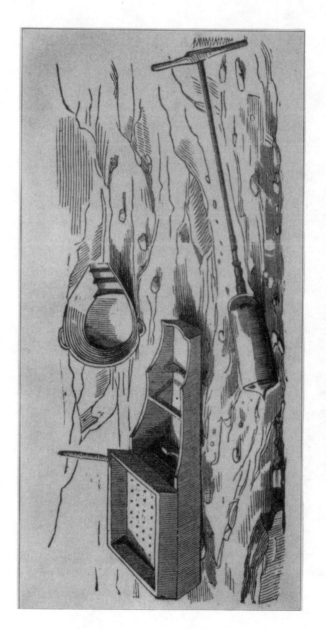

GOLD ROCKER, WASHING PAN, AND GOLD BORER

SCENE DURING THE RUSH TO THE GOLD MINES FROM SAN FRANCISCO. IN 1848

old scars became so angry and painful that we could scarcely hobble about the house. Many remedies were tried, to no purpose, the most severe being the early foot bath with floats of ice in the water. It chilled us through and through, and also made grandma keep us from the fire, lest the heat should undo the benefit expected from the cold. So, while we sat with shivering forms and chattering teeth looking across the room at the blazing logs under the breakfast pots and kettles, our string of cows was coming home in care of a new driver.

We were glad to be together, even in misery, and all things considered, were perhaps as useful in our crippled condition as before, for there was enough to keep our hands busy while our feet rested. Grandma thought she made our work lighter by bringing it to us, yet she came too often for it to seem easy to us.

First, the six brass candlesticks, with hoods, snuffers, and trays had to be brightened; and next, there were the small brass kettles in which she boiled the milk for coffee, to be polished inside and out. However, we did not dread the kettles much, unless burned, for there was always a spoon in the bottom to help to gather the scrapings, of which we were very fond.

But when she would come with a large pan of dried beans or peas to be picked over quickly, so that she could get them soaked for early cooking, we would measure its contents with critical eyes to make sure that it was not more than we had had the previous day. By the time we would get to the bottom of the pan, she would be ready to put before us a discouraging pile of iron knives, forks, and pewter spoons to scour with wood ashes. How we did hate those old black knives and forks! She said her sight was poor — but she could always see when we slighted any.

The redeeming work of the day was sorting the dried fruit for sauce or pies. We could take little nibbles as we handled it, and knew that we should get an extra taste vhen it was ready for use. And after she had put the upper crust on the pies, she would generally permit us to make the fancy print around the edges with a fork, and then prick a figure in the centre to let the steam escape while baking.

Sometimes she received a dollar apiece for these pies; and she had so many customers for them and for such loaves of bread as she could spare, that she often declared the farm was as good as a gold mine.

We were supposed not to play with dolls, consequently we durst not ask any one to step around and see how our little house in the back yard was weathering the storms, nor how the beloved nine in it were getting along. Though only bottles of different sizes, to us they were dear children, named after great personages whom the soldiers had taught us to honor.

The most distinguished had cork stoppers for heads, with faces marked on the sides, the rest, only wads of paper or cloth fastened on the ends of sticks that reached down into the bodies. A strip of cloth tied around each neck, below the bulge, served as make-believe arms, suitable for all ordinary purposes, and, with a little assistance, capable of saluting an officer or waving to a comrade.

We worried because they were clothed in fragments of cloth and paper too thin for the season; and the very first chance we got, we slipped out and found our darlings in a pitiable plight. Generals Washington and Jackson, and little Van Buren were mired at the foot of a land slide from the overhanging bank. Taylor, Webster, Clay, and Benton had been knocked down and buried almost out of sight. Martha Washington's white shawl and the chicken plumes in her hat were ruined; and Dandy Jim from North Carolina lay at her feet with a broken neck!

Such a shock! Not until we realized that everything could be restored was our grief assuaged — that is, everything but Dandy Jim. He was a serious loss, for he was our only black bottle and had always been kept to wait on Martha Washington.

We worked fast, and had accomplished so much before being called into the house that we might have put everything in order next day, had Georgia not waked up toward morning with a severe cold, and had grandma not found out how she caught it. The outcome was that our treasures were taken to the storeroom to become medicine and vinegar bottles, and we mourned like birds robbed of their young.

New duties were opened to me as soon as I could wear my shoes, and by the time Georgia was out again, I was a busy little dairymaid, and quite at home in the corrals. I had been decorated with the regulation salt bag, which hung close to my left side, like a fisher-man's basket. I owned a quart cup and could milk with either hand, also knew how to administer the pinch of salt which each cow expected. After a little practice I became able to do all the " stripping." In some cases it amounted to not more than half a pint from each animal. However, much or little, the strip-pings were of importance, and were kept separate, be-cause grandma considered them " good as cream in the cheese kettle."

When I could sit on the one-legged stool, which Jakie had made me, hold a pail between my knees and milk one or more cows, without help, they both praised my cleverness — a cleverness which fixed more outside responsibilities upon me, and kept me from Georgia a longer while each day. My work was hard, still I re-mained noticeably taller and stronger than she, who was assigned to lighter household duties. I felt that I had no reason to complain of my tasks, because every-body about me was busy, and the work had to be done.

If I was more helpful than my little sister, I was also a source of greater trouble, for I wore out my clothes faster, and they were difficult to replace, es-pecially shoes.

There was but one shoemaker in the town, and he was kept so busy that he took a generous measure of children's feet and then allowed a size or more, to guard against the shoes being too small by the time he should get them finished.

When my little stogies began to leak, he shook **his**

head thoughtfully, and declared that he had so many orders for men's boots that he could not possibly work for women or children until those orders were filled. Consequently, grandma kept her eye on my shoes, and as they got worse and worse, she became sorely perplexed. She would not let me go barefooted, because she was afraid of " snags " and ensuing lockjaw; she could not loan me her own, because she was saving them for special occasions, and wearing instead the heavy sabots she had brought from her native land. She tried the effect of continually reminding me to pick my way and save my shoes, which made life miserable for us both. Finally she upbraided me harshly for a playful run across the yard with Courage, and I lost my temper, and grumbled.

" I would rather go barefooted and get snags in my feet than have so much bother about old shoes that are worn out and no good anyway! "

I was still crying when Hendrik, a roly-poly Hollander, came along and asked the cause of my distress. Grandma told him that I was out of humor, because she was trying to keep shoes on my feet, while I was determined to run them off. He laughed, bade me cheer up, sang the rollicking sailor song with which he used to drive away storms at sea, then showed me a hole in the heel of the dogskin boots he wore, and told me that, out of their tops, he would make me a beautiful pair of shoes.

No clouds darkened my sky the morning that Hendrik came, wearing a pair of new cowhide boots then squeaked as though singing crickets were between the heavy soles; for he had his workbox and the dogskins under his arm, and we took seats under the oak tree, where he laid out his tools and went to work without more ado.

He had brought a piece of tanned cowhide for the soles of my shoes, an awl, a sailor's thimble, needles, coarse thread, a ball of wax, and a sharp knife. The hair on the inside of the boot legs was thick and smooth, and the colors showed that one of the skins had been taken from the body of a black and white dog, and the other from that of a tawny brindle. As Hendrik modelled and sewed, he told me a wondrous tale of the great North Polar Sea, where he had gone in a whaling vessel, and had stayed all winter among mountains of ice and snow. There his boots had worn out. So he had bought these skins from queer little people there, who live in snow huts, and instead of horses or oxen, use dogs to draw their sleds.

I liked the black and white skin better than the brindle, so he cut that for the right foot, and told me always to make it start first. And when I put the shoes on they felt so soft and warm that I knew I could never forget Hendrik's generosity and kindness.

The longer I wore them the more I became attached to them, and the better I understood the story he had told me; for in my musings they were not shoes, but "Spot" and "Brindle," live Eskimo dogs, that had drawn families of queer little people in sleds over the frozen sea, and had always been hungry and ready to fight over their scanty meals. At times I imagined that they wanted to race and scamper about as happy dogs do, and I would run myself out of breath to keep them going, and always stop with Spot in the lead.

When I needed shoestrings, I was sent to the shoe-maker, who only glanced up and replied, " Come to-morrow, and I 'll have a piece of leather big enough."

The next day, he made the same answer, " Come to-morrow," and kept pegging away as fast as he could on a boot sole. The third time I appeared before him, he looked up with the ejaculation, " Well, I 'll be damned, if she ain't here again!"

I was well aware that he should not have used that evil word, yet was not alarmed, for I had heard grandpa and others use worse, and mean no harm, nor yet intend to be cross. So I stood quietly, and in a trice he was up, had rushed across the shop, brought back two round pieces of leather not larger than cookies, and before I knew what he was about, had turned them into good straight shoestrings. He waxed them, and handed them to me with the remark, " Tell your grandma that since you had to wait so long, I charge her only twenty-five cents for them."

CHAPTER XXIV

MEXICAN METHODS OF CULTIVATION — FIRST STEAMSHIP
THROUGH THE GOLDEN GATE — "THE ARGONAUTS" OR
"BOYS OF '49" — A LETTER FROM THE STATES — JOHN
BAPTISTE — JAKIE LEAVES US — THE FIRST AMERICAN
SCHOOL IN SONOMA.

BY the first of March, 1849, carpenters had the frame of grandma's fine new two-story house enclosed, and the floors partly laid. Neighbors were hurrying to get their fields ploughed and planted, those without farming implements following the Mexican's crude method of ploughing the ground with wooden prongs and harrowing in the seed by dragging heavy brush over it.

They gladly turned to any tool that would complete the work by the time the roads to the mountains should be passable, and the diggings clear of snow. Their expectations might have been realized sooner, if a bluff old launch captain, with an eye to business for himself and San Francisco, had not appeared on the scene, shouting, " Ahoy " to everybody.

" I say, a steamship anchored in the Bay of San Francisco two days ago. She's the *California*. Steamed out of New York Harbor with merchandise. Stopped at Panama; there took aboard three hundred

and fifty waiting passengers that had cut across country — a mixture of men from all parts of the United
States, who have come to carry off the gold diggings,
root and branch! Others are coming in shiploads as
fast as they can. Now mark my words, and mark them
well: provisions is going to run mighty short, and if
this valley wants any, it had better send for them
pretty damn quick! "

By return boat, farmers, shopkeepers, and carpenters hastened to San Francisco. All were eager for
supplies from the first steamship that had entered the
Golden Gate — the first, it may be added, that most of
them, even those of a sea-going past, had ever seen.

During the absence of husbands, we little girls were
loaned separately nights to timid wives who had no
children to keep them company. Georgia went earlier
and stayed later than I, because grandma could not
spare me in the evenings until after the cows were
turned out, and she needed me in the mornings before
sunrise. Those who borrowed us made our stays so
pleasant that we felt at home in many different houses.

Once, however, I encountered danger on my early
homeward trip.

I had turned the bend in the road, could see the
smoke curling out of grandma's chimney, and knew
that every nearer house was closed. In order to avoid
attracting the attention of a suspicious-looking cow on
the road, I was running stealthily along a rail fence,
when, unexpectedly, I came upon a family of sleeping
swine, and before I was aware of danger from that

direction was set upon and felled to the ground by a vicious beast. Impelled, I know not how, but quick as thought, I rolled over and over and over, and when I opened my eyes I was on the other side of the fence, and an angry, noisy, bristling creature was glaring at me through the rails.

Quivering like a leaf and for a time unable to rise, I lay upon the green earth facing the morning sky. With strange sensations and wonderment, I tried to think what might have happened, if I had not rolled. What if that space between fence and ground had been too narrow to let my body through; what if, on the other hand, it had been wide enough for that enraged brute to follow?

Too frightened to cry, and still trembling, I made my way to the end of the field and climbed back over the fence near home. Grandma was greatly startled by my blanched face, and the rumpled and soiled condition of my clothes. After I related my frightful experience, she also felt that had it not been for that fence, I should have been torn to pieces. She explained, however, that I probably would not have been attacked had I not startled the old mother so suddenly that she believed her young in danger.

When our menfolk returned from San Francisco, they were accompanied by many excited treasure-seekers, anxious to secure pack animals to carry their effects to the mines. They were made welcome, and in turn furnished us news of the outer world, and distributed worn copies of American and foreign newspapers, which our hungry-minded pioneers read and re-read so long as the lines held together.

Those light-hearted newcomers, who danced and gayly sang,

> O Susannah, don't you cry for me!
> I 'm bound to Californy with a tin pan on my knee,

were the first we saw of that vast throng of gold-seekers, who flocked to our shores within a twelvemonth, and who have since become idealized in song and story as the " Argonauts," " the Boys of '49."

They were unlike either our pioneer or our soldier friends in style of dress and manner. Nor had they come to build homes or develop the country. They wanted gold to carry back to other lands. Some had expected to find it near the Bay of San Francisco; some, to scoop it up out of the river beds that crossed the valleys; and others, to shovel it from ravines and mountain-sides. When told of the difficulties before them, their impatience grew to be off, that they might prove to Western plodders what could be done by Eastern pluck and muscle.

Such packing as those men did! Mother's Bible, and wife and baby's daguerreotype not infrequently started to the mines in the coffee pot, or in the miner's boots, hanging across the mule's pack. The sweetheart's lock of hair, affectionately concealed beneath the hat lining of its faithful wearer, caught the scent of the old clay pipe stuck in the hat-band.

With the opening season all available Indians of both sexes were hired as gold-diggers, and trudged along behind their employers, and our town was again reduced to a settlement of white women and children. But what a difference in the feeling of our people! We now heard regularly from the Bay City, and entertained transients from nearly every part of the globe; and these would loan us books and newspapers, and frequently store unnecessary possessions with us until they should return from the mines.

San Francisco had a regular post office. One day its postmaster forwarded a letter, addressed to ex-Governor Boggs, which the latter brought out and read to grandma. She did not, as usual, put her head out of the window and call us, but came from the house wiping her eyes, and asked if we wanted to be put in a big ship and sent away from her and grandma and Jakie.

Greatly alarmed, we exclaimed, " No, no, grandma, no! "

Taking us by the hand, she led us into the house, seated herself and drew one of us to each side, then requested the Governor to read the letter again. We two did not understand all it said, but enough to know that it had been written by our own dear aunt, Elizabeth Poor, who wanted Governor Boggs to find her sister's three little orphaned girls and send them back to her by ship to Massachusetts. It contained the necessary directions for carrying out her wish.

Grandma assured the Governor that we did not want to leave her, nor would she give us up. She said she and her husband and Jakie had befriended us when we were poor and useless, and that we were

POST OFFICE, CORNER OF CLAY AND PIKE STREETS, SAN FRANCISCO, 1849

OLD CITY HOTEL, 1846, CORNER OF KEARNEY AND CLAY STREETS, THE FIRST HOTEL IN SAN FRANCISCO

now beginning to be helpful. Moreover, that they had prospered greatly since we had come into their home, and that their luck might change if they should part from us. She further stated that she already had riches in her own right, which we should inherit at her death.

The Governor spoke of schools and divers matters pertaining to our welfare, then promised to explain by letter to Aunt Elizabeth how fortunately we were situated.

This event created quite a flutter of excitement among friends. Grandpa and Jakie felt just as grandma did about keeping us. Georgia and I were assured that in not being allowed to go across the water, we had escaped great suffering, and, perhaps, drowning by shipwreck. Still, we did wish that it were possible for us to see Aunt Elizabeth, whom mother had taught us to love, and who now wanted us to come to her.

I told Georgia that I would learn to write as fast as I could, and send her a letter, so she would know all about us.

We now imagined that we were quite large girls, for grandma usually said before going away, " Children, you know what there is to do and I leave everything in your care." We did not realize that this was her little scheme, in part, to keep us out of mischief; but we knew that upon her return she would see, and call attention to what was left undone.

Once, when we were at home alone and talking about

" endless work and aching bones," as we had heard grown-up folks complain of theirs, we were interrupted by a bareback rider who did not " tie up " under the live oak, but came to the shade of the white oak in front of us at the kitchen door. After a cheery " Howdy do " and a hand shake, he exclaimed,

" I heard at Napa that you lived here, and my pony has made a hard run to give me this sight of you."

We were surprised and delighted, for the speaker was John Baptiste who had wintered with us in the Sierras. We asked him to dismount, take a seat under the tree, and let us bring him a glass of milk. He declined graciously, then with a pleased expression, drew a small brown-paper parcel from his trousers pocket and handed it to us, leaned forward, clasped his arms about his pony, rested his head on its neck, and smilingly watched Georgia unwrap it, and two beautiful bunches of raisins come to view,— one for each. He would not touch a single berry, nor let us save any. He asked us to eat them then and there so that he could witness our enjoyment of the luxury he had provided for this, our first meeting in the settlement.

Never had we seen raisins so large, translucent, and delicious. They seemed far too choice for us to have, and John was so poorly dressed and pinched in features that we hesitated about eating them. But he would have his way, and in simple language told us that he wanted them to soften the recollection of the hungry time when he came into camp empty-handed and discouraged. Also to fulfil his assurance to our mother that he would try to keep us in sight, and give us of the best that he could procure. His last injunctions were, " Be good little girls; always remember your mother and father; and don't forget John Baptiste."

He was gone when grandma got back; and she was very serious when told what had occurred in her absence. She rarely spoke to us of our mother, and feared it might lessen our affection for herself, if others kept the memory of the dead fresh in our minds.

There were many other happenings before the year closed, that caused me to think a great deal. Grandpa spent less time at the shop; he bought himself a fleet-footed horse which he named Antelope, and came home oftener to talk to grandma about money they had loaned Major Prudon to send to China for merchandise, also about a bar-room which he was fitting up near the butcher-shop, for a partner. Next, he bought faithful Charlie, a large bay horse, with friendly eyes, and long black mane and tail; also a small blue farm wagon in which Georgia and I were to drive about the fields, when sent to gather loose bark and dry branches for baking fires.

We were out for that purpose the day that we saw grandpa ride away to the mines, but we missed seeing Jakie steal off, with his bunch of cows. He felt too badly to say good-bye to us.

I was almost heart-broken when I learned that he was not coming back. He had been my comforter in most of my troubles, had taught me to ride and drive the horse, shown me the wood duck's nest in the hollow of our white oak tree, and the orioles' pretty home swinging from a twig in the live oak, also where the big white-faced owls lived. He had helped me to gather wild flowers, made me whistles from branches cut from the pussy willows, and had yodeled for me as joyfully as for loved ones in his Alpine home. Everything that he had said and done meant a great deal more to me now, and kept him in mind, as I went about alone, or with grandma, doing the things that had been his to do. She now moulded her cheeses in smaller forms, and we had fewer cows to milk.

When the season for collecting and drying herbs came, Georgia and I had opportunity to be together considerably. It was after we had picked the first drying of sage and were pricking our fingers on the saffron pods, that grandma, in passing, with her apron full of Castilian rose petals, stopped and announced that if we would promise to work well, and gather the sage leaves and saffron tufts as often as necessary, she would let us go to a " real school " which was about to open in town.

Oh, dear! to go to school, to have books and slate and pencil! What more could be wished? Yes, we would get up earlier, work faster before time to go, and hurry home after lessons were over. And I would carry the book Aunt Lucy had given me. It was all arranged, and grandma went to town to buy slates, pencils, speller, and a stick of wine-colored ribbon to tie up our hair.

When the anticipated hour came, there were great preparations that we might be neat and clean and ready on time. Our hair was parted in four equal divisions; the front braids, tied with ribbon, formed a U at the back of the neck; and we wore new calico dresses and sunbonnets, and carried lunch for two in a curious little basket, which grandma must have brought with her from Switzerland. Joyfully we started forth to the first American school opened in Sonoma.

Alas! it was not what our anticipations had pictured. The schoolroom was a dreary adobe, containing two rows of benches so high that, when seated, we could barely touch the earthen floor with our toes. The schoolmaster told us that we must hold our slates on our laps, and our open books in the right hand, and not look at the pictures, but study all the time, and not speak, even to each other, without permission. His face was so severe, his eyes so keen, and his voice so sharp that I was afraid of him.

He had a chair with a back to it, and a table to hold his books; yet he spent most of his time walking about with a narrow strap of rawhide in his hand, and was ever finding some one whose book drooped, or who was whispering; and the stinging bite of that strap would call the erring to order.

The Misses Boggs, Lewis, Smith, and Bone were pretty young ladies, and brought their own chairs and a table to sit around; and when they whispered, the master never saw them; and when they missed in lessons, he did n't keep them in, nor make them stand on the floor.

I learned my lessons well enough, but grandma was terribly shocked because I got strapped nearly every day. But then, I sat between Georgia and the other little girls in our row, and had to deliver messages from those on both sides of me, as well as to whisper a little on my own account. Finally, grandma declared that if I got a whipping next day, she would give me a second one after reaching home. So I started in the morning with the intention of being the best girl in school; but we had hardly settled in line for our first lesson, when Georgia whispered behind her book, "Eliza, see! Mary Jane Johnson has got my nice French card, with the double queens on it, and I can't get it."

Forgotten were my good resolutions. I leaned out of line, and whispered louder than I meant, "Mary Jane Johnson, that is my sister's card. and you must give it back to her."

She saw the master watching, but I did not, until he called me to hold out my hand. For once, I begged, "Please excuse me; I won't do it again." But he would n't, and I felt greatly humiliated, because I knew the large girls had heard me and were smiling.

After recess, a new boy arrived, little Willie Mc-Cracken, whom we had seen on the plains, and known at Sutter's Fort, and he knew us as soon as he reached his seat and looked around. In a short time, I nudged Georgia, and asked her if I had n't better roll him the little knot of dried apples that grandma had put in the basket for my lunch. She said, yes, if I wanted to. So I wiggled the basket from under the seat with my foot, and soon thereafter, my bit of hospitality was on its way to the friend I was glad to see again.

Instead of his getting it, however, the master stepped down and picked it up, with the hand that did n't have the strap in it. So, instead of being the best, I was the worst child in school, for not one had ever before received two strappings in a forenoon.

It must have been our bad day, for Georgia felt her very first bite from the strap that afternoon, and on the way home volunteered not to tell on me, if grandma did not ask. Yet grandma did, the first thing. And when Georgia reluctantly said, "Yes," grandma looked at me and shook her head despairingly; but when I announced that I had already had two strappings, and Georgia one, she burst out laughing, and said she thought I had had enough for one day.

A few weeks later, the large boys drove the master out of school on account of his cruelty to a little fellow who had played truant.

In that dingy schoolroom, Georgia and I later attended the first Protestant Sunday school and church service held in Sonoma.

CHAPTER XXV

A SHORT experience in the mines cured grandpa's "mining fever," but increased his rheumatism. The accounts he brought of sufferings he had witnessed in the camps prepared us for the approaching autumn's work, when many of the happy fellows who had started to the gold-fields in vigorous health and with great expectations returned haggard, sick, and out of luck.

Then was noble work done by the pioneer women. No door was closed against the needy. However small the house might be, its inmates had some comfort to offer the stranger. Many came to grandma, saying they had places to sleep but begging that she would give them food and medicine until they should be able to proceed to San Francisco.

Weary mortals dragged their aching limbs to the benches under her white oak tree, dropped upon them, with blankets still across their shoulders, declaring they could not go another rod. Often, she turned her face aside and murmured, " God help the poor wanderers "; but to them she would say encouragingly,

[226]

" You be not very sick, you will soon be rested. There be straw in the stack that we will bring for your bed, and me and the children will let you not go hungry."

Ere long, beds had to be made on the floor of the unfinished house. More were needed, and they were spread under the great white oak.

On a block beside each fever patient stood a tin cup, which Georgia and I were charged to keep full of cold water, and it was pitiful to see the eyes of the sick watch the cooling stream we poured. Our patients eagerly grasped the cup with unsteady hands, so that part of its contents did not reach the parched lips. Often, we heard the fervid prayer, " God bless the women of this land, and bless the children too! "

Soon we learned to detect signs of improvement, and were rejoiced when the convalescents smiled and asked for more to eat. Grandma carried most of the food to them and sent us later for the empty dishes.

Of the many who came to us that season, there was but one who never proceeded on his way. He was a young German, fair of face, but terribly wasted by disease. His gentle, boyish manner at once made him a favorite, and we not only gave him our best care, but when a physician drifted into town, grandma sent for him and followed his directions. I remember well the day that John seemed almost convalescent, relished his breakfast, wanted to talk a while, and before we left him, had us bring him a basin of warm water and his beflowered carpet bag, from which he took a change of clothing and his shaving outfit.

When we saw him later, his hair was smoothly combed; he looked neat and felt encouraged, and was sure that he should soon be up and doing for himself. At nightfall, grandma bade us wipe the dishes quickly as possible, at which Georgia proposed a race to see whether she could wash fast enough to keep us busy, and we got into a frolicsome mood, which grandma put an end to with the sobering remark:

" Oh, be not so worldly-minded. John ist very bad to-night. I be in a hurry to go back to him, and you must hold the candle."

We passed out into the clear cold starlight, with the burning candle sheltered by a milk pan, and picked our way between the lumber to the unfinished room where John lay. I was the last to enter, and saw grandma hurriedly give the candle to Georgia, drop upon her knees beside the bed, touch his forehead, lift his hand, and call him by name. The damp of death was on his brow, the organs of speech had lost their power. One long upward look, a slight quivering of the muscles of the face, and we were alone with the dead. I was so awed that I could scarcely move, but grandma wept over him, as she prepared his body for burial.

The next afternoon, we three and grandpa and a few friends followed him to his final resting-place. After he was gone, grandma remembered that she did not know his name in full, the land of his birth, nor the address of his people. Expecting his recovery, she had not troubled him with questions, and the few trinkets in his carpet bag yielded no identifying clue. So he lies in a nameless grave, like countless other youth of that period.

We had patients of every type, those who were appreciative and grateful, and those who rebelled against confinement, and swore at the pain which kept sleep from their eyes, and hurled their things about regardless of consequences. The most trying were the chronic grumblers, who did not know what they wanted, nor what they ought to have, and adopted the moody refrain:

> But the happy times are over,
>   I've only grief and pain,
> For I shall never, never see
>   Susannah dear again.

The entrance of Georgia and myself would occasionally turn their thoughts into homeward channels, and make them reminiscent of their little children and loved ones "back in the States." Then, again, our coming would set them to talking about our early disaster and such horrible recounts of happenings in the snow-bound camps that we would rush away, and poor Georgia would have distressing crying spells over what we had heard.

At first no tears dimmed my eyes, for I felt, with keen indignation, that those wounding tales were false; but there came hours of suffering for me later, when an unsympathetic soldier, nicknamed " Picayune Butler," engaged me in conversation and set me to thinking.

He was a great big man with eyes piercing as a hawk's, and lips so thin that they looked like red lines on his face, parting and snapping together as he repeated the horrible things he had read in *The California Star*. He insisted that the Donner Party was responsible for its own misfortune; that parents killed their babies and ate their bodies to keep themselves alive; cut off the heads of companions and called them good soup bones; and were as thievish as sneaking Indians, even stealing the strings from the snowshoes of those who had come to their rescue. He maintained that Keseberg had murdered my mother and mutilated my dead father's body; and that he himself felt that the miserable wretches brought from starvation were not worth the price it had cost to save them.

Too young, too ignorant, and too distressed to disprove the accusations or resent his individual views, I could only take refuge behind what I had heard and seen in camp, and declare, " I know it is not true; they were good people, and loved their babies, and were sorry for everybody."

How could I believe his cruel words? While I had come from the mountains remembering most clearly the sufferings from cold, hunger, thirst, and pitiful surroundings, I had also brought from there a child's mental picture of tenderest sympathies and bravest self-denials, evinced by the snowbound in my father's camp, and of Mrs. Murphy's earnest effort to soothe and care for us three little sisters after we had been deserted at the lake cabins by Cady and Stone; also her motherly watchfulness over Jimmie Eddy, Georgia Foster, and her own son Simon, and of Mr. Eddy's constant solicitude for our safety on the journey over the mountains to Sutter's Fort. Vain, however, my efforts to speak in behalf of either the dead or the absent; every attempt was met by the ready assertion, "You can't prove anything; you were not old enough to remember or understand what happened."

Oh, how I longed to be grown, to have opportunities to talk with those of the party who were considered old enough to remember facts, and would answer the questions I wanted to ask; and how firmly I resolved that when I grew to be a woman I would tell the story of my party so clearly that no one could doubt its truth!

CHAPTER XXVI

THANK OFFERINGS — MISS DOTY'S SCHOOL — THE BOND OF
KINDRED — IN JACKET AND TROUSERS — CHUM CHARLIE.

GRANDMA had a fixed price for table board, but
would not take pay for medicines, nor for attendance on the sick; consequently, many of her
patients, after reaching San Francisco, sent thank
offerings of articles useful and pleasing to her. Thus,
also, Sister Georgia and I came into possession of
pretty calico, Swiss, and delaine dresses, and shoes
that filled our hearts with pride, for they were of Mor-
occo leather, a red and a green pair for each. We had
seen finely dressed Spanish children wear such shoes,
but never supposed that we should be so favored.

After the first dresses were finished, there came a
Sunday when I was allowed to go to the Mission
Church with Kitty Purcell, the baker's little daughter,
and I felt wonderfully fine in my pink calico frock,
flecked with a bird's-eye of white, a sunbonnet to
match, and green shoes.

The brilliantly lighted altar, decked with flowers,
the priests in gorgeous vestments, the acolyte with the
swinging censer, and the intoned service in foreign
tongue, were bewildering to me. My eyes wandered
from the clergy to the benches upon which sat the rich

and the great, then back to the poor, among whom I was kneeling. Each humble worshipper had spread a bright-bordered handkerchief upon the bare floor as a kneeling mat. I observed the striking effect, then recollecting my shoes, put my hand back and drew up the hem of my dress, that my two green beauties might be seen by the children behind me. No seven-year-old child ever enjoyed finery more than I did those little shoes.

Gifts which grandma considered quite unsuitable came one day in two neat wooden boxes about thirty inches in length, and eight in width and depth. They were addressed to us individually, but in grandma's care. When she removed the cover and a layer of cotton batting from Georgia's, a beautiful French lady-doll was revealed, exquisitely dressed, with a spray of flowers in her hair, and another that looped one side of her lovely pink skirt sufficiently high to display an elaborately trimmed petticoat. She was so fine in lace and ribbons, yes, even watch and chain, that grandma was loath to let us touch her, and insisted she should be handled in the box.

My gift was a pretty young Swiss matron in holiday attire, really more picturesque, and quite as costly as Georgia's, but lacking that daintiness which made the lady-doll untouchable. I had her to hug and look at only a few moments; then both boxes with their precious contents were put away for safe keeping, and brought forth only on state occasions, for the inspection of special visitors.

Grandma did not want any nonsense put into our heads. She wished us to be practical, and often quoted maxims to the effect that, " As the twig is bent, the tree's inclined " ; " All work is ennobling if well done " ; " Much book-learning for girls is not conducive to happiness or success " ; and " The highest aim of a girl should be honesty, chastity, and industry."

Still, she was so pleased when I could write a little with ink and quill, that she dictated several letters to Jakie, who was in the dairy business near Stockton; and in an unguarded moment she agreed that I should attend Miss Doty's school. Then she hesitated. She wished to treat us exactly alike, yet could not spare both at the same time. Finally, as a way out of the difficulty, she decided that we should attend school alternate months, during the summer; and that my sister, being the elder, should begin the course.

It seemed to me that Georgia's month at school would never end. My own sped faster than I wished. Miss Doty helped me with my lessons during part of the noon hour, and encouragingly said, " Be patient, keep trying, and you will gain your reward."

While still her pupil, I wrote my long-planned letter to Aunt Elizabeth. Georgia helped to compose it, and when finished, we carried it to our friend, the postmaster. He banteringly held it in his hand, until we told its contents and begged that it go to Aunt Elizabeth as fast as possible. He must have seen that it was incorrectly addressed, yet he readily promised that if an answer should come addressed to " Miss

Georgia Ann Donner," or to " Miss Eliza Poor Donner," he would carefully save it for us.

After many fruitless trips to the post-office, we were one day handed a letter for grandma. It was not from our aunt, however, but from our sister Elitha, and bore the sad news that her husband, while on the range, had been thrown from his horse, and lived but a few moments after she reached him. She also stated that her little daughter Elisabeth and her sister Leanna were with her on the ranch, and that she was anxious to learn how Georgia and I were getting on.

By advice of short-sighted friends, grandma sent a very formal reply to the letter, and told us that she did not want Elitha to write again. Moreover, that we, in gratitude for what she had done for us, should take her name and call her " mother."

This endeavor to destroy personal identity and family connection, met with pathetic opposition. Of our own accord, we had called her grandma. But " mother " — that name was sacred to her who had taught our infant lips to give it utterance! We would bestow it on no other.

Under no circumstance was there difficulty in finding some one ready to advise or help to plan our duties. With the best of intentions? Yes, but often, oh, how trying to us, poor little waifs of misfortune!

One, like a thorn in the flesh, was apportioned to me at the approach of the Winter of 1849 and 1850. We needed more help in the dairy, but could get no one except Mr. Marsh, who lived in bachelor quarters half a mile south on the creek bank. He drove in the bunch of cows found in the mornings grazing on their homeward way, but was too old to follow after those on the range. Moreover, he did not know how to milk. Grandma, therefore, was obliged to give up going after the cows herself. She hesitated about sending us alone, for of late many stragglers had been seen crossing the valley, and also Indians loitering about. Furthermore, Georgia was again coughing badly.

At a loss what to do, she discussed the situation with a neighbor, who after reflection asked,

"Why not dress Eliza in boy's clothes and put her on old Charlie?"

Grandma threw up her hands at the bare suggestion. It was scandalous, improper! Why, she had even taught me to shun the boys of the village. However, she felt differently later in the day when she called me to her. But in vain was coaxing, in vain was scolding, I refused positively to don boy's clothing.

Then she told in strictest confidence that Georgia was very frail, would probably die young, certainly would not reach twenty-five; and I ought not to hesitate at what would make her life easier. Still, if I had no regard for my sister's comfort, she would be compelled to send us together afoot after the cows, and the exposure might be very bad for Georgia. This was enough. I would wear the hated clothes and my little sister should never learn from me the seriousness of her condition, lest it should hasten her death.

My suit of brown twill, red flannel shirt, boots, and sou'wester, with ear muffs attached, were ready for me before the heaviest winter storm. The jacket and trousers were modelled for a boy of nine, instead of a girl not yet eight, but grandma assured me that being all wool, the rain would soon shrink them to my size, also that the boots, which were too wide in the heel and hurt my toes, would shape themselves to my feet and prevent the old frost bites from returning.

I was very unhappy while she helped me to dress, and pinned up my braids, and hid them under my storm hat; and I was absolutely wretched when she kissed me and said,

" It would be hard to find a prettier little boy than you are."

After again admonishing me to let no one on the range know I was a girl, and to answer all questions civilly and ride on quickly after my string of cows, she promised that if I helped her thus through the short days of the rainy season, she would give back my " girl clothes " in the Spring, and never again ask me to wear others.

She led me to where Charlie was tied to a tree. I stepped on to a block, from there to a stump, put my foot into the stirrup, and clumsily raised myself into the seat of an old dragoon saddle. My eyes were too full of tears to see, but grandma put the reins in my hand and started me away. Away where? To drive up the cows? Yes,—and into wider fields of thought than she recked.

After I got beyond our road, I stopped Charlie, and made him turn his face toward mine, and told him all that had happened, and just how I felt. The good old horse seemed to understand, for no friend could be more faithful than Charlie thenceforth proved to me. He learned to separate our cows from the many strange ones on the plain; to move faster when it rained; to choose the crossings that were safe; and to avoid the branches that might scrape me from his back. Grandma was pleased to learn that drivers on the range, when inquiring about strays, addressed me as " Bubbie." My humiliation, however, was so great that, though Georgia and I were room-mates, and had secret day meetings, I never went near her when others were by.

She was allowed to play oftener with neighbors' children, and occasionally spent a week or more with Mrs. Bergwald, helping her to care for her little daughter. While away, she learned fine needlework, had fewer crying spells, and was more contented than at home with grandma.

This happiness in her life added much to mine, and it came to pass that the duty which had seemed such a bitter task, became a pleasure. As the days lengthened, chum Charlie and I kept earlier hours, and crept closer to the heart of nature. We read the signs of the day in the dawn tints; watched the coyotes and other night prowlers slink back to their lairs; saw where the various birds went to housekeeping, and how they cared for their young; knew them also by their call and song. We could show where Johnnie-jump-ups and baby-blue-eyes grew thickest; where the cream cups were largest; and where the wild forget-me-nots blossomed. We explored each nook and corner for miles around, and felt that everything that God had made and man had not put his mark upon was ours.

The aged boughs heaped by the wind in wild confusion about the maimed and storm-beaten tree-trunks seemed to assume fantastic shapes and expressions as we approached from different directions, or viewed them under light and shadow of changing weather. Gnarled and twisted, they became elves and goblins, and the huge piles of storm wreckage were transformed into weird old ruins and deserted castles like those which grandma had described to me in legends of the Rhine. At twilight I was often afraid to pass, lest giants and ghosts should show themselves between uncanny arches. Then all that was needed was a low cluck to Charlie, and off he would start on a run past imaginary dangers.

It was late in the Spring when grandma gave back my " girl clothes " and wearily told me she had hired a boy to drive in the cows, and a man to help to milk; and that Georgia was to look after the house, and I to take her own place in the corrals, because she was sick and would have to be cupped and bled before she could be better.

Grandpa came home early next day and everything was ready for the treatment immediately after the noon meal. Grandma looked so grave, and gave so many instructions about household and dairy matters, that Georgia and I feared that we might lose her. I verily believe we would have slipped away during the operation, had grandpa not commanded us to stay near, as he might need assistance. In dread we watched every movement, saw what made grandma's face pale, and where the sore spots were. Indeed our sympathies were so strained, our fingers fumbled awkwardly as we adjusted the covers about her weakened form.

As soon as her illness became known, neighbors came from far and near to help with the dairy work or nursing; and keen was their disappointment when she replied, "I thank you for your kind offers, but the children are handy and know my ways."

Regularly she asked me about the cows, and if the goats had been milked, the eggs gathered, and the pigs fed. She remembered and planned the work, but did not regain strength as rapidly as she wished; nor did she resume her place in the corrals, even after she was up and around, but had a way of coming unexpectedly to see if her instructions were being carried out.

One day she became quite angry on finding me talking with a stranger. He was well dressed and spoke like a gentleman, touched his hat as she drew near and remarked, "This little girl tells me she is an orphan, and that you have been very kind to her." Grandma was uncivil in her reply, and he went away. Then she warned me, "Beware of wolves in sheep's clothing,'' and insisted that no man wearing such fine clothes and having such soft hands could earn an honest living.   I did not repeat what he had told me of his little daughter, who lived in a beautiful home in New York, and was about my age, and had no sister; and his wish that I were there with her.   I could not understand what harm there was in his questions or my answers.   Did I not remind him of his own little girl? And had I not heard lonely miners tell of times when they gladly would have walked ten miles to shake hands and talk a few moments with a child?

CHAPTER XXVII

CAPT. FRISBIE — WEDDING FESTIVITIES — THE MASTERPIECE
OF GRANDMA'S YOUTH —SENORA VALLEJO — JAKIE'S RE-
TURN — HIS DEATH — A CHEROKEE INDIAN WHO HAD
STOOD BY MY FATHER'S GRAVE.

CAPTAIN FRISBIE spent much time in Sonoma after Company H was disbanded, and observing ones remarked that the attraction was Miss Fannie Vallejo. Yet, not until 1851 did the General consent to part with his first-born daughter. Weeks before the marriage day, friends began arriving at the bride's home, and large orders came to grandma for dairy supplies.

She anticipated the coming event with interest and pleasure, because the prolonged and brilliant festivities would afford her an opportunity to display her fancy and talent in butter modelling. For the work, she did not charge, but simply weighed the butter for the designs and put it into crocks standing in cold water in the adobe store-house where, in the evenings, after candle-light, we three gathered.

Her implements were a circular hardwood board, a paddle, a set of small, well pointed sticks, a thin-bladed knife, and squares of white muslin of various degrees of fineness. She talked and modelled, and we listening watched the fascinating process; saw her take the plastic substance, fashion a duck with ducklings on a pond, a lamb curled up asleep, and a couched lion with shaggy head resting upon his forepaws. We watched her press beads of proper size and color into the eye sockets; skilfully finish the base upon which each figure lay; then twist a lump of butter into a square of fine muslin, and deftly squeeze, until it crinkled through the meshes in form of fleece for the lamb's coat, then use a different mesh to produce the strands for the lion's mane and the tuft for the end of his tail.

In exuberant delight we exclaimed, " Oh, grandma, how did you learn to make such wonderful things? "

" I did not learn, it is a gift," she replied.

Then she spoke of her modelling in childhood, and her subsequent masterpiece, which had won the commendation of Napoleon and Empress Josephine.

At that auspicious time, she was but eighteen years of age, and second cook in the principal tavern of Neuchatel, Switzerland. Georgia and I sat entranced, as with animated words and gestures she pictured the appearance of the buglers and heralds who came weeks in advance to announce the date on which the Emperor and Empress would arrive in that town and dine at the tavern; then the excitement and enthusiastic preparations which followed. She described the consultations between the *Herr Wirth* and the *Frau Wirthin* and their maids; and how, finally, Marie's butter-piece for the christening feast of the child of the Herr Graf was remembered; and she, the lowly second cook, was told that a corner in the cellar would be set apart for her especial use, and that she should have her evenings to devote to the work, and three *groschen* (seven and a half cents) added to her week's wages, if she would produce a fitting centrepiece for the Emperor's table.

Five consecutive nights, she designed and modelled until the watchman's midnight cry drove her from work, and at three o'clock in the morning of the sixth day, she finished. And what a centrepiece it was! It required the careful handling of no less than three persons to get it in place on the table, where the Emperor might see at a glance the groups of figures along the splendid highway, which was spanned by arches and terminated with a magnificently wrought gateway, surmounted by His Majesty's coat of arms.

We scarcely winked as we listened to the rest of the happenings on that memorable day. She recounted how she had dropped everything at the sound of martial music and from the tiny open space at the window caught glimpses of the passing pageant — of the royal coaches, of the maids of honor, of Josephine in gorgeous attire, of the snow-white poodle snuggled close in the Empress's arms. Then she told how she heard a heavy thud by the kitchen fire, which made her rush back, only to discover that the head cook had fallen to the floor in a faint!

She gave the quick call which brought the Frau Wirthin to the scene of confusion, where in mute agony, she looked from servant to servant, until, with hands clasped, and eyes full of tears, she implored, "Marie, take the higher place for the day, and with God's help, make no mistake."

Then she went on to say that while the dinner was being served, the Emperor admired the butter-piece, and on hearing that it was the work of a young maid-servant in the house, commanded that she be brought in to receive commendation of himself and the Empress. Again the Frau Wirthin rushed to the kitchen in great excitement, and — knowing that Marie's face was red from heat of the fire, that she was nervous from added responsibilities, and not dressed for presentation — cried with quivering lips:

"Ah, Marie! the butter-piece is so grand, it brings us into trouble. The great Emperor asks to see thee, and thou must come!"

She told how poor, red-faced, bewildered Marie dropped her ladle and stared at the speaker, then rolled down her sleeves while the Frau Wirthin tied her own best white apron around her waist, at the same time instructing her in the manner in which she must hold her dress at the sides, between thumb and forefinger, and spread the skirt wide, in making a low, reverential bow. But Marie was so upset that she realized only that her heart was beating like a trip-hammer, and her form shaking like an aspen leaf, while being led before those august personages. Yet, after it was all over, she was informed that the Emperor and Empress had spoken kindly to her, and that she, herself, had made her bow and backed out of the room admirably for one in her position, and ought to feel that the great honor conferred upon her had covered with glory all the ills and embarrassments she had suffered.

To impress us more fully with the importance of that event, grandma had Georgia and me stand up on our cellar floor and learn to make that deferential bow, she by turns, taking the parts of the Frau Wirthin, the Emperor, and the Empress.

She now finished her modelling with a dainty centrepiece for the bride's table, and let me go with her when she carried it to the Vallejo mansion. It gave great satisfaction; and while the family and guests were admiring it, Señora Vallejo took me by the hand, saying in her own musical tongue, " Come, little daughter, and play while you wait."

She led me to a room that had pictures on the walls, and left me surrounded by toys. But I could not play. My eyes wandered about until they became riveted on one corner of the room, where stood a child's crib which looked like gold. Its head and foot boards were embellished with figures of angels; and a canopy of lace like a fleecy cloud hovered over them. The bed was white, but the pillows were covered with pink silk and encased in slips of linen lawn, exquisite with rare needlework. I touched it before I left the room, wondering what the little girl dreamed in that beautiful bed; and on the way home, grandma and I discussed all these things.

The linen pillow-slips were as fine as those Señorita

Isabella Fitch showed me, when she gave me the few highly prized lessons in simple drawn-work; and her cousin, Señorita Leese, had taught me hemming. These young ladies were related to the Vallejos and also lived in large houses facing the plaza, and were always kind to Georgia and me. In fact, some of my sweetest memories of Sonoma are associated with these three Spanish homes. Their people never asked unfeeling questions, nor repeated harrowing tales; and I did not learn until I was grown that they had been among the large contributors to the fund for the relief of our party.

I have a faint recollection of listening to the chimes of the wedding bells, and later, of hearing that Captain Frisbie had taken his bride away; but that is all, for about that time dear old Jakie returned to us in ill health, and our thoughts and care turned to him. He was so feeble and wasted that grandma sent for the French physician who had recently come among us. Even he said that he feared that Jakie had stayed away too long. After months of treatment, the doctor shook his head saying: " I have done my best with the medicines at hand. The only thing that remains to be tried is a tea steeped from the nettle root. That may give relief."

As soon as we could get ready after the doctor uttered those words, Georgia and I, equipped with hoe, large knife, and basket were on our way to the Sonoma River. We had a full two miles and a half to walk, but did not mind that, because we were going for something that might take Jakie's pains away. Georgia was to press down the nettle stems with a stick, while I cut them off and hoed up the roots.

The plants towered luxuriantly above our heads, making the task extremely painful. No sooner would I commence operations than the branches, slipping from under the stick, would brush Georgia's face, and strike my hands and arms with stinging force, and by the time we had secured the required number of roots, we were covered with fiery welts. We took off our shoes and stockings, waded into the stream and bathed our faces, hands, and arms, then rested and ate the lunch we had brought with us.

As we turned homeward, we observed several Indians approaching by the bushy path, the one in front staggering, and his squaw behind, making frantic motions to us to hurry over the snake fence near-by. This we did as speedily as possible, and succeeded none too soon; for as we reached the ground on the safe side, he stopped us, and angrily demanded the contents of our basket. We opened it, and when he saw what it contained he stamped his wabbling foot and motioned us to be off. We obeyed with alacrity, for it was our first experience with a drunken Indian, and greatly alarmed us.

The tea may have eased Jakie's pain, but it did not accomplish what we had hoped. One morning late in Summer, he asked grandpa to bring a lawyer and witnesses so that he could make his will. This request made us all move about very quietly and feel very serious. After the lawyer went away, grandma told us that Jakie had willed us each fifty dollars in gold, and the rest of his property to grandpa and herself. A few weeks later, when the sap ceased flowing to the branches of the trees, and the yellow leaves were falling, we laid Jakie beside other friends in the oak grove within sight of our house.

Grandma put on deep mourning, but Georgia and I had only black sunbonnets, which we wore with heartfelt grief. The following Spring grandpa had the grave enclosed with a white paling; and we children planted Castilian rose bushes at the head and foot of the mound, and carried water to them from the house, and in time their branches met and the grave was a bed of fragrant blossoms.

One day as I was returning from it with my empty pail, a tidy, black-eyed woman came up to me and said,

"I'm a Cherokee Indian, the wife of one of the three drovers that sold the Brunners them long-horned cattle that was delivered the other day. I know who you are, and if you'll sit on that log by me, I'll tell you something."

We took the seats shaded by the fence and she continued with unmistakable pride: "I can read and write quite a little, and me and the men belong to the same tribe. We drove our band of cattle across the plains and over the Sierras, and have sold them for more than we expected to get. We are going back the same road, but first I wanted to see you little girls. I heard lots about your father's party, and how you all suffered in the mountains, and that no one seems to remember what became of his body. Now, child, I tell the truth. I stood by your father's grave and read his name writ on the headboard, and come to tell you that he was buried in a long grave near his own camp in the mountains. I 'm glad at seeing you, but am going away, wishing you was n't so cut off from your own people.''

So earnest was she, that I believed what she told me, and was sorry that I could not answer all her questions. We parted as most people did in those days, feeling that the meeting was good, and the parting might be forever.

CHAPTER XXVIII

THE Spring-tide of 1852 was bewitchingly beautiful; hills and plain were covered with wild
flowers in countless shapes and hues. They were so
friendly that they sprang up in dainty clusters close
to the house doors, or wherever an inch of ground
would give them foothold.

They seemed to call to me, and I looked into their
bright faces, threw myself among them, and hugged
as many as my arms could encircle, then laid my ear
close to the ground to catch the low sound of moving
leaf and stem, or of the mysterious ticking in the
earth, which foretells the coming of later plants.
Sometimes in my ecstasy, I would shut my eyes and lie
still for a while, then open them inquiringly, to assure myself that all my favorites were around me
still, and that it was not all a day-dream.

This lovely season mellowed into the Summer which
brought a most unexpected letter from our sister
Frances, who had been living all these years with the
family of Mr. James F. Reed, in San Jose. Childlike,
she wrote:

I am happy, but there has not been a day since I left Sutter's Fort that I haven't thought of my little sisters and wanted to see them. Hiram Miller, our guardian, says he will take me to see you soon, and Elitha is going too.

After the first few days of wondering, grandma rarely mentioned our prospective visitors, nor did she show Georgia or me the letter she herself had received from Elitha, but we re-read ours until we knew it by heart, and were filled with delightful anticipations. We imagined that our blue-eyed sister with the golden curls would look as she did when we parted, and recalled many things that we had said and done together at the Fort.

I asked grandma what "guardian" meant, and after she explained, I was not pleased with mine, and dreaded his coming, for I had not forgotten how Mr. Miller had promised me a lump of sugar that night in the Sierras, and then did not have it for me after I had walked the required distance; nor could I quite forgive the severe punishment he administered next morning because I refused to go forward and cried to return to mother when he told me that I must walk as far as Georgia and Frances did that day.

Autumn was well advanced before the lumbering old passenger coach brought our long-expected guests from the *embarcadero*, and after the excitement of the meeting was over, I stealthily scanned each face and figure. Mr. Miller's stocky form in coarse, dark clothes, his cold gray eyes, uneven locks, stubby beard, and teeth and lips browned by tobacco. chewing, were not unfamiliar; but he looked less tired, more patient, and was a kindlier spoken man than I had remembered.

Elitha, well dressed, tall, slender, and regular of feature, had the complexion and sparkling black eyes which mark the handsome brunette. I was more surprised than disappointed, however, to see that the girl of twelve, who slipped one arm around Georgia and the other around me in a long, loving embrace, had nothing about her that resembled our little sister Frances, except her blue eyes and motherly touch.

The week of their visit was joyous indeed. Many courtesies were extended by friends with whom we had travelled from time to time on the plains. One never-to-be-forgotten afternoon was spent with the Boggs family at their beautiful home amid orchard and vineyard near the foothills.

On Sunday, the bell of the South Methodist Church called us to service. In those days, the men occupied the benches on one side of the building, and the women and children on the other; and I noticed that several of the young men found difficulty in keeping their eyes from straying in our direction, and after service, more than one came to inquire after grandma's health.

Mr. Miller passed so little time in our company that I remember only his arrival and his one serious talk with grandma, when he asked her the amount due her on account of the trouble and expense we two children had been since she had taken us in charge. She told him significantly that there was nothing to pay, because we were her children, and that she was abundantly able to take care of us. In proof, she handed him a daguerreotype taken the previous year.

It pictured herself comfortably seated, and one of us standing at either side with an elbow resting upon her shoulder, and a chubby face leaning against the uplifted hand. She was arrayed in her best cap, handsome embroidered black satin dress and apron, lace sleeve ruffs, kerchief, watch and chain. We were twin-like in lace-trimmed dresses of light blue dimity, striped with a tan-colored vine, blue sashes and hair ribbons; and each held a bunch of flowers in her hand. It was a costly trinket, in a case inlaid with pink roses, in mother of pearl, and she was very proud of it.

Grandma's answer to Mr. Miller was a death-knell to Elitha's hopes and plans in our behalf. Her little daughter had been dead more than a year. Sister Leanna had recently married and gone to a home of her own, and the previous week the place made vacant by the marriage had been given to Frances, with the ready approval of Hiram Miller and Mr. and Mrs. Reed. She had now come to Sonoma hoping that if Mr. Miller should pay grandma for the care we had been to her, she would consent to give us up in order that we four sisters might be reunited in one home. Elitha now foresaw that such a suggestion would not only result in failure, but arouse grandma's antagonism, and cut off future communication between us.

CHAPTER XXIX

GREAT SMALLPOX EPIDEMIC — ST. MARY'S HALL —
THANKSGIVING DAY IN CALIFORNIA — ANOTHER BROTH-
ER-IN-LAW.

MRS. BRUNNER has become too childish to
have the responsibility of young girls,"
had been frequently remarked before Elitha's visit;
and after her departure, the same friends expressed
regret that she had not taken us away with her.

These whispered comments, which did not improve
our situation, suddenly ceased, for the smallpox made
its appearance in Sonoma, and helpers were needed to
care for the afflicted. Grandma had had the disease
in infancy and could go among the patients without
fear. In fact, she had such confidence in her method
of treating it, that she would not have Georgia and me
vaccinated while the epidemic prevailed, insisting that
if we should take the disease she could nurse us
through it without disfigurement, and we would thenceforth be immune. She did not expose us during what
she termed the "catching-stage," but after that had
passed, she called us to share her work and become
familiar with its details, and taught us how to brew the
teas, make the ointments, and apply them.

I do not remember a death among her patients, and

only two who were badly disfigured. One was our pretty Miss Sallie Lewis, who had the dread disease in confluent form. Grandma was called hurriedly in the night, because the afflicted girl, in delirium, had loosened the straps which held her upon her bed, and while her attendant was out of the room had rushed from the house into the rain, and was not found until after she had become thoroughly drenched. Grandma had never before treated such serious conditions, yet strove heroically, and helped to restore Miss Sallie to health, but could not keep the cruel imprints from her face.

The other was our arch-enemy, Castle, who seemed so near death that one night as grandma was peering into the darkness for signal lights from the homes of the sick, she exclaimed impulsively, "Hark, children! there goes the Catholic bell. Count its strokes. Castle is a Catholic, and was very low when I saw him to-day." Together we slowly counted the knells until she stopped us, saying, "It's for somebody else; Castle is not so old."

She was right. Later he came to us to recuperate, and was the most exacting and profane man we ever waited on. He conceived a special grudge against Georgia, whom he had caught slyly laughing when she first observed the change in his appearance. Yet months previous, he had laid the foundation for her mirth.

He was then a handsome, rugged fellow, and particularly proud of the shape of his nose. Frequently had he twitted my sensitive sister about her little nose,

MRS. BRUNNER, GEORGIA AND ELIZA DONNER

ELIZA P. DONNER

S. O. HOUGHTON,
Member of Col. J. D. Stevenson's First Regiment
of N. Y. Volunteers

and had once made her very angry in the presence of others, by offering to tell her a story, then continuing: " God and the devil take turns in shaping noses. Now, look at mine, large and finely shaped. This is God's work; but when yours was growing, it was the devil's turn, and he shaped that little dab on your face and called it a nose."

Georgia fled, and cried in anger over this indignity, declaring that she hated Castle and would not be sorry if something should happen to spoil his fine nose. So when he came to us from the sick-room, soured and crestfallen because disease had deeply pitted and seamed that feature which had formerly been his pride, she laughingly whispered, " Well, I don't care, my nose could never look like his, even if I had the smallpox, for there is not so much of it to spoil."

Our dislike of the man became intense; and later, when we discovered that he was to be bartender at grandpa's bar, and board at our house, we held an indignation meeting in the back yard. This was more satisfaction to Georgia than to me, for she had the pleasure of declaring that if grandma took that man to board, she would be a Schweitzer child no longer, she would stop speaking German, make her clothes like American children's; and that she knew her friend Mrs. Bergwald would give her a home, if grandma should send her away.

Here the meeting was suddenly interrupted by the discovery that grandma was standing behind us. We did not know how long she had been there nor how much she had overheard, nor which she meant to strike with the switch she had in her hand. However, we were sitting close together and my left arm felt the sting, and it aroused in me the spirit of rebellion. I felt that I had outgrown such correction, nor had I deserved it; and I told her that she should never, never strike me again. Then I walked to the house alone.

A few moments later Georgia came up to our room, and found me dressing myself with greatest care. In amazement she asked, " Eliza, where are you going? " and was dumbfounded when I answered, " To find another home for us."

In the lower hall I encountered grandma, whose anger had cooled, and she asked the question Georgia had. I raised my sleeve, showed the welt on my arm, and replied, " I am going to see if I can't find a home where they will treat me kindly."

Poor grandma was conscience-stricken, drew me into her own room, and did not let me leave it until after she had soothed my hurts and we had become friends again.

Georgia went to Mrs. Bergwald's, and remained quite a while. When she came back speaking English, and insisting that she was an American, grandma became very angry, and threatened to send her away among strangers; then hesitated, as if realizing how fully Georgia belonged to me and I to her, and that we would cling together whatever might happen. In her perplexity, she besought Mrs. Bergwald's advice.

Now, Mrs. Bergwald was a native of Stockholm, a

lady of rare culture, and used the French language in conversing with grandma. She spoke feelingly of my little sister, said that she was companionable, willing, and helpful; anxious to learn the nicer ways of work, and ladylike accomplishments. She could see no harm in Georgia wishing to remain an American, since to love one's own people and country was natural.

Thereafter grandma changed her methods. She gave us our dolls to look at, and keep among our possessions, likewise most of our keepsakes. She also unlocked her carefully tended parlor and we three spent pleasant evenings there. Sometimes she would let us bring her, from under the sofa, her gorgeous prints, illustrating " Wilhelm Tell,'' and would repeat the text relating to the scenes as we examined each picture with eager interest.

We were also allowed to go to Sunday school oftener, and later, she sent me part of the term to the select school for girls recently established by Dr. Ver Mehr, an Episcopalian clergyman. In fact, my tuition was expected to offset the school's milk bill, yet that did not lessen my enthusiasm. I was eager for knowledge. I also expected to meet familiar faces in that great building, which had been the home of Mr. Jacob Leese. But upon entering I saw only finely dressed young ladies from other parts of the State promenading in the halls, and small girls flitting about in the yard like bright-winged butterflies. Some had received letters from home and were calling out the news; others were engaged in games that were strange to me.

The bell rang, I followed to the recitation hall, and was assigned a seat below the rest, because I was the only small Sonoma girl yet enrolled.

I made several life-long friends at that institute; still it was easy to see that " St. Mary's Hall " was established for pupils who had been reared in the lap of wealth and ease; not for those whose hands were rough like mine. Nor was there a class for me. I seemed to be between grades, and had the discouragement of trying to keep up with girls older and farther advanced.

My educational advantages in Sonoma closed with my half term at St. Mary's Hall, grandma believing that I had gone to school long enough to be able to finish my studies without teachers.

Georgia was more fortunate. When Miss Hutchinson opened " The Young Ladies' Seminary " in the Fall, grandma decided to lend it a helping hand by sending her a term as a day scholar. My delighted sister was soon in touch with a crowd of other little girls, and brought home many of their bright sayings for my edification.

One evening she rushed into the house bubbling over with excitement and joyously proclaimed: " Oh, Eliza, Miss Hutchinson is going to give a great dinner to her pupils on Thanksgiving Day; and I am to go, and you also, as her guest."

Grandma was pleased that I was invited, and declared that she would send a liberal donation of milk and cheese as a mark of appreciation.

I caught much of Georgia's spirit of delight, for I had a vivid recollection of the grand dinner given in commemoration of our very first legally appointed Thanksgiving Day in California; I had only to close my eyes, and in thought would reappear the longest and most bountifully spread table I had ever seen. Turkey, chicken, and wild duck, at the ends; a whole roasted pig in the centre, and more than enough delicious accompaniments to cover the spaces between. Then the grown folk dining first, and the flock of hungry children coming later; the speaking, laughing, and clapping of hands, with which the old home customs were introduced in the new land.

There, I wore a dark calico dress and sunbonnet, both made by poor Mrs. McCutchen of the Donner Party, who had to take in sewing for a livelihood; but to the Seminary, I should wear grandpa's gift, a costly alpaca, changeable in the sunlight to soft mingling bluish and greenish colors of the peacock. Its wide skirt reached to my shoetops, and the gathers to its full waist were gauged to a sharp peak in front. A wide open V from the shoulder down to the peak displayed an embroidered white Swiss chemisette. The sleeves, small at the wrist, were trimmed with folds of the material and a quilling of white lace at the hand.

On the all-important morning, grandma was anxious that I should look well; and after she had looped my braids with bows of blue ribbon and fastened my dress, she brought forth my dainty bonnet, her own gift. Deft fingers had shirred the pale-blue silk over a frame

which had been cut down from ladies' size, arranged
an exquisite spray of Maréchal Niel rosebuds and foliage on the outside, and quilled a soft white ruching
around the face, which emphasized the Frenchy style
and finish so pleasing to grandma.

Did I look old fashioned? Yes, for grandma said,
" Thou art like a picture I saw somewhere long ago."
Then she continued brightly, " Here are thy mits, and
thy little embroidered handkerchief folded in a square.
Carry it carefully so it won't get mussed before the
company see it, and come not back late for milking."

The Seminary playground was so noisy with chatter
and screams of joy, that it was impossible to remember all the games we played; and later the dining-room
and its offerings were so surprising and so beautifully
decorated that the sight nearly deprived me of my
appetite.

" Mumps. Bite a pickle and see if it ain't so! " exclaimed a neighbor to whom Georgia was showing her
painful and swollen face. True enough, the least taste
of anything sour produced the tell-tale shock. But the
most aggravating feature of the illness was that it
developed the week that sister Elitha and Mr. Benjamin W. Wilder were married in Sacramento; and when
they reached Sonoma on their wedding tour, we could
not visit with them, because neither had had the
disease.

They came to our house, and we had a hurried little
talk with a closed window between us, and were favor-

ably impressed by our tall "Brother Ben," who had very blue eyes and soft brown hair. He was the second of the three Wilder brothers, who had been among the early gold-seekers, and tried roughing it in the mines. Though a native of Rhode Island, and of Puritan ancestry, he was quite Western in appearance.

Though not a wealthy man, he had a competency, for he and his elder brother were owners of an undivided half of Ranchos de los Cazadores (three leagues of land in Sacramento Valley), which was well stocked with horned cattle and good horses. He was also interested in a stage line running between Sacramento and the gold regions. He encouraged Elitha in her wish to make us members of their household, and the home they had to offer us was convenient to public schools; yet for obvious reasons they were now silent on the subject.

CHAPTER XXX

A T the time of which I now speak, I was in my eleventh year, but older in feeling and thought. I had ideals and wanted to live up to them, and my way was blocked by difficulties. Often, in the cowyard, I would say to the dumb creatures before me,

" I shall milk you dry, and be kind to you as long as I stay; but I shall not always be here doing this kind of work."

These feelings had been growing since the beginning of grandpa's partnership in that bar-room. Neither he nor grandma saw harm in the business. They regarded it as a convenient place where men could meet and spend a social evening, and where strangers might feel at home. Yet, who could say that harm did not emanate from that bar? I could not but wish that grandpa had no interest in it. I did not want to blame him, for he was kind by nature, and had been more than benefactor to Georgia and me.

Fond recollection was ever bringing to mind joys he had woven into our early childhood. Especially tender and precious thoughts were associated with that night long ago when he hurried home to inspect a daguerreotype that had just been taken. Grandma

handed it to him with the complaisant remark, " Mine
and Georgia's sind fine; but Eliza's shows that she forgot herself and ist watching how the thing ist being
made."

Grandpa looked at it in silence, observing that
grandma's likeness was natural, and Georgia's perfect, in fact, pretty as could be; while I, not being tall
enough to rest my elbow comfortably upon grandma's
shoulder, stood awkwardly with my flowers drooping
and eyes turned, intently watching in the direction of
the operator. Regretfully, I explained:

" Grandpa, mine was best two times, for Georgia
moved in the first one, and grandma in the next, and
the pictureman said after each, ' We must try again.'
And he would have tried yet again, for me, but the sun
was low, and grandma said she was sorry but this
would have to do."

Lovingly, he then drew me to his side, saying,
" Never mind, *mein Schatz* (my treasure); let
grandma and Georgia keep this, and when that pictureman comes back, grandpa will sit for his picture, and
thou shalt stand at his knee. He 'll buy thee a long
gold chain to wear around thy neck, and thou shalt be
dressed all in white and look like an angel."

Being younger than grandma, and more fond of
amusements, he had taken us to many entertainments;
notably, Odd Fellows' picnics and dinners, where he
wore the little white linen apron, which we thought
would be cute for our dolls. He often reminded
grandma that she should teach us to speak the high

German, so that we might appear well among gentlefolk; and my cherished keepsakes included two wee gold dollars and a fifty-cent piece of the same bright metal, which he had given me after fortunate sales from the herds. But dearest of all is remembrance of the evening long ago when he befriended us at Sutter's Fort.

Still, not even those tender recollections could longer hold in check my resentment against the influences and associations which were filtering through that barroom, and robbing me of companions and privileges that I valued. More than once had I determined to run away, and then desisted, knowing that I should leave two lonely old people grieving over my seeming ingratitude. This question of duty to self and to those who had befriended me haunted my working hours, went with me to church and Sunday school, and troubled my mind when I was supposed to be asleep.

Strange, indeed, would it have seemed to me, could I then have known that before my thirtieth year, I should be welcomed in the home of the military chief of our nation. Strange, also, that the young Lieutenant, William Tecumseh Sherman, who when visiting in Sonoma, came with his fellow-officers to the Brunner farm, should have attained that dignity. Equally impossible would it have been then to conceive that in so short a time, I, a happy mother and the wife of a Congressional Representative, should be a guest at the brilliant receptions of the foreign diplomats and at the Executive Mansion in the city of Washington.

Is it any wonder that in later years when my mind reverted to those days, I almost questioned my identity?

Georgia's return from Mrs. Bergwald's before Christmas gave me a chance to talk matters over with her, and we decided that we must leave our present surroundings. Yet, how to get away, and when, puzzled us. Our only hope of escape seemed to be to slip off together some moonlight night.

"But," my sister remarked gravely, "we can't do it before Christmas! You forget the white flannel skirt that I am embroidering for grandma, the pillow-slips that you are hemstitching and trimming with lace for her; and the beautiful white shirt that you have for grandpa."

She was sure that not to stay and give them as we had planned, would be as bad as breaking a promise. So, we took out our work and hid ourselves to sew a while.

My undertaking was not so large or elaborate as hers, and when I finished, she still had quite a piece to do, and was out of floss. She had pin-pricked from an embroidered silk shawl on to strips of white paper, the outline of a vine representing foliage, buds, and blossoms; then basted the paper in place around the skirt. The colors were shaded green and pink. Unable to get the floss for the blossoms, she had bought narrow pink silk braid and outlined each rose and bud, then embroidered the foliage in green. Some might have thought it a trifle gaudy, but to me it seemed beautiful, and I was proud of her handiwork.

I washed, starched, and ironed the pillow-slips while grandma was from home, and they did look well, for I had taken great pains in doing my work. Several days before the appointed time, grandma, in great good humor, showed us the dresses she had been hiding from us; and then and there, like three children unable to keep their secrets longer, we exchanged gifts, and were as pleased as if we had waited until Christmas morning.

CHAPTER XXXI

ON the first of September, 1855, a widow, whom I shall call Stein, and her little son Johnnie, came to visit grandma. She considered herself a friend by reason of the fact that she and her five children had been hospitably entertained in our home two years earlier, upon their arrival in California. For grandpa in particular she professed a high regard, because her husband had been his bartender, and as such had earned money enough to bring his family from Europe, and also to pay for the farm which had come to her at his death.

Mother and son felt quite at home, and in humor to enjoy their self-appointed stay of two weeks. Despite her restless eye and sinister smile, she could be affable; and although, at first, I felt an indescribable misgiving in her presence, it wore away, and I often amused Johnnie while she and grandma talked.

As if to hasten events, Mrs. Bergwald had sent for Georgia almost at the beginning of the visit of the Steins; and after her departure, Mrs. Stein insisted on helping me with the chores, and then on my sitting with her during grandma's busiest hour.

She seemed deeply interested in California's early history, and when I would stop talking, she would ply me with questions. So I told her how poor everybody was before the discovery of gold; how mothers would send their boys to grandma's early morning fire for live coals, because they had no matches or tinder boxes; how neighbors brought their coffee and spices to grind in her mills; how the women gathered in the afternoons under her great oak tree, to talk, sew, and eagerly listen to the reading of extracts from letters and papers that had come from friends away back in the States. I told her how, in case of sickness, one neighbor would slip over and cook the family breakfast for the sick woman, others would drop in later, wash the dishes, and put the house in order; and so by turns and shares, the washing, ironing, and mending would be done, and by the time the sick woman would be up and around, she would have no neglected work to discourage her. Also we talked of how flags were used for day signals and lights by night, in calls for help.

Our last talk was on Saturday morning between work. She questioned me in regard to the amount, and location of the property of the Brunners, then wanted to hear all about my sisters in Sacramento, and wondered that we did not go to live with them. I explained that Elitha had written us several times asking us to come, but, knowing that grandma would be displeased, we had not read her those parts of the letters, lest she forbid our correspondence entirely. I added that we were very sorry that she could not like those who were dear to us.

Finally, having exhausted information on several subjects, Mrs. Stein gave me a searching glance, and after a marked silence, continued: " I don't wonder that you love grandpa and grandma as much as you tell me, and it is a pity about these other things that aren't pleasant. Don't you think it would be better for you to live with your sister, and grandma could have some real German children to live here? She is old, and can't help liking her own kind of people best.''

I did not have an unkind thought in mind, yet I did confess that I should like to live well and grow up to be like my mother. In thoughtless chatter I continued, that more nice people came to visit grandma and to talk with us before the town filled with strangers, and before Americans lived in the good old Spanish houses, and before the new churches and homes were built.

She led me to speak of mother, then wondered at my vivid recollections, since I had parted from her so young. She was very attentive as I told how Georgia and I spoke of her when we were by ourselves, and that friends did not let us forget her. I even cited a recent instance, when the teacher had invited us, and two other young girls, to go to the Vallejo pear orchard for all the fruit we wished to eat, and when he offered the money in payment, the old Spanish gentleman in charge said, '' Pay for three.''

" But we are five," said the teacher.

Then the Don blessed himself with the sign of the cross, and pointing to Georgia and me, replied, " Those two are daughters of a sainted mother, and are always welcome! "

At noon grandma told me that she and the Steins would be ready to go down town immediately after dinner, and that I must wash the dishes and finish baking the bread in the round oven. We parted in best of humor, and I went to work. The dishes and bread received first attention. Then I scrubbed the brick floor in the milk-house; swept the store-room and front yard; gathered the eggs, fed the chickens, and rebuilt the fire for supper. I fancied grandma would be pleased with all I had accomplished, and laughed to myself as I saw the three coming home leaning close to each other in earnest conversation.

To my surprise, the Steins went directly to their own room; and grandma did not speak, but closed her eyes as she passed me. That was her way, and I knew that it would be useless to ask what had offended her. So I took my milk pails, and, wondering, went to the cow corrals. I could not imagine what had happened, yet felt hurt and uncomfortable.

Returning with the milk, I saw Johnnie playing by the tree, too near the horse's feet, and warned him. As he moved, grandma stepped forward and stood in front of me, her face white with rage. I set my buckets down and standing between them listened as she said in German:

" Oh, false one, thou didst not think this morning that I would so soon find thee out. Thou wast not smart enough to see that my friend, Mrs. Stein, was studying thee, so that she could let me know what kind of children I had around me. And thou, like a snake in the grass, hast been sticking out thy tongue behind my back. Thou pretendest that thou art not staying here to get my money and property, yet thou couldst tell her all I had. Thou wouldst not read all in the letters from thy fine sisters? Thou wouldst rather stay here until I die and then be rich and spend it with them ! "

She stopped as if to catch her breath, and I could only answer, " Grandma, I have not done what thou sayest."

She continued : " I have invited people to come here this night, and thou shalt stand before them and listen while I tell what I have done for thee, and how thou hast thanked me. Now, go, finish thy work, eat thy supper, and come when I call thee."

I heard her call, but don't know how I got into the room, nor before how many I stood. I know that my head throbbed and my feet almost refused to support my body, as I listened to grandma, who in forceful language declared that she had taken me, a starveling, and reared me until I was almost as tall as she herself ; that she had loved and trusted me, and taught me everything I knew, and that I had that day blackened the home that had sheltered me, wounded the hand that had fed me, and proved myself unworthy the love that

[273]

had been showered upon me. Mrs. Stein helped her through an account of our morning chat, misconstruing all that had passed between us.

I remained silent until the latter had announced that almost the first thing that she had noticed was that we children were of a selfish, jealous disposition, and that Georgia was very cross when her little Johnnie came home wearing a hat that grandpa had bought him. Then I turned upon her saying, " Mrs. Stein, you forget that Georgia has not seen that hat. You know that grandma bought it after Georgia went away."

She sprang toward me, then turned to grandma, and asked if she was going to let an underling insult a guest in her house.

I did not wait for the reply. I fled out into the dark and made my way to the weird old tree-trunk in the back yard. Thence, I could see the lights from the windows, and at times hear the sound of voices. There, I could stand in the starlight and look up to the heavens. I had been there before, but never in such a heartsick and forlorn condition. I was too overwrought to think, yet had to do something to ease the tension. I moved around and looked toward Jakie's grave, then returned to the side of the tree-trunk which had escaped the ravages of fire, and ran my finger up and down, feeling the holes which the red-headed woodpecker had bored and filled with acorns.

A flutter in the air aroused me. It was the old white-faced owl leaving the hollow in the live oak for the night's hunt. I faced about and saw her mate fly after her. Then in the stillness that followed, I stretched both arms toward heaven and cried aloud, " O God, I 'm all alone; take care of me! "

The spell was broken. I grew calmer and began to think and to plan. I pictured Georgia asleep in a pretty house two miles away, wondered how I could get word to her and what she would say when told that we would go away together from Sonoma, and not take anything that grandpa or grandma had given us.

I remembered that of the fund which we had started by hemming new, and washing soiled handkerchiefs for the miners, there still remained in her trunk seven dollars and eighty-five cents, and in mine seven dollars and fifty cents. If this was not enough to take us to Sacramento, we might get a chance as Sister Leanna had, to work our way.

I was still leaning against the tree-trunk when the moon began to peep over the eastern mountains, and I vowed by its rising that before it came up in its full, Georgia and I should be in Sacramento.

I heard grandma's call from the door, which she opened and quickly closed, and I knew by experience that I should find a lighted candle on the table, and that no one would be in the room to say good-night. I slept little, but when I arose in the morning I was no longer trouble tossed. I knew what I would say to grandma if she should give me the chance.

Grandpa, who had come home very late, did not know what had happened, and he and I breakfasted with the men, and grandma and the Steins came after we left the room. No one offered to help me that morning, still I got through my duties before grandma called me to her. She seemed more hurt than angry, and began by saying:

" On account of thy bad conduct, Mrs. Stein is going to shorten her stay. She is going to leave on Tuesday, and wants me to go with her. She says that she has kept back the worst things that thou hast told about me, but will tell them to me on the road.''

Trembling with indignation, I exclaimed, " Oh, grandma, thou hast always told us that it is wrong to speak of the faults of a guest in the house, but what dost thou think of one who hath done what Mrs. Stein hath done? I did say some of the things she told thee, but I did not say them in that way. I did n't give them that meaning. I did n't utter one unkind word against thee or grandpa. I have not been false to thee. To prove it, I promise to stay and take care of everything while thou goest and hearest what more she hath to tell, but after the home-coming, I leave. Nothing that thou canst say will make me change my mind. I am thankful for the home I have had, but will not be a burden to thee longer. I came to thee poor, and I will go away poor.''

The Brunner conveyance was at the door on Tuesday morning when grandma and her guest came out to begin their journey. Grandpa helped grandma and the widow on to the back seat. While he was putting Johnnie in front with the driver, I stepped close to the vehicle, and extended my hand to grandma, saying, "Good-bye, don't worry about the dairy while thou art gone, for everything will be attended to until thy return; but remember — then I go."

On the way back to the house grandpa asked why I did not treat the widow more friendly, and I answered, "Because I don't believe in her." To my surprise, he replied, " I don't either, but grandma is like a little child in her hands."

I felt that I ought to tell him I should soon go away, but I had never gone to him with home troubles, and knew that it would not be right to speak of them in grandma's absence; so he quietly went to his duties and I to mine. Yet I could not help wondering how grandma could leave me in full charge of her possessions if she believed the stories that had been told her. I felt so sure that the guilty one would be found out that it made me light-hearted.

Mrs. Blake came and spent the night with me, and the following morning helped to get the breakfast and talked over the cleaning that I wished to do before grandma's return on the coming Saturday morning. But

> God moves in a mysterious way
> His wonders to perform,

and unseen hands were shaping a different course for me! I had the milk skimmed, and a long row of clean pans in the sunshine before time to hurry the dinner for grandpa and the three men. I was tired, for I had carried most of the milk to the pig troughs after having finished work which grandma and I had always done together; so I sat down under the tree to rest and meditate.

My thoughts followed the travellers with many questions, and the wish that I might hear what Mrs. Stein had to say. I might have overstayed my time, if the flock of goats had not come up and smelled my hands, nibbled at the hem of my apron, and tried to chew the cape of my sun-bonnet. I sprang up and with a shout and clap of my hands, scattered them, and entered the log kitchen, reclosing the lower section of the divided door, to keep them from following me within.

I prepared the dinner, and if it lacked the flavor of grandma's cooking, those who ate it did not tell me. Grandpa lingered a moment to bestow a meed of praise on my work, then went off to the back corral to slaughter a beef for the shop. I began clearing the table, and was turning from it with a vegetable dish in each hand when I caught sight of the shadow of a tall silk hat in the open space above the closed half door. Then the hat and its wearer appeared.

Leaning over the edge of the door, he gazed at me standing there as if I were nailed to the floor. I was speechless with amazement, and it seemed a long while before he remarked lightly, " You don't seem to know me."

" Yes, you are Mr. Wilder, my brother-in-law," I stammered. " Where is Elitha? "

He informed me that she and their little daughter

SACRAMENTO CITY IN THE EARLY FIFTIES

FRONT STREET, SACRAMENTO CITY, 1850

were at the hotel in town, where they had arrived about noon, and that she wanted Georgia and me to be prompt in coming to her at four o'clock. I told him that we could not do so, because Georgia was at Mrs. Bergwald's, grandma on a journey beyond Bodego, and I at home in charge of the work.

In surprise he listened, then asked, "But aren't you at all anxious to see your sister and little niece?"

Most earnestly, I replied that I was. Nevertheless, as grandma was away, I could not leave the place until after the day's work was done. Then I enumerated what was before me. He agreed that there was quite enough to keep me busy, yet insisted that I ought to keep the appointment for four o'clock. After his departure, I rushed out to grandpa, told him who had come and gone, and what had passed between us. He too, regretted the situation, but promised that I should spend the evening at the hotel.

I fairly flew about my work that afternoon, and my brain was as active as my hands and feet. I was certain that brother and sister had come for us, and the absorbing query was, "How did they happen to arrive at this particular time?" I also feared there was more trouble before me, and remembered my promise to grandma with twinges of regret.

At half-past four, I was feeding the hens in the yard, and, looking up, saw a strange carriage approaching. Instantly, I guessed who was in it, and was at the gate before it stopped. Elitha greeted me kindly, but not cordially. She asked why I had not come as requested, and then said, "Go, bring the silver thimble Frances left here, and the coral necklace I gave you."

In my nervous haste I could not find the thimble, but carried out the necklace. She next bade me take the seat beside her, thus disclosing her intention of carrying me on, picking up Georgia and proceeding to Sacramento. She was annoyed by my answer and disappointed in what she termed my lack of pride. Calling my attention to my peculiar style of dress and surroundings, to my stooped shoulders and callous hands, she bade me think twice before I refused the comfortable home she had to offer.

When assured that I would gladly go on Saturday, but was unwilling to leave in grandma's absence, she did not urge further, simply inquired the way to Georgia, and left me.

I was nursing my disappointment and watching the disappearing carriage, when Mr. Knipp, the brewer, with his load of empty kegs drew up, and asked what I was thinking about so hard. It was a relief to see his jolly, good-natured face, and I told him briefly that our people were in town and wished to take us home with them. He got down from his wagon to say confidentially:

"Thou must not leave grandpa and grandma, because the old man is always kind to thee, and though she may sometimes wag a sharp tongue, she means well. Be patient, by-and-by thou wilt have a nice property, the country will have more people for hire, and thou wilt not have so hard to work."

When I told him that I did not want the property, and that there were other things I did care for, he continued persuasively:

"Women need not so much learning from books. Grandma would not know how to scold so grandly if she remembered not so many fine words from ' Wilhelm Tell ' and the other books that she knoweth by heart." And he climbed back and drove off, believing that he had done me a good turn.

To my great satisfaction, Georgia arrived about dark, saying that Benjamin had brought her and would call for us later to spend the evening with them. When we reached the hotel, Elitha received us affectionately, and did not refer to the disappointments of the afternoon. The time was given up to talk about plans for our future, and that night when we two crept into bed, I felt that I had been eased of a heavy burden, for Benjamin was willing to await grandma's return.

He also told us that early next morning he would go to Santa Rosa, the county seat, and apply to be made our guardian in place of Hiram Miller, and would also satisfy any claim grandma might have to us, or against us, adding that we need not take anything away with us, except our keepsakes.

CHAPTER XXXII

MEANWHILE, grandma and her friends had reached Bodego and spent the night there. She had not learned anything more terrible that I had said about her, and at breakfast told Mrs. Stein that she had had a dream foreboding trouble, and would not continue the journey to the Stein home. The widow coaxed and insisted that she go the few remaining miles to see her children. Then she waxed indignant and let slip the fact that she considered it an outrage that American, instead of European born children should inherit the Brunner property, and that she had hoped that grandma would select two of her daughters to fill the places from which Georgia and I should ·be expelled.

Grandma took a different view of the matter, and started homeward immediately after breakfast.

That very afternoon, on the Santa Rosa road, whom should she pass but our brother Ben. They recognized each other, but were too astonished to speak. Grandma ordered her driver to whip up, saying that she had just seen the red-whiskered imp of darkness who had troubled her sleep, and she must get to town as fast as possible.

FAREWELL TO THE FARM

She stopped first at the butcher shop. Before grandpa could express surprise at her unexpected return, she showered him with questions in regard to happenings at home, and being informed, took him to task for having permitted us to visit our people at the hotel. He innocently remarked that he knew of no reason why we should not see our relatives; that Georgia was spending the day with them; and that we both had his permission to go again in the evening. In conclusion he said that I had been a faithful, hard working little housekeeper, and she would find everything in order at home.

Grandma arrived at home before sunset, too excited to be interested in dairy matters. She told me all about her trip, even to the name she had called my brother-in-law, adding that she knew he was " not red-whiskered, but he was next door to it." Later, when he came, she did not receive him pleasantly, nor would she let us go to Elitha. Brusquely, she demanded to know if I had written to him to come for us, and would not believe him when he assured her that neither he nor our sisters had received letter or message from us in months.

After his departure, I could see that she was no longer angry, and I dreaded the ensuing day, which was destined to be my last on that farm.

It came with a rosy dawn, and I was up to meet it, and to say good-bye to the many dumb creatures that I had cared for. The tension I was under lent me strength to work faster than usual. When the breakfast call sounded, I had finished in the corrals, and was busy in the hen houses, having taken care to keep out of grandpa's sight; for I knew how he would miss me, and I did not want to say the parting words. After he and the men were gone, grandma came, and watched me finish my task, then said kindly,

"Come, Eliza, and eat thy breakfast."

I looked up and replied,

"Grandma, I ate my last meal in thy house last night. Dost thou not remember, I told thee that I would take care of everything until thy return, and then would not be a burden to thee longer? I have kept my word, and am going away this morning."

"Thou are mine, and canst not go; but if thou wilt not eat, come and help me with the dishes," she replied nervously.

I had planned to slip off and change my dress before meeting her, but now, after a breath of hesitation, I went to dry the dishes, hoping that our talk would soon be over. I knew it would be hard for both of us, for dear, childish grandma was ready to forgive and forget what she termed our little troubles. I, however, smarting under the wrong and injustice that had been done me, felt she had nothing to forgive, and that matters between us had reached the breaking-point.

She was still insisting on her right to keep me, when a slight sound caused us both to turn, and meeting Georgia's anxious, listening gaze, grandma appealed to her, saying,

"Thou hast heard thy sister's talk, but thou hast not been in this fuss, and surely wilt not leave me?"

"Yes, I am going with Eliza," was the prompt answer, which had no sooner left her lips, than grandma resorted to her last expedient: she ordered us both to our room, and forbade us to leave it until she should hear from grandpa.

What message she sent him by the milker we never learned. Georgia, being already dressed for the journey, and her trunk containing most of her possessions being at Mrs. Bergwald's, had nothing to do but await results.

I quickly changed my working suit for a better one, which had been given me by a German friend from San Francisco. Then I laid out my treasured keepsakes. In my nervous energy, nothing was forgotten. I took pains that my clothes against the wall should hang in straight rows, that the folded ones should lie in neat piles in my pretty Chinese trunk, and that the bunch of artificial flowers which I had always kept for a top centre mark, should be exactly in the middle; finally, that the gray gauze veil used as a fancy covering of the whole should be smoothly tucked in around the clothing. This done, I gave a parting glance at the dainty effect, dropped the cover, snapped the queer little brass padlock in place, put the key on the table, and covered the trunk so that its embossed figures of birds and flowers should be protected from harm.

We had not remembered to tell Elitha about the hundred dollars which Jakie had willed us, so decided to let grandma keep it to cover some of the expense we had been to her, also not to ask for our little trinkets stored in her closet.

With the bundle containing my keepsakes, I now sat down by Georgia and listened with bated breath to the sound of grandma's approaching footsteps. She entered and hastily began,

" Grandpa says, if you want to go, and your people are here to take you, we have no right to keep you; but that I am not to part with you bad friends. So I came to shake hands and say good-bye. But I don't forgive you for going away, and I never want to see you or hear from you again!"

She did not ask to see what we were taking away, nor did her good-bye seem like parting.

The fear that something might yet arise to prevent our reaching brother and sister impelled us to run the greater part of the distance to the hotel, and in less than an hour thereafter, we were in the carriage with them on the way to Mrs. Bergwald's, prior to taking the road to Sacramento.

Off at last, without a soul in the town knowing it!

Georgia, who had neither said nor done anything to anger grandma, was easier in mind and more comfortable in body, than I, who, fasting, had borne the trials of the morning. I could conceal the cause, but not the faint and ill feeling which oppressed me during the morning drive and continued until I had had something to eat at the wayside inn, and a rest, while the horses were enjoying their nooning.

I had also been too miserable to feel any interest in what occurred at Mrs. Bergwald's after we stopped to let Georgia get her keepsakes. But when the day's travel was over, and we were comfortably housed for the night, Georgia and I left our brother and sister to their happy hour with their child, and sat close together on the outer doorsteps to review the events of the day. Our world during that solemn hour was circumscribed, reaching back only to the busy scenes of the morning, and forward to the little home that should open to us on the morrow.

When we resumed travel, we did not follow the pioneers' trail, once marked by hoof of deer, elk, and antelope, nor the winding way of the Spanish *cabellero*, but took the short route which the eager tradesman and miner had hewn and tramped into shape.

On reaching the ferry across the Sacramento River, I gazed at the surrounding country in silent amazement. Seven and a half years with their marvellous influx of brawn and brain, and their output of gold, had indeed changed every familiar scene, except the snow-capped Sierras, wrapped in their misty cloak of autumnal blue. The broad, deep river had given up both its crystal floods and the wild, free song which had accompanied it to the sea, and become a turbid waterway, encumbered with busy craft bringing daily supplies to countless homes, and carrying afar the long hidden wealth of ages.

The tule flat between the water front and Sutter's Fort had become a bustling city. The streets running north and south were numbered from first to twenty-eighth, and those east and west lettered from A to Z, and thriving, light-hearted throngs were pursuing their various occupations upon ground which had once seemed like a Noah's ark to me. Yes, this was the very spot where with wondering eyes I had watched nature's untamed herds winding through the reedy paths to the river bank, to quench their morning and evening thirst.

As we crossed from J Street to K, brother remarked, " Our journey will end on this street; which of you girls will pick out the house before we come to it? "

Elitha would not help us, but smiled, when, after several guesses, I said that I wished it to be a white house with brownish steps and a dark door with a white knob. Hence, great was my satisfaction when near the southeast corner of Eighteenth and K streets, we halted in front of a cottage of that description; and it was regarded as a lucky omen for me, that my first wish amid new scenes should be realized.

The meeting with Sister Frances and the novelty of the new situation kept up a pleasurable excitement until bed-time. Then in the stillness of the night, in the darkness of the new chamber, came the recollection that at about that hour one week ago, I, sorrowing and alone, had stood by a weird old tree-trunk in Sonoma, and vowed by the rising moon that before it should come up again in its full, Georgia and I would be in Sacramento. I did not sleep until I had thanked the good Father for sending help to me in my time of need.

CHAPTER XXXIII

THE PUBLIC SCHOOLS OF SACRAMENTO — A GLIMPSE OF GRANDPA — THE RANCHO DE LOS CAZADORES — MY SWEETEST PRIVILEGE — LETTERS FROM THE BRUNNERS.

I T is needless to say that we were grateful for our new home, and tried to express our appreciation in words and by sharing the household duties, and by helping to make the neat clothing provided for us.

The first Monday in October was a veritable red-letter day. Aglow with bright anticipations, we hurried off to public school with Frances. Not since our short attendance at the pioneer school in Sonoma had Georgia and I been schoolmates, and never before had we three sisters started out together with books in hand; nor did our expectations overreach the sum of happiness which the day had in store for us.

The supposition that grandpa and grandma had passed out of our lives was soon disproved; for as I was crossing our back yard on the Saturday of that first week of school, I happened to look toward Seventeenth Street, and saw a string of wagons bringing exhibits from the fair grounds. Beside the driver of a truck carrying a closed cage marked, "Buffalo," stood grandpa. He had risen from his seat, leaned back against the front of the cage, folded his arms and was looking at me. My long black braids had been cut off, and my style of dress changed, still he had recognized me. I fled into the house, and told Elitha what I had seen. She, too, was somewhat disquieted, and replied musingly,

"The old gentleman is lonely, and may have come to take you girls back with him."

His presence in Sacramento so soon after our reaching there did seem significant, because he had bought that buffalo in 1851, before she was weaned from the emigrant cow that had suckled and led her in from the great buffalo range, and he had never before thought of exhibiting her.

The following afternoon, as we were returning from Sunday school, a hand suddenly reached out of the crowd on J Street and touched Georgia's shoulder, then stopped me. A startled backward glance rested on Castle, our old enemy, who said,

" Come. Grandpa is in town, and wants to see you." We shook our heads. Then he looked at Frances, saying, " All of you, come and see the large seal and other things at the fair."

But she replied, emphatically, " We have not permission," and grasping a hand of each, hurried us homeward. For days thereafter, we were on the alert guarding against what we feared might happen.

Our alarm over, life moved along smoothly. Elitha admonished us to forget the past, and prepare for the future. She forbade Georgia and me to use the German language in speaking with each other, giving as

Photograph by Lynwood Abbott.

PINES OF THE SIERRAS

COL. J. D. STEVENSON

GENERAL JOHN A. SUTTER

a reason that we should take Frances into our confidence and thoughts as closely as we took one another.

I was never a morbid child, and the days that I did not find a sunbeam in life, I was apt to hunt for a rainbow. But there, in sight of the Sierras, the feeling again haunted me that perhaps my mother did not die, but had strayed from the trail and later reached the settlement and could not find us. Each middle-aged woman that I saw ahead of me on the street would thrill me with expectation, and I would quicken my steps in order to get a view of her face. When I gave up this illusion, I still prayed that Keseberg would send for me some day, and let me know her end, and give me a last message. I wanted his call to me to be voluntary, so that I might know that his words were true. These hopes and prayers were sacred, even from Georgia.

On the twenty-fourth of March, 1856, brother Ben took us all to pioneer quarters on Rancho de los Cazadores, where their growing interests required the personal attention of the three brothers. There we became familiar with the pleasures, and also the inconveniences and hardships of life on a cattle ranch. We were twenty miles from town, church, and school; ten miles from the post office; and close scrutiny far and wide disclosed but one house in range. Our supply of books was meagre, and for knowledge of current events, we relied on *The Sacramento Union,* and on the friends who came to enjoy the cattleman's hospitality.

My sweetest privilege was an occasional visit to

cousin Frances Bond, my mother's niece, who, with her husband and child, had settled on a farm about twelve miles from us. She also had grown up a motherless girl, but had spent a part of her young ladyhood at our home in Illinois. She had helped my mother to prepare for our long journey and would have crossed the plains with us had her father granted her wish. She was particularly fond of us "three little ones" whom she had caressed in babyhood. She related many pleasing incidents connected with those days, and spoke feelingly, yet guardedly, of our experiences in the mountains. Like Elitha, she hoped we would forget them, and as she watched me cheerfully adapting myself to new surroundings, she imagined that time and circumstances were dimming the past from my memory.

She did not understand me. I was light-hearted because I was old enough to appreciate the blessings that had come to me; old enough to look ahead and see the pure, intelligent womanhood opening to me; and trustful enough to believe that my expectations in life would be realized. So I gathered counsel and comfort from the lips of that sympathetic cousin, and loved her word pictures of the home where I was born.

Nor could change of circumstances wean my grateful thoughts from Grandpa and Grandma Brunner. At times, I seemed to listen for the sound of his voice, and to hear hers so near and clear that in the night, I often started up out of sleep in answer to her dream calls. Finally I determined to disregard her parting words, and write her. Georgia was sure that I would get a severe answer, but Elitha's ready permission made the letter easier to write. Weeks elapsed without a reply, and I had about given up looking for it, when late in August, William, the youngest Wilder brother, saddled his horse, and upon mounting, called out,

" I 'm off to Sacramento, Eliza, to bring you that long-expected letter. It was misdirected, and is advertised in *The Sacramento Union's* list of uncalled-for mail."

He left me in a speculative mood, wondering if it was from grandma; which of her many friends had written it for her; and if it was severe, as predicted by Georgia. Great was my delight when the letter was handed me, and I opened it and read:

SONOMA, *July 3, 1856*

To MISS ELIZA P. DONNER:
  CASADOR RANCHO, CONSUMNE RIVER
        NEAR SACRAMENTO CITY.

DEAR ELIZA:
Your letter of the fifteenth of June came duly to hand, giving me great satisfaction in regard to your health, as well as keeping me and grandfather in good memory.

I have perused the contents of your letter with great interest. I am glad to learn that you enjoy a country life. We have sold lately twelve cows, and are milking fifteen at present. You want to know how Flower is coming on: had you not better come and see for yourself? Hard feelings or ill will we have none against you; and why should I not forgive little troubles that are past and gone by?

I know that you saw grandfather in Sacramento; he saw you and knew you well too. Why did you not go and speak to him?

The roses you planted on Jacob's grave are growing beautifully, and our garden looks well. Grandfather and myself enjoy good health, and we wish you the same for all time to come. We give you our love, and remain,

In parental affection,

MARY AND CHRISTIAN BRUNNER.

(Give our love also to Georgia.)

Georgia was as much gratified by the contents of the letter as I, and we each sent an immediate answer, addressed to grandpa and grandma, expressing our appreciation of their forgiving words, regret for trouble and annoyances we had caused them, thanks for their past kindness, and the hope that they would write to us again when convenient. We referred to our contentment in our new home, and avoided any words which they might construe as a wish to return.

There was no long waiting for the second letter, nor mistake in address. It was dated just three days prior to the first anniversary of our leaving Sonoma, and here speaks for itself:

SONOMA, *Sept. 11, 1856*

GEORGIA AND ELIZA DONNER.

MY DEAR CHILDREN:

Your two letters dated August thirty-first reached us in due season.

We were glad to hear from you, and it is our wish that you do well. Whenever you are disposed to come to us again our doors shall be open to you, and we will rejoice to see you.

We are glad to see that you acknowledge your errors, **for** it shows good hearts, and the right kind of principles; for you should always remember that in showing respect to old age you are doing yourself honor, and those who know you will respect you. All your cows are doing well.

I am inclined to think that the last letter we wrote you, you did not get. We mention this to show you that we **always** write to you.

Your mother desires to know if you have forgotten the

[294]

time when she used to have you sleep with her, each in one arm, showing the great love and care she had for you; she remembers, and can't forget.

Your grandfather informs you that he still keeps the butcher shop, and bar-room, and that scarcely a day passes without his thinking of you. He still feels very bad that you did not, before going away, come to him and say "Goodbye, grandfather." He forgives you, however, and hopes you will come and see him. When you get this letter you must write.   Yours affectionately,

CHRISTIAN BRUNNER,
MARY BRUNNER.

Letters following the foregoing assured us that grandma had become fully satisfied that the stories told her by Mrs. Stein were untrue. She freely acknowledged that she was miserable and forlorn without us, and begged us to return to the love and trust which awaited us at our old home. This, however, we could not do.

Before the close of the Winter, Frances and Georgia began preparations for boarding school in Sacramento, and I being promised like opportunities for myself later, wrote all about them to grandma, trusting that this course would convince her that we were permanently separated from her, and that Elitha and her husband had definite plans for our future. I received no response to this, but Georgia's first communication from school contained the following paragraph:

I saw Sallie Keiberg last week, who told me that her mother had a letter from the old lady (Grandma Brunner) five weeks ago. A man brought it. And that the old lady had sent us by him some jewellery, gold breast-pins, earrings, and wristlets. He stopped at the William Tell Hotel. And that is all they know about him and the presents.

CHAPTER XXXIV

TRAGEDY IN SONOMA — CHRISTIAN BRUNNER IN A PRISON
CELL — ST. CATHERINE'S CONVENT AT BENICIA — RO-
MANCE OF SPANISH CALIFORNIA — THE BEAUTIFUL ANGEL
IN BLACK — THE PRAYER OF DONA CONCEPCION ARGU-
ELLO REALIZED — MONASTIC RITES.

TIME passed. Not a word had come to me from Sonoma in months, when Benjamin handed me the *Union,* and with horror I read the headlines to which he pointed: " TRAGEDY IN SONOMA. CHRISTIAN BRUNNER, AN OLD RESIDENT, SLAYS HIS OWN NEPHEW! "

From the lurid details published, I learned that the Brunners had asked this nephew to come to them, and had sent him money to defray his expenses from Switzerland to California. Upon his arrival in Sonoma, he had settled himself in the proffered home, and at once begun a life of extravagance, at the expense of his relatives. He was repeatedly warned against trifling with their affection, and wasting their hard-earned riches. Then patience ceased, and he was forbidden the house of his uncle.

Meanwhile, his aunt became seriously ill, and the young man visited her secretly, and prevailed upon her to give him, in the event of her death, certain cattle and other property which stood in her name.

She, however, recovered health; and he in the presence of his uncle, insisted that she had given him the property outright, and he wanted possession. This made trouble between the old couple, and the wife took refuge with friends in San Francisco. The night after her departure, the husband entered his own room and found the nephew in his bed. Thoroughly enraged, he ordered him up and out of his sight, and was insolently told by the young man that he was owner of that property and in rightful possession of the same. At this, his uncle snatched his pistol from the table at the bedside, and fired the fatal shot.

This almost incredible news was so harrowing that I could scarcely think of anything, except grandpa chained in a prison cell, grandma in hiding away from home, and excited groups of people gathering about the thoroughfares of Sonoma discussing the tragedy.

I was not sorry that at this time an epidemic of measles broke out in Sacramento, and Georgia became one of its early victims. This brought both girls back to the ranch, and during Georgia's convalescence, we had many serious talks about the Brunners' troubles. We wrote to grandma, but received no answer, and could only wait to learn what would be done with grandpa. He was arraigned and held; but the date set for trial was not fixed before Benjamin took Frances and Georgia to Benicia, to enter the September term of St. Catherine's Convent School.

Upon Ben's return, I observed that he and Elitha were keeping from me some mysterious but pleasurable secret. It came out a few days later when Elitha began making a black and a white uniform which would fit no one except me. When ready to try them on, she informed me that we would have to sew early and late, that I might be ready to enter the convent by the first of October, and thereby reap the benefit of the institution's established custom — "That when more than two of a family become pupils the same term, the third one shall be received free of charge (except incidentals) with the understanding that the family thus favored shall exert its influence toward bringing an additional pupil into the school."

Friends who had religious prejudices advised Ben against putting us under Catholic influence, but he replied good-naturedly: "The school is excellent, the girls are Protestants, and I am not afraid. Besides, I have told them all the horrible and uncanny stories that I have heard about convents, and they will not care to meddle with anything outside of the prescribed course of study."

He was twenty years older than I, and had such conservative and dignified ways, that I often stood in awe of him. So when he let the convent gate close behind us with a loud click and said, "Now, you are a goner," I scanned his face apprehensively, but seeing nothing very alarming, silently followed him through the massive door which was in charge of a white-robed nun of the Dominican order.

Presently Mother Mary Superior and my two sisters came to us in the reception room and my brother

ST. CATHERINE'S CONVENT AT BENICIA, CALIFORNIA

CHAPEL, ST. CATHERINE'S CONVENT

deposited the fund for my school incidentals, and after a brief conversation, departed. The preparations in connection with my coming had been so rapidly carried out that I had had little time in which to question or anticipate what my reception at the convent might be. Now, however, Mother Mary, with open watch in hand, stood before me, saying,

" Your sister Georgia cried twice as long as expected when she came; still I will allow you the regular five minutes."

" I don't wish to cry," was my timid response.

" But," she insisted, " you must shed a few entrance tears to — " Before she finished her sentence, and without thinking that it would be overreaching a stranger's privilege, I impulsively threw my arms around her neck, laid my cheek against hers, and whispered, " Please don't make me cry."

She drew me closer to her, and her lips touched my forehead, and she said, " No, child, you need not." Then she bade me go with my sisters and become acquainted with my new surroundings.

I was at once made to feel that I was welcome to every advantage and privilege accorded to Frances and Georgia. The following Monday, soon after breakfast, I slipped unobserved from the recreation room and made my way to the children's dormitory, where Sister Mary Joseph was busily engaged. I told her that I had come to help make beds and that I hoped she would also let me wash or wipe the silverware used at the noon and evening meals. She would not accept my services until she became thoroughly satisfied that I had not offered them because I felt that I was expected to do so, but because I earnestly desired to do whatever I could in return for the educational and cultural advantages so freely tendered me by the convent.

By the end of the week I knew the way to parts of the buildings not usually open to pupils. Up in the clothes room, I found Sister Mary Frances, and on assuring her that I only wanted occupation for part of my leisure time, she let me help her to sort and distribute the clothing of the small girls, on Saturdays. Sister Rose let me come to her in the kitchen an hour on Sundays, and other light tasks were assigned me at my request.

Then did I eat the bread of independence, take a wholesome interest in my studies, and enjoy the friends I gained!

My seat in the refectory was between my sister Georgia and Miss Cayitana Payñe, a wealthy Spanish girl. Near neighbors were the two Estudillo sisters, who were prouder of their Castilian lineage than of the princely estate which they had inherited through it. To them I was in a measure indebted for pleasing conversation at table. My abundant glossy black hair and brunette type had first attracted their attention, and suggested the probability of Spanish blood in my veins. After they had learned otherwise, those points of resemblance still awoke in them an unobtrusive interest in my welfare. I became aware of its depth one evening in the recreation room while Georgia was home for a month on sick leave.

I was near Miss Dolores Estudillo, and overheard her say quietly to her sister, in Spanish, " Magdalena, see how care-free the young girl at my side seems to-night. The far-away look so often in her eyes leads me to think that our dear Lord has given her many crosses to bear. Her hands show marks of hard work and her clothing is inexpensive, yet she appears of good birth and when I can throw pleasure in her way, I mean to do it."

Whereupon Miss Magdalena turned to me and asked, " Do you live in Sacramento, Miss Donner? "

" No, I live on a ranch twenty miles from the city."

" Do your parents like it there? "

" I have no parents, they died when I was four years old."

She did not ask another question, nor did she know that I had caught the note of sympathy in her apology as she turned away. From that time on, she and her coterie of young friends showed me many delicate attentions.

While still a new pupil, I not infrequently met Sister Dominica resting at the foot of the steps after her walk in the sunshine, and with a gracious, " Thank you," she would permit me to assist her up the flight of stairs leading to her apartment. Bowed by age, and wasted by disease, she was patiently awaiting the final summons. I became deeply interested in her before I learned that this wan bit of humanity was the once winsome daughter of Commandante Arguello, and the heroine of a pathetic romance of Spanish California's day.*

The hero was Rezanoff, an officer of high repute, sent by Russia in 1806 to inspect its establishment at the port of Sitka, Alaska. Finding the colony there in almost destitute condition, he had embarked on the first voyage of a Russian vessel to the port of San Francisco, California. There being no commercial treaty between the two ports, Rezanoff made personal appeal for help to Governor Arrillago, and later to Commandante Arguello. After many difficulties and delays, he succeeded in obtaining the sorely needed supplies.

Meanwhile, the young officer frequently met in her father's house the vivacious Doña Concepcion Arguello, and Cupid soon joined their hearts with an immortal chain.

After their betrothal, Rezanoff hastened back to the destitute colony with supplies. Then he sped on toward St. Petersburg, buoyant with a lover's hope of obtaining his sovereign's sanction to his marriage, and perhaps an appointment to Spain, which would enable him to give his bride a distinguished position in the country of her proud ancestors. Alas, death overtook the lover *en route* across the snows of Siberia.

When Doña Concepcion learned of her bereavement, her lamentations were tearless, her sorrow inconsolable. She turned from social duties and honors, and,

*The subject of a poem by Bret Harte, and of a novel by Mrs. Gertrude Atherton.

clad in mourning weeds, devoted her time and means to the poor and the afflicted, among whom she became known and idolized as "the beautiful angel in black." After the death of her parents, she endowed St. Catherine's Convent with her inheritance, took the vows of the Dominican nun, and the world saw her no more.

Early in her sorrow, she had prayed that death might come to her in the season when the snow lay deep on Siberia's plain; and her prayer was realized, for it was on a bleak winter morning that we pupils gathered in silence around the breakfast table, knowing that Sister Dominica lay upon her bier in the chapel.

The meal was nearly finished when Sister Amelda entered, and spoke to a couple of the Spanish young ladies, who bowed and immediately withdrew. As she came down the line selecting other Spanish friends of the dead, she stopped beside me long enough to say:

"You also may go to her. You comforted her in life, and it is fitting that you should be among those who keep the last watch, and that your prayers mingle with theirs."

After her burial, which was consecrated by monastic rites, I returned to the schoolroom with reverential memories of Sister Dominica, the once "beautiful angel in black."

The school year closed in July, 1858, and I left the convent with regret. The gentle, self-sacrificing conduct of the nuns had destroyed the effect of the prejudicial stories I had heard against conventual life. The tender, ennobling influences which had surrounded me had been more impressive than any I had experienced during orphanhood, and I dreaded what the noisy world might again have in store for me.

My sister Frances and William R. Wilder, who had been betrothed for more than a year, and had kept their secret until we three returned from the convent, were married November 24, 1858, and soon thereafter moved to a pleasant home of their own on a farm adjoining Rancho de los Cazadores. The following January, Georgia and I entered public school in Sacramento, where we spent a year and a half in earnest and arduous study.

CHAPTER XXXV

THE CHAMBERLAIN FAMILY, COUSINS OF DANIEL WEBSTER
— JEFFERSON GRAMMAR SCHOOL — FURTHER CONFLICT-
ING ACCOUNTS OF THE DONNER PARTY — PATERNAL AN-
CESTRY — S. O. HOUGHTON — DEATH TAKES ONE OF THE
SEVEN SURVIVING DONNERS.

OUR school home in Sacramento was with friends who not only encouraged our desire for knowledge, but made the acquirement pleasant. The head of the house was Mr. William E. Chamberlain, cashier of D. O. Mills's bank. His wife, Charlotte, was a contributor to *The Sacramento Union* and leading magazines. Their daughter, Miss Florence, taught in the public schools; and their son, William E., Jr., was a high-school student, preparing for Harvard.

In addition to their superior personal attainments, Mr. and Mrs. Chamberlain, each — for they were cousins — had the distinction of being first cousins to Daniel Webster, and this fact also served to bring to their home guests of note and culture. Georgia and I were too closely occupied with lessons to venture often beyond the school-girl precinct, but the intellectual atmosphere which pervaded the house, and the books to which we had access, were of inestimable advantage. Furthermore, the tuition fees required of non-resident pupils entitled them to choice of district, and we fortunately had selected Jefferson Grammar School, No. 4, in charge of Mr. Henry A. White, one of the ablest educators in the city.

Several resident families had also taken advantage of this privilege, and elected to pay tuition and place their children under his instruction, thus bringing together forty-nine energetic boys and girls to whet each other's ambition and incite class rivalry. Among the number were the five clever children of the Hon. Tod Robinson; three sons of Judge Robert Robinson; Colonel Zabriskie's pretty daughter Annie; Banker Swift's stately Margaret; General Redding's two sons; Dr. Oatman's son Eugene; beloved Nelly Upton, daughter of the editor of *The Sacramento Union;* Daniel Yost; Agnes Toll, the sweet singer; and Eliza Denison, my chum.

At the end of the term, *The Daily Union* closed its account of the public examination of Jefferson Grammar School with the following statement: "Among Mr. White's pupils are two young ladies, survivors of the terrible disaster which befell the emigration of 1846 among the snows of the California mountains."

Even this cursory reference was a matter of regret to Georgia and me. We had entered school silent in regard to personal history, and did not wish public attention turned toward ourselves even in an indirect way, fearing it might lead to a revival of the false and sensational accounts of the past, and we were not prepared to correct them, nor willing they should be spread. Pursued by these fears, we returned to the ranch, where Elitha and her three black-eyed little daughters welcomed our home-coming and brightened our vacation.

Almost coincident, however, with the foregoing circumstance, Georgia came into possession of " What I Saw in California," by Edwin Bryant; and we found that the book did contain many facts in connection with our party's disaster, but they were so interwoven with wild rumors, and the false and sensational statements quoted from *The California Star*, that they proved nothing, yet gave to the untrue that appearance of truth which is so difficult to correct.

The language employed in description seemed to us so coarse and brutal that we could not forgive its injustice to the living, and to the memory of the dead. We could but feel that had simple facts been stated, there would have been no harrowing criticism on account of long unburied corpses found in the lake cabins. Nor would the sight of mutilated dead have suggested that the starving survivors had become " gloating cannibals, preying on the bodies of their companions." Bare facts would have shown that the living had become too emaciated, too weak, to dig graves, or to lift or drag the dead up the narrow snow steps, even had open graves awaited their coming. Aye, more, would have shown conclusively that mutilation of the bodies of those who had perished was never from choice, never cannibalistic, but dire necessity's last resort to ease torturing hunger, to prevent loss of reason, to save life. Loss of reason was more dreaded than death by the starving protectors of the helpless.

Fair statements would also have shown that the First Relief reached the camps with insufficient provision to meet the pressing needs of the unfortunate. Consequently, it felt the urgency of haste to get as many refugees as possible to Bear Valley before storms should gather and delays defeat the purpose of its coming; that it divided what it could conscientiously spare among those whom it was obliged to leave, cut wood for the fires, and endeavored to give encouragement and hope to the desponding, but did not remain long enough to remove or bury the dead.

Each succeeding party actuated by like anxieties and precautions, departed with its charges, leaving pitiable destitution behind; leaving mournful conditions in camp,— conditions attributable as much to the work of time and atmospheric agencies as to the deplorable expedients to which the starving were again and again reduced.

With trembling hand Georgia turned the pages, from the sickening details of the *Star* * to the personal observations of Edwin Bryant, who in returning to the United States in the Summer of 1847, crossed the Sierra Nevadas with General Kearney and escort, reached the lake cabins June 22, and wrote as follows:

A halt was called for the purpose of interring the remains. Near the principal lake cabin I saw two bodies entire, except the abdomens had been cut open and entrails extracted. Their flesh had been either wasted by famine or

*See Appendix for extract from *The California Star.*

evaporated by exposure to dry atmosphere, and presented the appearance of mummies. Strewn around the cabins were dislocated and broken skulls (in some instances sawed asunder with care for the purpose of extracting the brains). Human skeletons, in short, in every variety of mutilation. A more appalling spectacle I never witnessed. The remains were, by order of General Kearney, collected and buried under supervision of Major Sword. They were interred in a pit dug in the centre of one of the cabins for a cache. These melancholy duties to the dead being performed, the cabins, by order of Major Sword, were fired and, with everything surrounding them connected with the horrible and melancholy tragedy, consumed.

The body of (Captain) George Donner was found in his camp about eight miles distant. He had been carefully laid out by his wife, and a sheet was wrapped around the corpse. This sad office was probably the last act she performed before visiting the camp of Keseberg. He was buried by a party of men detailed for that purpose.

I knew the Donners well; their means in money and merchandise which they had brought with them were abundant. Mr. Donner was a man of about sixty, and was at the time of leaving the United States a highly respectable citizen of Illinois, a farmer of independent means. Mrs. Donner was considerably younger than her husband, an energetic woman of refined education.

After Georgia left me, I reopened the book, and pondered its revelations, many of them new to us both; and most of them I marked for later investigation.

Bryant found no human bones at Donner's camp. His description of that camp was all-important, proving that my father's body had not been mutilated, but lay in his mountain hut three long months, sacred as when left by my little mother, who had watched over him to the pitiful end, had closed his eyes, folded his arms across his breast, and wrapped the burial sheet about his precious form. There, too, was proof of his last resting-place, just as had been told me in sight of Jakie's grave, by the Cherokee woman in Sonoma.

The book had also a copy of Colonel McKinstrey's letter to the General Relief Committee in San Francisco, reporting the return of the first rescuers with refugees. In speaking of the destitution of the unfortunates in camp, he used the following words sympathically:

When the party arrived at camp, it was obliged to guard the little stock of provisions it had carried over the mountains on its back on foot, for the relief of the poor beings, as they were in such a starving condition that they would have immediately used up all the little store. They even stole the buckskin strings from the party's snowshoes and ate them.

I at once recognized this friendly paragraph as the one which had had its kindness extracted, and been abbreviated and twisted into that cruel taunt which I had heard in my childhood from the lips of " Picayune Butler."

A careful study of Bryant's work increased my desire to sift that of Thornton, for I had been told that it not only contained the " Fallon Diary," but lengthier extracts from the *Star,* and I wanted to compare and analyze those details which had been published as " Thrilling Events in California History." I was unable to procure the book then, but resolved to do so when opportunity should occur. Naturally, we who see history made, are solicitous that it be accurately recorded, especially when it vitally concerns those near to us.

THE CROSS AT DONNER LAKE

Shortly before school reopened, Georgia and I spent the day with cousin Frances E. Bond; and in relating to her various incidents of our life, we spoke of the embarrassment we had felt in class the day that Mr. White asked every pupil whose ancestors had fought in the war of the American Revolution to rise, and Georgia and I were the only ones who remained seated. My cousin regarded us a moment and then said:

" Your Grandfather Eustis, although a widow's only son, and not yet sixteen years of age, enlisted when the Revolutionary War began. He was a sentinel at Old South Church, and finally, a prisoner aboard the *Count d'Estang.*"

She would have stopped there, but we begged for all she knew about our mother's people, so she continued, mingling advice with information:

" I would rather that you should not know the difference between their position in life and your own; yet, if you must know it, the Eustis and the Wheelwright families, from whom you are descended, are among the most substantial and influential of New England. Their reputation, however, is not a prop for you to lean on. They are on the Atlantic coast, you on the Pacific; so your future depends upon your own merit and exertions."

This revelation of lineage, nevertheless, was an added incentive to strive for higher things; an inheritance more enduring than our little tin box and black silk stockings which had belonged to mother.

An almost indescribable joy was mine when, at a

gathering of the school children to do honor to the citizens who had inaugurated the system of public instruction in Sacramento, I beheld on the platform Captain John A. Sutter. Memories both painful and grateful were evoked. It was he who had first sent food to the starving travellers in the Sierra Nevada Mountains. It was he who had laid his hand on my head, when a forlorn little waif at the Fort, tenderly saying, " Poor little girl, I wish I could give back what you have lost! "

To me, Captain Sutter had long been the embodiment of all that was good and grand; and now I longed to touch his hand and whisper to him gratitude too sacred for strangers' ears. But the opportunity was withheld until riper years.

During our last term at school, Georgia's health was so improved that my life was more free of cares and aglow with fairer promises. Miss Kate Robinson and I were rivals for school honors, and I studied as I never had studied before, for in the history, physiology, and rhetoric classes, she pressed me hard. At the close of the session the record showed a tie. Neither of us would accept determination by lot, and we respectfully asked the Honorable Board of Education to withhold the medal for that year.

About this time Georgia and I enjoyed a rare surprise. On his return from business one day, Mr. Chamberlain announced that a distinguished-appearing young lawyer, S. O. Houghton by name, had stopped at the bank that afternoon, to learn our address and say that he would call in the evening. We, knowing that he was the husband of our "little cousin Mary," were anxious to meet him and to hear of her, whom we had not seen since our journey across the snow. He came that evening, and told us of the cozy home in San Jose to which he had taken his young wife, and of her wish that we visit them the coming July or August.

Although letters had passed between us, up to this time we had known little of Mary's girlhood life. After we parted, in 1847, she was carried through to San Francisco, then called Yerba Buena, where her maimed foot was successfully treated by the surgeon of the United States ship *Portsmouth*. The citizens of that place purchased and presented to her the one hundred *vara* lot Number 38, and the lot adjoining to her brother George. Mr. Reed was appointed her guardian and given charge of her apportionment of funds realized from the sale of goods brought from her father's tents. She became a member of the Reed household in San Jose, and her life must have been cast in pleasant lines, for she always spoke of Mr. and Mrs. Reed with filial affection. Moreover, her brother had been industrious and prosperous, and had contributed generously to her comfort and happiness.

Some weeks later, we took Mr. Houghton's report home to Elitha. We also showed her a recent letter from Mary, sparkling with bright anticipations — anticipations never to be realized; for we girls were hardly settled on the ranch before a letter came from cousin George Donner, dated Sacramento, June 20, 1860. From this we learned that he had on that day been summoned to the bedside of his dying sister, and had come from his home on Putah Creek as fast as horse could carry him, yet had failed to catch the bay steamer; and while waiting for the next boat, was writing to us who could best understand his state of mind.

Next, a note from San Jose informed us that Mrs. Mary M. Houghton died June 21, 1860, leaving a namesake, a daughter two weeks old, and that her brother had reached there in time for the funeral.

Of the seven Donners who had survived the disaster, she was the first called by death, and we deeply mourned her loss, and grieved because another little Mary was motherless. The following August, Mr. Houghton made his first visit to Rancho de los Cazadores, and with fatherly pride, showed the likeness of his little girl, and promised to keep us all in touch with her by letter.

Mr. Houghton was closely identified with pioneer affairs, and we had many friends in common, especially among officers and soldiers of the Mexican War. He had enlisted in Company A of Stevenson's Regiment of New York Volunteers when barely eighteen years of age; and sailed with it from his native State on the twenty-sixth of September, 1846. After an eventful voyage by way of Cape Horn, the good ship *Loo Choo,* which bore him hither, cast anchor in the Bay of San Francisco, March 26, 1847, about the time the

Third Relief was bringing us little girls over the mountains. His company being part of the detachment ordered to Mexico under Colonel Burton, he went at once into active service, was promoted through intermediate grades, and appointed lieutenant, and adjutant on the staff of Colonel Burton, before his twentieth year. Following an honorable discharge at the close of the war, and a year's exciting experiences in the gold fields, he settled in San Jose in November, 1849, then the capital city. His knowledge of the Spanish and French languages fitting him specially therefor, he turned his attention to legislative and municipal matters. As clerk of the Senate Judiciary Committee of the first session of the California Legislature, he helped to formulate statutes for enactment, they being promulgated in Spanish as well as English at that time. During the period between 1851 and 1860 he held several official positions, among them that of president of the City Council; and on his twenty-fifth birthday he was elected Mayor of San Jose. Meanwhile he had organized the Eagle Guard, one of the first independent military companies in the State, and had also been successively promoted from adjutant to ordnance officer, with the rank of lieutenant-colonel, on Major-General Halleck's staff of the State Militia. Moreover, he had completed the study of law in the office of Judge W. T. Wallace, been admitted to the bar, and was now actively engaged in the practice of his profession.

CHAPTER XXXVI

MORE than two years had elapsed since we had heard directly from Sonoma, when, on the day before Thanksgiving, 1860, Judge Robert Robinson and wife, of Sacramento, came to the ranch, and he, in his pleasing way, announced that he and Mrs. Robinson had a little story to tell, and a message to deliver, which would explain why they had arrived unexpectedly to spend the national holiday with us. Then seating himself, he bowed to his wife, and listened in corroborative silence while she related the following incident:

" Last Summer when the Judge went on his circuit, he took the carriage, and I accompanied him on his travels. One day we stopped for dinner at the stage station between Sonoma and Santa Rosa. After we had registered, the proprietor approached us, saying: ' I see you are from Sacramento, and wonder if you know anything about a couple of young girls by the name of Downie, who spent some time there in the public school? ' He seemed disappointed when we replied, ' We know Donners, but not Downies.' ' Well,' he continued, ' they are strangers to me; but I am interested in them on account of their former connection

[316]

with an unfortunate little old German woman who frequently comes in on the stage that runs between Sonoma and Santa Rosa. She carries their pictures in her hand-bag and tells a touching story about her happiness when they lived with her.' Just then the stage stopped before the door, and he, looking out, exclaimed, ' Why, she is among the passengers to-day! With your permission, I 'll bring her to you.'

" He introduced her as Mrs. Brunner, told her where we were from, and asked her to show us the picture of her little girls. After shaking hands with us, she took the seat offered, and nervously drew from her reticule a handsomely inlaid case, which she opened and handed to us. An expression of pride and tenderness lighted her worn features as Judge and I at once exclaimed, pointing to one and then the other, ' Why, this is Georgia, and this, Eliza Donner. We know them well and call them " our girls " in Sacramento ! ' "

" She sprang from her seat, and stood with one hand on Judge's shoulder, and the other on mine, saying earnestly,

" ' Yes! You do know my children? Be they well, and doing well? '

" We had to talk fast in order to answer all her questions, and a number of listeners drew nearer and were considerably affected as the poor old soul said, ' Please shake hands with me again for them, and tell them that you talked with their old Grandma

Brunner, that loves them now just the same as when they was little.'

"Judge and I assured her that we would deliver her messages in person, as soon as we should get time to look you up. After dinner we saw her reseated in the stage, and the black silk reticule containing the picture was upon her lap as the stage carried her homeward."

We learned from them further that grandpa had been convicted of manslaughter and sentenced to San Quentin Prison for a term of eleven years, and that grandma had been granted a divorce, and awarded all the property, but was having great trouble because it had since become involved and was being frittered away in litigation.

The information given by the Robinsons increased our uneasiness for our trouble-worn friends. Since the tragedy, Georgia and I had often spoken of them to one another, but to no one else. We knew that few could understand them as we did, and we refrained from exposing them to unnecessary criticism. Anxious as we were to comfort them, it was not in our power to do more than endeavor again to reach them by letter. The first was despatched to grandma at Sonoma, the day after the departure of our guests; and shortly before Christmas I posted one to grandpa. The former was answered quickly, and so pathetically that brother Ben offered to take us to Sonoma for a visit in the early Spring and then to see what could be done for grandma.

The letter to grandpa did not reach him until January 27, 1861, but his reply left San Quentin by Wells-Fargo Express on the twenty-eighth of January. It was a brave letter, closing with the following mystifying paragraph:

Though I may be confined by prison walls, I wish those dear to me to be happy and joyous as they can, and I trust in God to open a way for me out of here, when I can see you all; which will make us all very happy.

Your affectionate grandfather,

CHRISTIAN BRUNNER.

His next communication contained a thrilling surprise which cleared the lurking mystery of his former letter, and expressed such joyous appreciation of his regained privileges that I once more quote his own words, from the letter yellowed by age, which lies before me.

SONOMA, *March 25, 1861*

DEAR ELIZA AND GEORGIA:

Your kind and friendly letter reached me about ten days ago, and I would have responded to the same right away, but waited a few days, so that I could give you some good news, over which you, my dear little girls, will surely rejoice, as you take so much interest in everything which myself concerns. This news is that I am free again.

Last Tuesday I received, through the influence of friends, from the Governor of the State of California, a full pardon, and am again in Sonoma; and as soon as I have my business affairs in such a way settled that I can leave for a week or two, I will come up and see you. I have much to tell you which you will better understand through a personal interview than by writing.

Yours friendly,

C. BRUNNER

Georgia and I felt this news was almost too good to be true. We wondered how soon he would come to see us; wondered also, if he and grandma had met, and were glad that we had not taken the side of either against the other.

"What next?" was the pertinent question uppermost in our minds. We found the answer in *The Sacramento Daily Union*, early in April, under title of "Romance in Real Life." After a brief review of the troubles of the Brunners, and reference to their divorcement, the article announced their recent remarriage.

This gratifying circumstance made our long intended trip to Sonoma unnecessary, especially since the reunited couple seemed to have retained the sympathy and loyalty of those who had known them in their days of prosperity and usefulness.

CHAPTER XXXVII

I HAPPENED to be in Sacramento on the thirteenth day of April, 1861, and found the city full of irrepressible excitement. Men on gayly caparisoned horses galloping hither and thither, unfurled flags, and a general air of expectancy on eager faces everywhere betokened an occasion of rare moment. At times hats were swung aloft and cheers rang out tumultuously, only to be hushed by the disappointing murmur, "Not yet." But an instant's quiet, and there was a mad rush of the populace toward Sutter's Fort; then again enthusiasm died, and the crowds ebbed back up J Street, which, some eight or ten feet higher than any other street in the city, extended straight as an arrow from the fort to where the bay steamer lightly hugged the water front, puffing and impatient to be off to San Francisco.

So the anxious waiting continued until the day was well on to its close, when suddenly, vociferous cheers again rent the air, and this time knew no cessation. What a din! With leap and outcry, all faced Sutter's Fort. That was a spectacle to be remembered.

Pony! The pony, hurrah, hurrah! We see a dark

speck in the distance. It grows, as up J Street it comes. Now, the pony foams before us; now, swift as the wind, it is gone. It passes reception committee, passes escort. It reaches the water front; down the gang-plank it dashes; the band plays, the whistle blows, the bell rings, the steamer catches the middle of the stream and is off, leaving a trail of sparks and smoke in the twilight, and bearing away the first "Pony Express," memorable in history.

The baffling problem is solved; the dream of years is realized; expeditious mail service with the East is an accomplished fact.

No wonder the people cheered! It was a gigantic scheme, well conceived, magnificently executed. Think of it, a stretch of two thousand miles of mountain wild and desert plain covered in twelve days!

How was it done? Horses were tested and riders selected by weight and power of endurance. The latter were boys in years — Bill Cody, the youngest, said to be only fourteen years of age. The pouch was light, its contents were limited — but how gladly five dollars per letter was paid for those precious missives.

Every detail was carefully arranged. The first mount left St. Joseph, Missouri, April 2; relay camps were established ten miles apart, with a horse ever in readiness for instantaneous exchange, and a fresh rider, mounted for the next run, was waiting at each successive hundred-mile station along the entire route.

Small wonder those pioneers were beside themselves

with enthusiastic excitement. The minds of many reverted to personal experiences with ox team, or jog-trot of horses or mule train. Here was the Overland Stage outdone; even the speed with which Monk Hanks brought Horace Greeley over the mountains was at discount.

CHAPTER XXXVIII

THE Summer of 1861, now well advanced, was rife
with war and rumors of war, and foreshadowings
of coming events. The old and the young were flushed
with patriotism, each eager to help his country's cause.
I, remembering grandma's training, was ready to give
my services to hospital work. Earnest as was this
desire, however, I was dissuaded from taking definite
steps in that direction by those who knew that my
slender physique and girlish appearance would defeat
my purpose before the board of appointing physicians.
Moreover, Mr. Houghton's visits and frequent letters
were changing my earlier plans for the future, and
finally led to my naming the tenth of October, 1861, as
our wedding day.

The ceremony was solemnized by the Rev. J. A.
Benton, of Sacramento. The event is also noteworthy
as being the occasion of the first reunion of the five
Donner sisters since their parting at Sutter's Fort in
June, 1847. Georgia's place was by my side, while
Elitha, Leanna, and Frances each grouped with hus-
band and children in front among friends, who had
come to witness the plighting of vows between my hero

and me. Not until I had donned my travelling suit, and my little white Swiss wedding dress was being packed, did I fully realize that the days of inseparable companionship between Georgia and me were past. She had long been assured that in my new home a welcome would be ever ready for her, yet she had thoughtfully answered, " No, I am not needed there, and I feel that I am needed here."

Nature's wedding gift to us was a week of glorious weather, and its first five days we passed in San Francisco, the bustling, historic city, which I knew so well, yet had never seen before. Then we boarded the afternoon boat up the bay, expecting to spend the evening and following morning in Sonoma with Grandpa and Grandma Brunner, but the vessel failed to reach Lakeside Landing in time to connect with the northbound coach. This mischance necessitated our staying overnight at the only hostelry in the place.

The cry, "All aboard for Sonoma!" hurried us from the table next morning, and on reaching the sidewalk, we learned that the proprietor of the hotel had bespoken the two best seats in the coach for us.

I was too happy to talk until after we crossed the Sonoma River, shaded by grand old oak, sycamore, and laurel trees, and then onward, I was too happy to remain silent. Before us lay the valley which brought back memories of my childhood, and I was in a mood to recall only the brightest, as we sped on to our destination. My companion shared my delight and gave heed to each scene I called to his attention.

The coach stopped in front of the hotel, and we alighted upon almost the same spot from which I had climbed into the carriage to leave Sonoma six years earlier. But, oh, how changed was everything! One sweeping glance at the little town revealed the fact that it had passed its romantic age and lost its quickening spirit. Closed were the homes of the old Spanish families; gone were the *caballeros* and the bright-eyed *señoritas;* grass-grown was the highway to the mines; the flagstaff alone remained flushed with its old-time dignity and importance. In subdued mood, I stepped into the parlor until our names should be registered. When my husband returned, I said,

" The carpet on this floor, the chairs in this room, and the pictures on these walls were in place in grandma's home when I left her — perhaps she is no longer living."

He left me again to make inquiry concerning those whom we had come to see, and ascertained that the Brunners had remarried for the purpose of facilitating the readjustment of their property rights, and of rescuing them from the hands of a scheming manager, who, with his family, was now living on the estate, and caring for grandma, but would not permit grandpa to enter the house.

After sending a messenger to find grandpa, I led the way to the open door of the old home, then slipped aside to let my husband seek admission. He rapped.

I heard a side door open, uneven footsteps in the hall, and him saying quietly, " I think the old lady her-

GENERAL VALLEJO'S CARRIAGE, BUILT IN ENGLAND IN 1832

GENERAL VALLEJO'S OLD JAIL

self is coming, and you had better meet her alone." I crossed the threshold, opened my arms, and uttered the one word, " Grandma! "

She came and rested her head against my bosom and I folded my arms about her just as she had enfolded me when I went to her a lonely child yearning for love. She stirred, then drew back, looked up into my face and asked, " Who be you? "

Touched by her wistful gaze, I exclaimed, " Grandma, don't you know me? "

" Be you Eliza? " she asked, and when I had given answer, she turned from me in deepest emotion, murmuring, " No, no, it can't be my little Eliza! " She would have tottered away had I not supported her to a seat in the well-remembered living room and caressed her until she looked up through her tears, saying, " When you smile, you be my little Eliza, but when you look serious, I don't know you."

She inquired about Georgia, and how I came to be there without her. Then she bade me call my husband, and thanked him for bringing me to her. Forgetting all the faults and shortcomings that once had troubled her sorely, she spoke of my busy childhood and the place I had won in the affections of all who knew me.

A tender impulse took her from us a moment. She returned, saying, " Now, you must not feel bad when you see what I have in the hand behind me," and drawing it forth continued, " This white lace veil which I bought at Sutter's Fort when your mother's things were sold at auction, is to cover my face when I am dead; and this picture of us three is to be buried in the coffin with me. I want your husband to see how you looked when you was little."

She appeared proudly happy; but a flame of embarrassment burned my cheeks, as she handed him the picture wherein I showed to such disadvantage, with the question, "Now, does n't she look lovely?" and heard his affirmative reply.

Upon the clock lay a broken toy which had been mine, and in childlike ecstasy she spoke of it and of others which she had kept ever near her. When invited to go to luncheon with us, she brought first her bonnet, next her shawl, for me to hold while she should don her best apparel for the occasion. Instead of going directly, she insisted on choosing the longer road to town, that we might stop at Mrs. Lewis's to see if she and her daughter Sallie would recognize me. Frequently as we walked along, she hastened in advance, and then faced about on the road to watch us draw near. When we reached Mrs. Lewis's door, she charged me not to smile, and clapped her hands when both ladies appeared and called me by name.

As we were taking leave, an aged horseman drew rein at the gate and dismounted, and Mrs. Lewis looking up, exclaimed, "Why, there is Mr. Brunner!"

It did not take me long to meet him part way down the walk, nor did I shrink from the caress he gave me, nor know how much joy and pain that meeting evoked in him, even after he turned to Mr. Houghton saying

fervently, " Do not be angry because I kiss your wife
and put my arms around her, for she is my child come
back to me. I helped raise her, and we learned her
to do all kinds of work, what is useful, and she was
my comfort child in my troubles."

My husband's reply seemed to dispel the recollections which had made the reunion distressing, and
grandpa led his horse and walked and talked with us
until we reached the turn where he bade us leave him
while he disposed of Antelope preparatory to joining
us at luncheon. Proceeding, we observed an increasing crowd in front of the hotel, massed together as if
in waiting. As we drew nearer, a way was opened for
our passage, and friends and acquaintances stepped
forth, shook hands with me and desired to be introduced to my husband. It was apparent that the message which we had sent to grandpa early in the day,
stating the hour we would be at the hotel, had spread
among the people, who were now assembled for the
purpose of meeting us.

Strangers also were among them, for I heard the
whispered answer many times, " Why, that is little
Eliza Donner, who used to live with the Brunners,
and that is Mr. Houghton, her husband — they can
only stay until two o'clock." The hotel table, usually
more than ample to accommodate its guests, was not
nearly large enough for all who followed to the dining-room, so the smiling host placed another table
across the end for many who had intended to lunch
at home that day.

Meantime, our little party was seated, with Mr. Houghton at the head of the table, I at his right; grandpa opposite me, and grandma at my right. She was supremely happy, would fold her hands in her lap and say, " If you please," and " Thank you," as I served her; and I was grateful that she claimed my attention, for grandpa's lips were mute.

He strove for calm, endeavoring to eat that he might the better conceal the unbidden tears which coursed down his cheeks. Not until we reached a secluded retreat for our farewell talk, did his emotion express itself in words. Grasping my husband's hand he said:

" My friend, I must leave you. I broke bread and tasted salt with you, but I am too heartsick to visit, or to say good-bye. You bring back my child, a bride, and I have no home to welcome her in, no wedding feast, or happiness to offer. I must see and talk with her in the house of strangers, and it makes me suffer more than I can bear! But before I go, I want you both to make me the promise that you will always work together, and have but one home, one purse, one wish in life, so that when you be old, you will not have to walk separately like we do. You will not have bitter thoughts and blame one another."

Here grandma interrupted meekly, " I know I did wrong, but I did not mean to, and I be sorry."

The pause which followed our given promise afforded me the opportunity to clasp their withered hands together between mine, and gain from grandpa an earnest pledge that he would watch over and be kind to her, who had married him when he was poor and in ill health; who had toiled for him through the long years of his convalescence; who had been the power behind the throne, his best aid and counsellor, until time had turned her back in its tide, and made her a child again.

My husband followed him from the room to bestow the sympathy and encouragement which a strong man can give to a desponding one.

When the carriage was announced, which would take us to Benicia in time to catch the Sacramento steamer to San Francisco, I tied on grandma's bonnet, pinned her shawl around her shoulders, and told her that we would take her home before proceeding on our way, but she crossed her hands in front and artlessly whispered:

" No; I 'd like to stay in town a while to talk with friends; but I thank you just the same, and shall not forget that I am to go to you, after you be settled in the new home, and his little daughter has learned to call you ' mother.' "

We left her standing on the hotel piazza, smiling and important among the friends who had waited to see us off; but grandpa was nowhere in sight.

The steamer was at the landing when we reached Benicia so we hurriedly embarked and found seats upon the deck overlooking the town. As the moonlight glistened on the white spray which encircled our departing boat, the sound of the Angelus came softly, sweetly, prayerfully over the water; and I looking up and beyond, saw the glimmering lights of Saint Catherine's Convent, fitting close to scenes of my childhood, its silver-toned bells cheering my way to long life, honors, and many blessings!

APPENDIX

Though the mills of God grind slowly, yet they grind
   exceeding small;
Though with patience He stands waiting, with exact-
   ness grinds He all.

FRIEDRICH VON LOGAU.

I

ARTICLES PUBLISHED IN *The California Star* — STATIS-
TICS OF THE PARTY — NOTES OF AGUILLA GLOVER — EX-
TRACT FROM THORNTON — RECOLLECTIONS OF JOHN
BAPTISTE TRUBODE.

IN honor to the State that cherishes the landmark;
in justice to history which is entitled to the truth;
in sympathetic fellowship with those who survived the
disaster; and in reverent memory of those who suffered and died in the snowbound camps of the Sierra
Nevadas, I refute the charges of cruelty, selfishness,
and inhumanity which have been ascribed to the
Donner Party.

In this Appendix I set forth some of the unwar-
ranted statements to which frequent reference has been
made in the foregoing pages, that they may be examined and analyzed, and their utter unreliability dem-
onstrated by comparison with established facts and
figures. These latter data, for the sake of brevity,
are in somewhat statistical form. A few further incidents, which I did not learn of or understand until
long after they occurred, are also related.

The accounts of weather conditions, of scarcity of
food and fuel, also the number of deaths in the camps
before the first of March, 1847, are verified by the care-

fully kept " Diary of Patrick Breen, One of the Donner Party," which has recently been published by the Academy of Pacific Coast History.

The following article, which originally appeared in *The California Star,* April 10, 1847, is here quoted from " The Life and Days of General John A. Sutter," by T. J. Schoonover:

A more shocking scene cannot be imagined than was witnessed by the party of men who went to the relief of the unfortunate emigrants in the California Mountains. The bones of those who had died and been devoured by the miserable ones that still survived were around their tents and cabins; bodies of men, women, and children with half the flesh torn from them lay on every side. A woman sat by the side of the body of her dead husband cutting out his tongue; the heart she had already taken out, broiled, and eaten. The daughter was seen eating the father; and the mother, that [*viz.* body] of her children; children, that of father and mother. The emaciated, wild, and ghastly appearance of the survivors added to the horror of it. Language can not describe the awful change that a few weeks of dire suffering had wrought in the minds of the wretched and pitiable beings. Those who one month before would have shuddered and sickened at the thought of eating human flesh, or of killing their companions and relatives to preserve their own lives, now looked upon the opportunity the acts afforded them of escaping the most dreadful of deaths as providential interference in their behalf.

Calculations were coldly made, as they sat around their gloomy camp fires, for the next succeeding meals. Various expedients were devised to prevent the dreadful crime of murder, but they finally resolved to kill those who had least claims to longer existence. Just at this moment some of them died, which afforded the rest temporary relief. Some sank into the arms of death cursing God for their miserable fate, while the last whisperings of others were prayers and songs of praise to the Almighty. After the first few deaths, but the one all-absorbing thought of individual self-preservation prevailed. The fountains of natural affection were dried up. The chords that once vibrated with connubial, parental, and filial affection were torn asunder, and each one seemed resolved, without regard to the fate of others, to escape from impending calamity.

So changed had the emigrants become that when the rescuing party arrived with food, some of them cast it aside, and seemed to prefer the putrid human flesh that still remained. The day before the party arrived, one emigrant took the body of a child about four years of age in bed with him and devoured the whole before morning; and the next day he ate another about the same age, before noon.

This article, one of the most harrowing to be found in print, spread through the early mining-camps, and has since been quoted by historians and authors as an authentic account of scenes and conduct witnessed by the first relief corps to Donner Lake. It has since furnished style and suggestion for other nerve-racking stories on the subject, causing keener mental suffering to those vitally concerned than words can tell. Yet it is easily proved to be nothing more or less than a perniciously sensational newspaper production, too utterly false, too cruelly misleading, to merit credence. Evidently, it was written without malice, but in ignorance, and by some warmly clad, well nourished person, who did not know the humanizing effect of suffering and sorrow, and who may not have talked with either a survivor or a rescuer of the Donner Party.

When the Donner Party ascended the Sierra Nevadas on the last day of October, 1846, it comprised eighty-one souls; namely, Charles Berger,* Patrick Breen, Margaret Breen (his wife), John Breen, Edward

*Died while in the mountain camps.

Breen, Patrick Breen, Jr., Simon Breen, James Breen, Peter Breen, Isabella Breen, Jacob Donner,* Elizabeth Donner * (his wife), William Hook,† Solomon Hook, George Donner, Jr., Mary Donner, Isaac Donner,† Lewis Donner,* Samuel Donner,* George Donner, Sr.,* Tamsen Donner * (his wife), Elitha Donner, Leanna C. Donner, Frances Eustis Donner, Georgia Anna Donner, Eliza Poor Donner, Patrick Doland,† John Denton,† Milton Elliot,* William Eddy, Eleanor Eddy (his wife), Margaret Eddy,* and James Eddy,* Jay Fosdick † and Sarah Fosdick (his wife), William Foster, Sarah Foster (his wife) and George Foster,* Franklin W. Graves, Sr.,† Elisabeth Graves † (his wife), Mary Graves, William C. Graves, Eleanor Graves, Lovina Graves, Nancy Graves, Jonathan B. Graves, Franklin W. Graves, Jr.,† and Elizabeth Graves, Jr., Noah James, Lewis S. Keseberg, Philippine Keseberg (his wife), Ada Keseberg † and Lewis S. Keseberg, Jr.,* Mrs. Lovina Murphy * (a widow), John Landrum Murphy,* Lemuel Murphy,† Mary Murphy, William G. Murphy and Simon Murphy, Mrs. Amanda McCutchen and Harriet McCutchen,* Mrs. Harriet Pike (widow), Nioma Pike and Catherine Pike,* Mrs. Margaret Reed, Virginia Reed, Martha J. Reed, James F. Reed, Jr., and Thomas K. Reed, Joseph Rhinehart,* Charles Stanton,† John Baptiste Trubode, August Spitzer,* James Smith,* Samuel Shoemaker, Bailis Williams * and Eliza Williams (his sister), Mrs. Wool-

*Died while in the mountain camps.
†Died *en route* over the mountains to the settlements in California.

finger (widow), Antonio (a Mexican) and Lewis and Salvador (the two Indians sent with Stanton by General Sutter).

Stated in brief, the result of the disaster to the party in the mountains was as follows:

The total number of deaths was thirty-six, as follows: fourteen in the mountains while *en route* to the settlement; fourteen at camp near Donner Lake; and eight at Donner's Camp.

The total number who reached the settlement was forty-five; of whom five were men, eight were women, and thirty-two were children.

The family of James F. Reed and that of Patrick Breen survived in unbroken numbers. The only other family in which all the children reached the settlement was that of Captain George Donner.

Fourteen of the eighty-one souls constituting the Donner Party were boys and girls between the ages of nineteen and twelve years; twenty-six ranged from twelve years to a year and a half; and seven were nursing babes. There were only thirty-four adults, — twenty-two men and twelve women.

Of the first-named group, eleven survived the disaster. One youth died *en route* with the Forlorn Hope; one at the Lake Camp; and one at Bear Valley in charge of the First Relief.

Twenty of the second-named group also reached the settlements. One died *en route* with the First Relief; two at Donner's Camp (in March, 1847); two at

Starved Camp, in charge of the Second Relief; and one at the Lake Camp (in March).

Two of the seven babes lived, and five perished at the Lake Camp. They hungered and slowly perished after famine had dried the natural flow, and infant lips had drawn blood from maternal breasts.

The first nursling's life to ebb was that of Lewis Keseberg, Jr., on January 24, 1847.* His grief-stricken mother could not be comforted. She hugged his wasted form to her heart and carried it far from camp, where she dug a grave and buried it in the snow.

Harriet McCutchen, whose mother had struggled on with the Forlorn Hope in search of succor, breathed her last on the second of February, while lying upon the lap of Mrs. Graves; and the snow being deep and hard frozen, Mrs. Graves bade her son William make the necessary excavation near the wall within their cabin, and they buried the body there, where the mother should find it upon her return. Catherine Pike died in the Murphy cabin a few hours before the arrival of food from the settlement and was buried on the morning of February 22.†

Those were the only babes that perished before relief came. Does not the fact that so many young children survived the disaster refute the charges of parental selfishness and inhumanity, and emphasize the immeasurable self-sacrifice, love, and care that kept so

*Report brought by John Baptiste to Donner's Camp, after one of his trips to the lake.
†Incident related by William C. Graves, after he reached the settlement.

Photograph by Lynwood Abbott.

ALDER CREEK

DENNISON'S EXCHANGE AND THE PARKER HOUSE, SAN FRANCISCO

many of the little ones alive through that long, bitter siege of starvation?

Mrs. Elinor Eddy, who passed away in the Murphy cabin on the seventh of February, was the only wife and mother called by death, in either camp, before the arrival of the First Relief. Both Patrick Breen's diary and William G. Murphy, then a lad of eleven years, assert that Mrs. Eddy and little Margaret, her only daughter, were buried in the snow near the Murphy cabin on the ninth of February. Furthermore, the Breen Diary and the death-list of the Donner Party show that not a husband or father died at the Lake Camp during the entire period of the party's imprisonment in the mountains.*

How, then, could that First Relief, or either of the other relief parties see — how could they even have imagined that they saw — " wife sitting at the side of her husband who had just died, mutilating his body," or " the daughter eating her father," or " mother that of her children," or " children that of father and mother "? The same questions might be asked regarding the other revolting scenes pictured by the *Star.*

The seven men who first braved the dangers of the icy trail in the work of rescue came over a trackless, rugged waste of snow, varying from ten to forty feet in depth,† and approached the camp-site near the

*Franklin W. Graves and Jay Fosdick perished in December, 1846, while *en route* to the settlement with the Forlorn Hope.

†One of the stumps near the Breen-Graves cabin, cut for fuel while the snow was deepest, was found by actual measurement to be twenty-two feet in height. It is still standing.

lake at sunset. They halloed, and up the snow steps came those able to drag themselves to the surface. When they descended into those cabins, they found no cheering lights. Through the smoky atmosphere, they saw smouldering fires, and faced conditions so appalling that words forsook them; their very souls were racked with agonizing sympathy. There were the famine-stricken and the perishing, almost as wasted and helpless as those whose sufferings had ceased. Too weak to show rejoicing, they could only beg with quivering lips and trembling hands, "Oh, give us something to eat! Give us something to drink! We are starving!"

True, their hands were grimy, their clothing tattered, and the floors were bestrewn with hair from hides and bits of broken bullock bones; but of connubial, parental, or filial inhumanity, there were no signs.

With what deep emotion those seven heroic men contemplated the conditions in camp may be gathered from Mr. Aguilla Glover's own notes, published in Thornton's work:

Feb. 19, 1847. The unhappy survivors were, in short, in a condition most deplorable, and beyond power of language to describe, or imagination to conceive.

The emigrants had not yet commenced eating the dead. Many of the sufferers had been living on bullock hides for weeks and even that sort of food was so nearly exhausted that they were about to dig up from the snow the bodies of their companions for the purpose of prolonging their wretched lives.

Thornton's work contains the following statement by a member of one of the relief corps:

JOHN BAPTISTE TRUBODE'S STORY

On the morning of February 20,* Racine Tucker, John Rhodes, and Riley Moutrey went to the camp of George Donner eight miles distant, taking a little jerked beef. These sufferers (eighteen) had but one hide remaining. They had determined that upon consuming this they would dig from the snow the bodies of those who had died from starvation. Mr. Donner was helpless, Mrs. Donner was weak but in good health, and might have come to the settlement with this party; yet she solemnly but calmly determined to remain with her husband and perform for him the last sad offices of affection and humanity. And this she did in full view that she must necessarily perish by remaining behind. The three men returned the same day with seven refugees† from Donner Camp.

John Baptiste Trubode has distinct recollections of the arrival and departure of Tucker's party, and of the amount of food left by it.

He said to me in that connection:

" To each of us who had to stay in camp, one of the First Relief Party measured a teacupful of flour, two small biscuits, and thin pieces of jerked beef, each piece as long as his first finger, and as many pieces as he could encircle with that first finger and thumb brought together, end to end. This was all that could be spared, and was to last until the next party could reach us.

" Our outlook was dreary and often hopeless. I don't know what I would have done sometimes without the comforting talks and prayers of those two women, your mother and Aunt Elizabeth. Then even-

*Thornton's dates are one day later than those in the Breen Diary. Breen must have lost a day *en route.*

†The First Relief Corps took six, instead of seven, refugees from Donner Camp, and set out from the lake cabins with twenty-three, instead of twenty-four, refugees.

ings after you children went to sleep, Mrs. George Donner would read to me from the book* she wrote in every day. If that book had been saved, every one would know the truth of what went on in camp, and not spread these false tales.

"I dug in the snow for the dead cattle, but found none, and we had to go back to our saltless old bullock hide, days before the Second Relief got to us, on the first of March."

*The journal, herbarium, manuscript, and drawings of Mrs. George Donner were not among the goods delivered at the Fort by the Fallon Party, and no trace of them was ever found.

O N the third of March, 1847, the Reed-Greenwood,
or Second Relief Corps (excepting Nicholas
Clark) left camp with the following refugees: Patrick
Breen, Margaret Breen (his wife), Patrick Breen, Jr.,
Simon Breen, James Breen, Peter Breen, Isabella
Breen, Solomon Hook, Mary Donner, Isaac Donner,
Mrs. Elizabeth Graves, Nancy Graves, Jonathan B.
Graves, Franklin W. Graves, Jr., Elizabeth Graves, Jr.,
Martha J. Reed, and Thomas K. Reed. The whole
party, as has been already told, were forced into camp
about ten miles below the summit on the west side of
the Sierras, by one of the fiercest snow-storms of the
season.

All credit is due Mr. and Mrs. Breen for keeping
the nine helpless waifs left with them at Starved
Camp alive until food was brought them by members
of the Third Relief Party. Mr. Breen's much prized
diary does not cover the experiences of that little band
in their struggle across the mountains, but concludes
two days before they started. After he and his family
succeeded in reaching the Sacramento Valley, he gave

his diary (kept at Donner Lake) to Colonel George McKinstry for the purpose of assisting him in making out his report to Captain Hall, U. S. N., Sloop of War *Warren*, Commander Northern District of California.

James F. Reed of the Reed-Greenwood Party, the second to reach the emigrants, has been adversely criticised from time to time, because he and six of his men returned to Sutter's Fort in March with no more than his own two children and Solomon Hook, a lad of twelve years, who had said that he could and would walk, and did.

Careful investigation, however, proves the criticism hasty and unfair. True, Mr. Reed went over the mountains with the largest and best equipped party sent out, ten well furnished, able-bodied men. But returning he left one man at camp to assist the needy emigrants.

The seventeen refugees whom he and nine companions brought over the summit comprised three weak, wasted adults, and fourteen emaciated young children. The prospect of getting them all to the settlement, even under favorable circumstances, had seemed doubtful at the beginning of the journey. Alas, one of the heaviest snow-storms of the season overtook them on the bleak mountain-side ten miles from the tops of the Sierra Nevadas. It continued many days. Food gave out, death took toll. The combined efforts of the men could not do more than provide fuel and keep the fires. All became exhausted. Rescuers and refugees might have perished there together had the nine men not followed what seemed their only alternative. Who would not have done what Reed did? With almost superhuman effort, he saved his two children. No one felt keener regret than he over the fact that he had been obliged to abandon at Starved Camp the eleven refugees he had heroically endeavored to save.

In those days of affliction, it were well nigh impossible to say who was most afflicted; still, it would seem that no greater destitution and sorrow could have been meted to any one than fell to the lot of Mrs. Murphy at the lake camp. The following incidents were related by her son, William G. Murphy, in an address to a concourse of people assembled on the shore of Donner Lake in February, 1896:

I was a little more than eleven years of age when we all reached these mountains, and that one-roomed shanty was built, where so many of us lived, ate, and slept. No! — Where so many of us slept, starved, and died! It was constructed for my mother and seven children (two being married) and her three grandchildren, and William Foster, husband of her daughter Sarah.

Early in December when the Forlorn Hope was planned, we were almost out of provisions; and my mother took the babes from the arms of Sarah and Harriet (Mrs. Pike) and told them that she would care for their little ones, and they being young might with William (Foster) and their brother Lemuel reach the settlement and return with food. And the four became members of that hapless band of fifteen.

Mr. Eddy being its leader, his wife and her two children came to live with us during his absence. When my eldest brother, on whom my mother depended, was very weak and almost at death's door, my mother went to the Breens and begged a little meat, just a few mouthfuls — I remember well that little piece of meat! My mother gave half of it to my dying brother; he ate it, fell asleep with a hollow death gurgle. When it ceased I went to him — he was dead — starved to death in our presence. Although starving herself, my mother said that if she had known that Landrum was going to die she would have given him the balance of the meat. Little Margaret Eddy lingered until February 4, and her mother until the seventh. Their bodies lay two days and nights longer in the room with us before we could find assistance able to bury them in the snow. Some days earlier Milton Elliot, weak and wandering around, had taken up his abode with us. We shared with him the remnant of our beef hides. We had had a lot of that glue-making material. But mark, it would not sustain life. Elliot soon starved to death, and neighbors removed and interred the body in the snow beside others.

Catherine Pike, my absent sister's baby, died on the eighteenth of February, only a few hours before the arrival of the First Relief. Thus the inmates of our shanty had been reduced to my mother, my sister Mary, brother Simon, Nioma Pike, Georgie Foster, myself, and little Jimmy Eddy.

When the rescuers decided they would carry out Nioma Pike, and that my sister Mary and I should follow, stepping in the tracks made by those who had snowshoes, strength seemed to come, so that I was able to cut and carry to my mother's shanty what appeared to me a huge pile of wood. It was green, but it was all I could get.

We left mother there with three helpless little ones to feed on almost nothing, yet in the hope that she might keep them alive until the arrival of the next relief.

Many of the survivors remember that after having again eaten food seasoned with salt, the boiled, saltless hides produced nausea and could not be retained by adult or child.

I say with deep reverence that flesh of the dead was used to sustain the living in more than one cabin near the lake. But it was not used until after the pittance of food left by the First Relief had long been consumed; not until after the wolves had dug the snow from the graves. Perhaps God sent the wolves to show Mrs. Murphy and also Mrs. Graves where to get sustenance for their dependent little ones.

Both were widows; the one had three, and the other four helpless children to save. Was it culpable, or cannibalistic to seek and use the only life-saving means left them? Were the acts and purposes of their unsteady hands and aching hearts less tender, less humane than those of the lauded surgeons of to-day, who infuse human blood from living bodies into the arteries of those whom naught else can save, or who strip skin from bodies that feel pain, to cover wounds which would otherwise prove fatal?

John Baptiste Trubode and Nicholas Clark, of the Second Relief, were the last men who saw my father alive. In August, 1883, the latter came to my home in San Jose.

This was our second meeting since that memorable morning of March 2, 1847, when he went in pursuit of the wounded mother bear, and was left behind by the relief party. We spoke long and earnestly of our experience in the mountains, and he wished me to deny the statement frequently made that, " Clark carried a pack of plunder and a heavy shotgun from Donner's Camp and left a child there to die." This I can do positively, for when the Third Relief Party took Simon Murphy and us "three little Donner girls " from the mountain camp, not a living being remained, except Mrs. Murphy and Keseberg at the lake camp, and my father and mother at Donner's Camp. All were helpless except my mother.

The Spring following my interview with Nicholas Clark, John Baptiste came to San Jose, and Mr. Mc-Cutchen brought him to talk with me. John, always a picturesque character, had become a hop picker in hop season, and a fisherman the rest of the year. He could not restrain the tears which coursed down his bronzed cheeks as he spoke of the destitution and suffering in the snow-bound camps; of the young unmarried men who had been so light-hearted on the plains and brave when first they faced the snows. His voice trembled as he told how often they had tried to break through the great barriers, and failed; hunted, and found nothing; fished, and caught nothing; and when rations dwindled to strips of beef hide, their strength waned, and death found them ready victims. He declared,

The hair and bones found around the Donner fires were those of cattle. No human flesh was used by either Donner family. This I know, for I was there all winter and helped get all the wood and food we had, after starvation threatened us. I was about sixteen years old at the time. Our four men died early in December and were buried in excavations in the side of the mountain. Their bodies were never disturbed. As the snows deepened to ten and twelve feet, we lost track of their location.

When saying good-bye, he looked at me wistfully and exclaimed: " Oh, little Eliza, sister mine, how I suffered and worked to help keep you alive. Do you think there was ever colder, stronger winds than them that whistled and howled around our camp in the Sierras? "

He returned the next day, and in his quaint, earnest way expressed keenest regret that he and Clark had not remained longer in camp with my father and mother.

" I did not feel it so much at first; but after I got married and had children of my own, I often fished and cried, as I thought of what I done, for if we two men had stayed, perhaps we might have saved that little woman."

His careworn features lightened as I bade him grieve no more, for I realized that he was but a boy, over-burdened with a man's responsibilities, and had done his best, and that nobly. Then I added what I have always believed, that no one was to blame for the misfortunes which overtook us in the mountains. The dangers and difficulties encountered by reason of taking the Hastings Cut-off had all been surmounted — two weeks more and we should have reached our destination in safety. Then came the snow! Who could foresee that it would come earlier, fall deeper, and linger longer, that season than for thirty years before? Everything that a party could do to save itself was done by the Donner Party; and certainly everything that a generous, sympathizing people could do to save the snow-bound was done by the people of California.

III

THE following is the report of Thomas Fallon, leader of the fourth party to the camps near Donner Lake:

Left Johnson's on the evening of April 13, and arrived at the lower end of Bear River Valley on the fifteenth. Hung our saddles upon trees, and sent the horses back, to be returned again in ten days to bring us in again. Started on foot, with provisions for ten days and travelled to head of the valley, and camped for the night; snow from two to three feet deep. Started early in the morning of April 15 and travelled twenty-three miles. Snow ten feet deep.

April 17. Reached the cabins between twelve and one o'clock. Expected to find some of the sufferers alive. Mrs. Donner and Keseberg * in particular. Entered the cabins, and a horrible scene presented itself. Human bodies terribly mutilated, legs, arms, and skulls scattered in every direction. One body supposed to be that of Mrs. Eddy lay near the entrance, the limbs severed off, and a frightful gash in the skull. The flesh was nearly consumed from the bones, and a painful stillness pervaded the place. The supposition was, that all were dead, when a sudden shout revived our hopes, and we flew in the direction of the sound. Three Indians who had been hitherto concealed, started from the ground, fled at our approach, leaving behind their bows and arrows. We delayed two hours in searching the cabins, during which we were obliged to witness sights from which we would have fain turned away, and which are too dreadful to put on

*Should be spelled Keseberg.

[352]

record. We next started for Donner's camp, eight miles distant over the mountains. After travelling about halfway, we came upon a track in the snow which excited our suspicion, and we determined to pursue. It brought us to the camp of Jacob Donner, where it had evidently left that morning. There we found property of every description, books, calicoes, tea, coffee, shoes, percussion caps, household and kitchen furniture, scattered in every direction, and mostly in water. At the mouth of the tent stood a large iron kettle, filled with human flesh cut up. It was from the body of George Donner. The head had been split open, and the brain extracted therefrom; and to the appearance he had not been long dead — not over three or four days, at most. Near-by the kettle stood a chair, and thereupon three legs of a bullock that had been shot down in the early part of winter, and snowed upon before it could be dressed. The meat was found sound and good, and with the exception of a small piece out of the shoulder, whole, untouched. We gathered up some property, and camped for the night.

April 18. Commenced gathering the most valuable property, suitable for our packs; the greater portion had to be dried. We then made them up, and camped for the night.

April 19. This morning Foster, Rhodes, and J. Foster started, with small packs, for the first cabins, intending from thence to follow the trail of the person that had left the morning previous. The other three remained behind to cache and secure the goods necessarily left there. Knowing the Donners had a considerable sum of money we searched diligently but were unsuccessful. The party for the cabins were unable to keep the trail of the mysterious personage, owing to the rapid melting of the snow; they therefore went directly to the cabins and upon entering discovered Keseberg lying down amid the human bones, and beside him a large pan full of fresh liver and lights. They asked him what had become of his companions; whether they were alive, and what had become of Mrs. Donner. He answered them by stating that they were all dead. Mrs. Donner, he said, had, in attempting to cross from one cabin to another, missed the trail and slept out one night; that she came to his camp the next night very much fatigued. He made her a cup of coffee, placed her in bed, and rolled her well in the blankets; but next morning she was dead. He ate her body and found her flesh the best he had ever tasted. He further stated that he obtained from her body at least four pounds of fat. No trace of her body was found, nor of the body of Mrs. Murphy either. When the last company left the camp, three weeks previous, Mrs. Donner was in perfect health, though unwilling to leave her husband there, and offered $500.00 to any person or persons who would come out and bring them in, saying this in the presence of Keseberg, and that she had plenty of tea and coffee. We suspected that it was she who had taken the piece from the shoulder of beef on the chair before mentioned. In the cabin with Keseberg were found two kettles of human blood, in all, supposed to be over two gallons. Rhodes asked him where he had got the blood. He answered, '' There is blood in dead bodies.'' They asked him numerous questions, but he appeared embarrassed, and equivocated a great deal; and in reply to their asking him where Mrs. Donner's money was, he evinced confusion, and answered that he knew nothing about it, that she must have cached it before she died. '' I have n't it,'' said he, '' nor money nor property of any person, living or dead.'' They then examined his bundle, and found silks and jewellery, which had been taken from the camp of Donners, amounting in value to about $200.00. On his person they discovered a brace of pistols recognized to be those of George Donner; and while taking them from him, discovered something concealed in his waistcoat, which on being opened was found to be $225.00 in gold.

Before leaving the settlement, the wife of Keseberg had told us that we would find but little money about him; the men therefore said to him that they knew he was lying to them, and that he was well aware of the place of concealment of the Donners' money. He declared before Heaven he knew nothing concerning it, and that he had not the property of any one in his possession. They told him that to lie to them would effect nothing; that there were others back at the cabins who unless informed of the spot where the treasure was hidden would not hesitate to hang him upon the first tree. Their threats were of no avail. He still affirmed his ignorance and innocence. Rhodes took him aside and talked to him kindly, telling him that if he would give the information desired, he should receive from their hands the best of treatment, and be in every way assisted; otherwise, the party back at Donner's Camp would, upon arrival, and his refusal to discover to them the place where he had deposited this money, immediately put him to death. It was all to no purpose, however, and they prepared to return to us, leaving him in charge of the packs, and assuring him of their determination to visit him in the morning; and that he must make up his mind during the night. They started back and joined us at Donner's Camp.

April 20. We all started for Bear River Valley, with packs of one hundred pounds each; our provisions being nearly consumed, we were obliged to make haste away. Came within a few hundred yards of the cabins and halted to prepare breakfast, after which we proceeded to the cabin. I now asked Keseberg if he was willing to disclose to me where he had concealed that money. He turned somewhat pale and again protested his innocence. I said to him, "Keseberg, you know well where Donner's money is, and damn you, you shall tell me! I am not going to multiply words with you or say but little about it. Bring me that rope!" He then arose from his hot soup and human flesh, and begged me not to harm him; he had not the money nor goods; the silk clothing and money which were found upon him the previous day and which he then declared belonged to his wife, he now said were the property of others in California. I told him I did not wish to hear more from him, unless he at once informed us where he had concealed the money of those orphan children; then producing the rope I approached him. He became frightened, but I bent the rope around his neck and as I tightened the cord, and choked him, he cried out that he would confess all upon release. I then permitted him to arise. He still seemed inclined to be obstinate and made much delay in talking. Finally, but without evident reluctance, he led the way back to Donner's Camp, about ten miles distant, accompanied by Rhodes and Tucker. While they were absent we moved all our packs over the lower end of the lake, and made all ready for a start when they should return. Mr. Foster went down to the cabin of Mrs. Murphy, his mother-in-law, to see if any property remained there worth collecting and securing; he found the body of young Murphy who had been dead about three months with his breast and skull cut open, and the brains, liver, and lights taken out; and this accounted for the contents of the pan which stood beside Keseberg when he was found. It appeared that he had left at the other camp the dead bullock and horse, and on visiting this camp and finding the body thawed out, took therefrom the brains, liver, and lights.

Tucker and Rhodes came back the next morning, bringing $273.00 that had been cached by Keseberg, who after disclosing to them the spot, returned to the cabin. The money had been hidden directly underneath the projecting limb of a large tree, the end of which seemed to point precisely to the treasure buried in the earth. On their return and passing the cabin, they saw the unfortunate man within devouring the remaining brains and liver left from his morning repast. They hurried him away, but before leaving, he gathered together the bones and heaped them all in a box he used for the purpose, blessed them and the cabin and said, " I hope God will forgive me what I have done. I could not help it; and I hope I may get to heaven yet! " We asked Keseberg why he did not use the meat of the bullock and horse instead of human flesh. He replied he had not seen them. We then told him we knew better, and asked him why the meat on the chair had not been consumed. He said, " Oh, it is too dry eating; the liver and lights were a great deal better, and brains made good soup! " We then moved on and camped by the lake for the night.

April 21. Started for Bear River Valley this morning. Found the snow from six to eight feet deep; camped at Yuma River for the night. On the twenty-second travelled down Yuma about eighteen miles, and camped at the head of Bear River Valley. On the twenty-fifth moved down to lower end of the valley, met our horses, and came in.

The account by Fallon regarding the fate of the last of the Donners in their mountain camp was the same as that which Elitha and Leanna had heard and had endeavored to keep from us little ones at Sutter's Fort.

VIEW IN THE GROUNDS OF THE HOUGHTON HOME
IN SAN JOSE

THE HOUGHTON RESIDENCE IN SAN JOSE, CALIFORNIA

It is self-evident, however, that the author of those statements did not contemplate that reliable parties * would see the Donner camps before prowling beasts, or time and elements, had destroyed all proof of his own and his party's wanton falsity.

It is also plain that the Fallon Party did not set out expecting to find any one alive in the mountains, otherwise would it not have taken more provisions than just enough to sustain its own men ten days? Would it not have ordered more horses to meet it at the lower end of Bear Valley for the return trip? Had it planned to find and succor survivors would it have taken it for granted that all had perished, simply because there was no one in the lake cabins, and would it have delayed two precious hours in searching the lake camp for valuables before proceeding to Donner's Camp?

Had the desire to rescue been uppermost in mind, would not the sight of human foot-tracks on the snow half way between the two camps have excited hope, instead of " suspicion," and prompted some of the party to pursue the lone wanderer with kindly intent? Does not each succeeding day's entry in that journal disclose the party's forgetfulness of its declared mission to the mountains? Can any palliating excuse be urged why those men did not share with Keseberg the food they had brought, instead of permitting him to continue that which famine had forced upon him, and which later they so righteously condemned?

Is there a single strain of humanity, pathos, or rev-

*General Kearney and escort, accompanied by Edwin Bryant.

erence in that diary, save that reflected from Keseberg's last act before being hurried away from that desolate cabin? Or could there be a falser, crueler, or more heartless account brought to bereaved children than Fallon's purported description of the father's body found in Donner's Camp?

Here is the statement of Edwin Bryant, who with General Kearney and escort, *en route* to the United States, halted at the deserted cabins on June 22, 1847, and wrote:

> The body of (Captain) George Donner was found in his own camp about eight miles distant. He had been carefully laid out by his wife, and a sheet was wrapped around the corpse. This sad office was probably the last act she performed before visiting the camp of Keseberg.*

After considering what had been published by *The California Star,* by Bryant, Thornton, Mrs. Farnham, and others, I could not but realize Keseberg's peculiarly helpless situation. Without a chance to speak in his own defence, he had been charged, tried, and adjudged guilty by his accusers; and an excited people had accepted the verdict without question. Later, at Captain Sutter's suggestion, Keseberg brought action for slander against Captain Fallon and party. The case was tried before Alcalde Sinclair,† and the jury gave Keseberg a verdict of one dollar damages. This verdict, however, was not given wide circulation, and prejudice remained unchecked.

*McGlashan's " History of the Donner Party " (1879).
† The old Alcalde records are not in existence, but some of the survivors of the party remember the circumstance; and Mrs. Samuel Kybert, now of Clarkville, Eldorado County, was a witness at the trial. C. F. McGlashan, 1879.

QUESTIONS CONCERNING KESEBERG

There were other peculiar circumstances connected with this much accused man which were worthy of consideration, notably the following: If, as reported, Keseberg was in condition to walk to the settlement, why did the First Relief permit him to remain in camp consuming rations that might have saved others?

Messrs. Reed and McCutchen of the Second Relief knew the man on the plains, and had they regarded him as able to travel, or a menace to life in camp, would they have left him there to prey on women and little children, like a wolf in the fold?

Messrs. Eddy and Foster of the Third Relief had travelled with him on the plains, starved with him in camp, and had had opportunities of talking with him upon their return to the cabins too late to rescue Jimmy Eddy and Georgia Foster. Had they believed that he had murdered the children, would those two fathers and the rest of their party have taken Simon Murphy and the three little Donner girls and left Keseberg *alive* in camp with lone, sick, and helpless Mrs. Murphy — Mrs. Murphy who was grandmother of Georgia Foster, and had sole charge of Jimmy Eddy?

IV

IN March, 1879, while collecting material for his "History of the Donner Party," Mr. C. F. McGlashan, of Truckee, California, visited survivors at San Jose, and coming to me, said:

"Mrs. Houghton, I am sorry that I must look to you and your sisters for answers to the most delicate and trying questions relating to this history. I refer to the death of your mother at the hand of Keseberg."

He was so surprised and shocked as I replied, "I do not believe that Keseberg was responsible for my mother's death," that he interrupted me, lost for a moment the manner of the impartial historian, and with the directness of a cross-questioning attorney asked:

"Is it possible that Mrs. George Donner's daughter defends the murderer of her mother?"

And when I replied, "We have no proofs. My mother's body was never found," he continued earnestly,

"Why, I have enough evidence in this note book to convict that monster, and I can do it, or at least arouse such public sentiment against him that he will have to leave the State."

Very closely he followed my answering words, " Mr. McGlashan, from little girlhood I have prayed that Lewis Keseberg some day would send for me and tell me of my mother's last hours, and perhaps give a last message left for her children, and I firmly believe that my prayer will be granted, and I would not like you to destroy my opportunity. You have a ready pen, but it will not be used in exact justice to all the survivors, as you have promised, if you finish your work without giving Keseberg also a chance to speak for himself."

After a moment's reflection, he replied, " I am amazed; but your wish in this matter shall be respected."

The following evening he wrote from San Francisco:

You will be glad to know that I have put Harry N. Morse's detective agency of Oakland upon the track of Keseberg, and if found, I mean to take steps to obtain his confession.

In less than a week after the foregoing, came a note from him which tells its own story.

SACRAMENTO, *Midnight, April 4, 1879*

MRS. E. P. HOUGHTON,
    DEAR MADAM :—

Late as it is, I feel that I ought to tell you that I have spent the evening with Keseberg. I have just got back, and return early to-morrow to complete my interview. By merest accident, while tracing, as I supposed, the record of his death, I found a clue to his whereabouts. After dark I drove six miles and found him. At first he declined to tell me anything, but somehow I melted the mood with which he seemed enwrapped, and he talked freely.

He swears to me that he did not murder your mother. He declares it so earnestly that I cannot doubt his veracity.

[361]

To-morrow I intend plying him closely with questions, and by a rigid system of cross examination will detect the falsehood, if there is one, in his statement. He gives chapter after chapter that others never knew. I cannot say more to-night, but desire that you write me (at the Cosmopolitan) any questions you might wish me to ask Keseberg, and if I have not already asked them, I will do so on my return from San Francisco.   Yours respectfully,

C. F. McGLASHAN.

After his second interview with Keseberg and in response to my urgent appeal for full details of everything relating to my parents, Mr. McGlashan wrote:

I wish you could see him. He will talk to either you or me at any time, unless other influences are brought to bear upon him. If I send word for him to come to Sacramento, he will meet me on my return. If you and your husband could be there on Thursday or Friday of this week, I could arrange an interview at the hotel that would be all you could wish. I asked him especially if he would talk to you, and he said, " Yes."

I dared not tell you about my interview until I had your permission. Even now, I approach the task tremblingly.

Your mother was not murdered. Your father died, Keseberg thinks, about two weeks after you left. Your mother remained with him until the last and laid him out tenderly, as you know.

The days — to Keseberg — were perfect blanks. Mrs. Murphy died soon after your departure with Eddy, and he was left alone — alone in his cabin — alone with the dead bodies which he could not have lifted from the floor, because of his weakness, even had he desired. The man sighs and shudders, and great drops of agony gather upon his brows as he endeavors to relate the details of those terrible days, or recall their horrors. Loneliness, desolation was the chief element of horror. Alone with the mutilated dead!

One night he sprang up in affright at the sound of something moving or scratching at a log outside his cabin. It was some time before he could understand that it was wolves trying to get in.

LETTER FROM MR. McGLASHAN

One night, about two weeks after you left, a knock came at his door, and your mother entered. To this lonely wretch her coming seemed like an angel's. She was cold and wet and freezing, yet her first words were, that she must see her children. Keseberg understood that she intended to start out that very night, and soon found that she was slightly demented. She kept saying, "O God! I must see my children. I must go to my children!" She finally consented to wait until the morning, but was determined that nothing should then prevent her lonely journey. She told Keseberg where her money was concealed, she made him solemnly promise that he would get the money and take it to her children. She would not taste the food he had to offer. She had not tasted human flesh, and would hardly consent to remain in his foul and hideous den. Too weak and chilled to move, she finally sank down on the floor, and he covered her as best he could with blankets and feather bed, and made a fire to warm her; but it was of no avail, she had received her death-chill, and in the morning her spirit had passed heavenward.

I believe Keseberg tells the truth. Your mother watched day and night by your father's bedside until the end. At nightfall he ceased to breathe, and she was alone in the desolate camp, where she performed the last sad ministrations, and then her duty in the mountains was accomplished. All the smothered yearnings of maternal love now burst forth with full power. Out into the darkness and night she rushed, without waiting for the morning. "My children, I must see my children!"

She arrived at Keseberg's cabin, overwrought mentally, overtaxed physically, and chilled by the freezing night air. She was eager to set forth on her desperate journey without resting a moment. I can see her as he described her, wringing her hands and exclaiming over and over again, "I must see my children!"

The story told by Mrs. Farnham and others about finding your mother's remains, and that of Thornton concerning the pail of blood, are unquestionably false. She had been dead weeks, and Keseberg confessed to me that no part of her body was found by the relief (Fallon) party.

My friend, I have attempted to comply with your request. More than once during this evening I have burst into tears.

THE EXPEDITION OF THE DONNER PARTY

I am sorry almost that I attempted so mournful a task, but you will pardon the pain I have caused.

Keseberg is a powerful man, six feet in height, with full bushy beard, thin brown locks, and high forehead. He has blue eyes that look squarely at you while he talks. He is sometimes absent-minded and at times seems almost carried away with the intensity of his misery and desolation.

He speaks and writes German, French, Spanish, and English; and his selection of words proves him a scholar. When I first asked him to make a statement which I could reduce to writing he urged: "What is the use of making a statement? People incline to believe the most horrible reports concerning a man; they will not credit what I say in my own defence. My conscience is clear. I am an old man, and am calmly awaiting my death. God is my judge, and it long ago ceased to trouble me that people shunned and slandered me."

He finally consented to make the desired statement, and in speaking of your family he continued: "Some time after Mrs. George Donner's death, I thought I had gained sufficient strength to redeem the pledge I had made her before her death. I went to Alder Creek Camp to get the money. I had a difficult journey. The wagons of the Donners were loaded with tobacco, powder, caps, school-books, shoes, and dry goods. This stock was very valuable. I spent the night there, searched carefully among the bales and bundles of goods, and found five hundred and thirty-one dollars. Part of this sum was gold, part silver. The silver I buried at the foot of a pine tree, a little way from camp. One of the lower branches of another tree reached down close to the ground, and appeared to point to the spot. I put the gold in my pocket, and started back to my cabin; got lost, and in crossing a little flat the snow suddenly gave way, and I sank down almost to my arm-pits. After great exertion I raised myself out of a snow-covered stream, and went round on a hillside and continued my journey. At dark, and completely exhausted, and almost dead, I came in sight of the Graves's cabin, and sometime after dark staggered into my own. My clothes were wet, and the night was so cold that my garments were frozen stiff. I did not build a fire nor get anything to eat, just rolled myself up in the bed-clothes, and shivered; finally fell asleep, and did not waken until late in the morning. Then I saw my camp was in most inexplicable confusion; everything about the cabin was torn up and scattered about, trunks broken open; and my wife's jewellery, my cloak, my pistol and ammunition was missing. I thought Indians had been there. Suddenly I heard human voices. I hurried up to the surface of the snow, and saw white men approaching. I was overwhelmed with joy and gratitude. I had suffered so much and so long, that I could scarcely believe my senses. Imagine my astonishment upon their arrival to be greeted, not with a ' Good-morning ' or a kind word, but with a gruff, insolent demand, 'Where is Donner's money?'

" I told them they ought to give me something to eat, and that I would talk with them afterwards; but no, they insisted that I should tell them about Donner's money. I asked who they were, and where they came from, but they replied by threatening to kill me if I did not give up the money. They threatened to hang or shoot me. At last I told them that I had promised Mrs. Donner that I would carry her money to her children, and I proposed to do so, unless shown some authority by which they had a better claim. This so exasperated them that they acted as though they were going to kill me. I offered to let them bind me as a prisoner, and take me before Alcalde Sinclair at Sutter's Fort, and I promised that I would then tell all I knew about the money. They would listen to nothing, however, and finally I told them where they would find the silver, and gave them the gold. After I had done this they showed me a document from Alcalde Sinclair, by which they were to receive a certain proportion of all moneys and properties which they rescued. Those men treated me with great unkindness. Mr. Tucker was the only one who took my part or befriended me. When they started over the mountains, each man carried two bales of goods. They had silks, calicoes, and delaines from the Donners, and other articles of great value. Each man would carry one bundle a little way, lay it down, and come back and get the other bundle. In this way they passed over the snow three times. I could not keep up with them, because I was so weak, but managed to come up to their camp every night."

Upon receipt of this communication I wrote Mr. McGlashan from San Jose that I was nerved for the ordeal, but that he should not permit me to start on that momentous journey if his proposed arrangements were at all doubtful, and that he should telegraph me at once.

Alas! my note miscarried; and, believing that his proposal had not met my approval, Mr. and Mrs. McGlashan returned to Truckee a day earlier than expected. Two weeks later he returned the envelope, its postmarks showing what had happened.

It was not easy to gain the consent of my husband to a meeting with Keseberg. He dreaded its effect on me. He feared the outcome of the interview.

However, on May 16, 1879, he and I, by invitation, joined Mr. and Mrs. McGlashan at the Golden Eagle Hotel in Sacramento. The former then announced that although Keseberg had agreed by letter to meet us there, he had that morning begged to be spared the mortification of coming to the city hotel, where some one might recognize him, and as of old, point the finger of scorn at him. After some deliberation as to how I would accept the change, Mr. McGlashan had acceded to the old man's wish, that we drive to the neat little boarding house at Brighton next morning, where we could have the use of the parlor for a private interview. In compliance with this arrangement we four were at the Brighton hotel at the appointed time.

Mr. McGlashan and my husband went in search of Keseberg, and after some delay returned, saying:

" Keseberg cannot overcome his strong feeling against a meeting in a public house. He has tidied up a vacant room in the brewery adjoining the house where he lives with his afflicted children. It being Sunday, he knows that no one will be about to disturb us. Will you go there? "

I could only reply, " I am ready."

My husband, seeing my lips tremble and knowing the intensity of my suppressed emotion, hastened to assure me that he had talked with the man, and been impressed by his straightforward answers, and that I need have no dread of meeting or talking with him.

When we met at his door, Mr. McGlashan introduced us. We bowed, not as strangers, not as friends, nor did we shake hands. Our thoughts were fixed solely on the purpose that had brought us together. He invited us to enter, led the way to that room which I had been told he had swept and furnished for the occasion with seats for five. His first sentence made us both forget that others were present. It opened the way at once.

" Mr. McGlashan has told me that you have questions you wish to ask me yourself about what happened in the mountain cabin."

Still standing, and looking up into his face, I replied: " Yes, for the eye of God and your eyes witnessed my mother's last hours, and I have come to ask you, in the presence of that other Witness, when, where, and how she died. I want you to tell me all, and so truly that there shall be no disappointment for me, nor remorse and denials for you in your last hour. Tell it now, so that you will not need to send for me to hear a different story then."

I took the chair he proffered, and he placed his own opposite and having gently reminded me of the love and respect the members of the Donner Party bore their captain and his wife, earnestly and feelingly, he told me the story as he had related it to Mr. McGlashan.

Then, before I understood his movement, he had sunk upon his knees, saying solemnly,

" On my knees before you, and in the sight of God, I want to assert my innocence."

I could not have it thus. I bade him rise, and stand with me in the presence of the all-seeing Father. Extending my upturned hand, I bade him lay his own right hand upon it, then covering it with my left, I bade him speak. Slowly, but unhesitatingly, he spoke:

" Mrs. Houghton, if I had murdered your mother, would I stand here with my hand between your hands, look into your pale face, see the tear-marks on your cheeks, and the quiver of your lips as you ask the question? No, God Almighty is my witness, I am innocent of your mother's death! I have given you the facts as I gave them to the Fallon Party, as I told them at Sutter's Fort, and as I repeated them to Mr. McGlashan. You will hear no change from my death-bed, for what I have told you is true."

There, with a man's honor and soul to uncover, I had scarcely breathed while he spoke. I watched the expression of his face, his words, his hands. His eyes did not turn from my face; his hand between mine lay as untrembling as that of a child in peaceful sleep; and so, unflinchingly Lewis Keseberg passed the ordeal which would have made a guilty man quake.

I felt the truth of his assertion, and told him that if it would be any comfort to him at that late day to know that Tamsen Donner's daughter believed him innocent of her murder, he had that assurance in my words, and that I would maintain that belief so long as my lips retained their power of speech.

Tears glistened in his eyes as he uttered a heartfelt " Thank you! " and spoke of the comfort the recollection of this meeting would be to him during the remaining years of his life.

Before our departure, Mr. McGlashan asked Keseberg to step aside and show my husband the scars left by the wound which had prevented his going to the settlement with the earlier refugees. There was a mark of a fearful gash which had almost severed the heel from the foot and left a troublesome deformity. One could easily realize how slow and tedious its healing must have been, and Keseberg assured us that walking caused excruciating pain even at the time the Third Relief Corps left camp.

His clothing was threadbare, but neat and clean. One could not but feel that he was poor, yet he courteously but positively declined the assistance which, privately, I offered him. In bidding him good-bye, I remarked that we might not see one another again on earth, and he replied pathetically, "Don't say that, for I hope this may not be our last meeting."

I did not see Keseberg again. Years later, I learned that he had passed away; and in answer to inquiries I received the following personal note from Dr. G. A. White, Medical Superintendent of the Sacramento County Hospital:

Lewis Keseberg died here on September 3, 1895; aged 81 years. He left no special message to any one. His death was peaceful.

THE END

INDEX

INDEX

Academy of Pacific Coast History, 336.
Altemera, Padre, 187.
American Fur Company, 27.
American Tract Society, 10.
Arguello, Dona Concepcion, 302, 303.

Bartlett, Washington A., 93, 94.
Benton, Rev. J. A., 324.
Benton, Thomas H., 1.
Boggs, ex-Governor of Missouri, 9, 14, 2u, 218.
Bond, Frances, 292, 311.
Boone, Alphonso, 9.
Breen, Patrick, 32, 119; diary of, 68, 336, 345.
Brenheim, Adolph, 97.
Brunner, Christian, 150, 173, 296, 297, 318-320.
Brunner, "Grandma," 147-149, 317, 327; and Napoleon, 243-246.
Bryant, Edwin, 1z, 16, 27, 30, 307-310, 358.

Cady, Charles, 104.
California Star, 140, 307, 336.
Camp of Death, 83.
Chamberlain, Charlotte (Mrs. Wm. E.), 305.
Chamberlain, William E., 305.
Church, Mission service, 233.
Civil War, 324.
Clark, Nicholas, 104, 349.
Cody, Bill, 322.
Coffemeir, Edward, 97, 134.
Coon, William, 97.
Curtis, James, 97.

Del, John, 134.
Denison, Eliza, 306.
"Diary of Patrick Breen, One of the Donner Party," 336.

Dofar, Matthew, 104.
Doland, Patrick, 33, 73, 80, 81.
Donner, Elitha, 3, 132-137, 145, 253, 262.
Donner, Frances, 3, 251, 304.
Donner, George, 2, 4, 25, 137, 250, 309.
Donner, Mrs. George, 2, 5, 33, 102, 111, 137, 309; letters, 24-26.
Donner, Georgia, 3, 161.
Donner, Jacob, 2, 4, 8, 60, 68, 69.
Donner, Leanna, 3, 132-137, 153, 254.
Donner, Mary, 128, 313.
Donner Party, 32, 33, 337, 338.
Dozier, Tamsen Eustis, *see* Donner, Mrs. George.

Eddy, William, 32, 73, 78, 97, 119.

Fallon, Thomas, 134; diary, 310, 352-356.
Fitch, Capt., 184.
"Forlorn Hope" Party, 73, 76-90.
Fortune, Padre, 187.
Fosdick, Jay, 35, 73, 87.
Foster, John, 97.
Foster, William, 32, 73, 119; 134.
Francis, Allen, 4, 6, 8, 23.
Frémont, John C., 1, 4.
Frisbie, Capt., 195, 242; marriage of, 247.
Fuller, John, 94.

Glover, Aguilla, 76, 342.
Gold, discovery, 192; early minings, 204-206; seekers, 217.
Graves, W. F., 35, 79-81, 134.
Grayson, Mrs. Andrew J., 169, 170.
Great Overland Caravan, 4.
Greenwood, "Old Trapper," 94, 95.

INDEX

Halloran, Luke, 33, 36, 37.
Hardcoop, ——, 33, 50.
Hastings, Lansford W., 4, 31.
Herron, Walter, 33, 49.
Hook, Solomon, 117.
Hooker, Capt. Joe, 195.
Houghton, S. O., 312, 314, 315, 324.

Independence, Mo., 8, 10, 11.
Indians, as guides, 15; Sioux, 26, 28; on raids, 54; as saviours, 88; at "grub-feast," 162-164.

James, Noah, 70.
Jondro, Joseph, 104.
Josephine, Empress, 243.

Kerns, Capt., 92.
Keseberg, Lewis, 32, 136, 139-141, 230, 355, 360-370.

Land-grants, Mexican, 5.
Leese, Jacob, 184.
"Life and Days of General John A. Sutter," 336.

Maps of territory, 1, 3.
Maury, William L., 95.
M'Coon, Perry, 145.
McCutchen, William, 32, 37, 66.
McGlashan, C. F., 360-369.
McKinstrey, Col. George, 310, 346.
Mervine, Capt., 93, 95.
Mexican War, 93, 193.
Miller, Hiram, 104, 119, 141, 251.
Moutrey, R. S., 96.
Murphy, Mrs. Lavina, 32, 110.
Murphy, William G., 347.

Napoleon, 243.

Oakley, Howard, 119.
Oatman, Eugene, 306.
"Oregon and California," 17.

Packwood, Mr. and Mrs., 157.
Pike, William, 32, 36, 57.
Pony Express, first, 321-323.
Poor, Elizabeth, 218; letter to, 234.
Prudon, Major, 184.

Reed, James F., 4, 8, 48, 66, 313.
Relief Party, First, 97, 341.

Relief Party, Fourth, 134.
Relief Party, Second, 104, 345.
Relief Party, Third, 119.
Rhinehart, Joseph, 33, 68.
Rhodes, Daniel, 97.
Rhodes, John, 97, 134.
Richardson, ——, 93.
Richey, D., 97.
Richey, Col. M. D., 89.
Robinson, Kate, 312.
Robinson, Judge Robert, 306, 316.
Robinson, Hon. Tod, 306.
Russell, Col., 9, 10, 12, 25-27.

Sacramento, 288.
Sacramento Union, 291, 296, 305, 306, 320.
School, first in California, 223, 225; Miss Doty's, 234; St. Mary's Hall, 260; Miss Hutchinson's, 260; St. Catherine's, 297; Jefferson Grammar, 306.
Schoonover, T. J., 336.
Sherman, Gen. Wm. T., 266.
Shoemaker, Samuel, 33, 68.
Sinclair, John, 91, 96, 145.
Sloat, Commodore, 188.
Smallpox, 255-257.
Smith, General, 197.
Smith, James, 33, 69.
Snyder, John, 35, 48.
Sonoma, 187-191; last visit to, 326-331.
Springfield Journal, 4, 8, 23.
Stanton, Charles, 33, 36, 37, 79.
Stark, John, 118, 134.
Starved Camp, 119.
Stone, Charles, 104, 119.
Sutter, Captain John A., 37, 38, 92, 96, 311.
Sutter's Fort, 131-138.
Swift, Margaret, 306.

Thanksgiving celebration, 261, 262.
Thornton, J. Q., 9, 16; extracts from journal, 39, 54, 85, 87, 89, 95, 121, 342.
"Thrilling Events in California History," 310.
Toll, Agnes, 306.
"Topographical Report, with Maps Attached," 4.
"Travels Among the Rocky Mountains, Through Oregon and California," 4, 32.

INDEX

Trubode, John Baptiste, 34, 62, 220, 343, 349, 350.
Tucker, Daniel, 134.
Tucker, George, 97.
Tucker, Racine, 97.
Turner, John, 104.

Upton, Nellie, 306.

Vallejo, Mariano G., 95, 184, 187.

Webster, Daniel, 305.

"What I Saw in California," 12, 307.
White, Dr. G. A., 370.
White, Henry A., 306.
Wolfinger, ——, 33, 55.
Woodworth, Midshipman, 94, 116, 127.

Yost, Daniel, 306.
Yount, George, 94.

Zabriskie, Annie, 306.